39.50

MISSION COLL
LEARNING RESOUF

D0354443

FOR REFERENCE

Do Not Take From This Room

VIOLENCE
AND THE MEDIA

A Reference Handbook

Other Titles in ABC-CLIO's
CONTEMPORARY
WORLD ISSUES
Series

Books in the Contemporary World Issues series address vital issues in today's society such as terrorism, sexual harassment, homelessness, AIDS, gambling, animal rights, and air pollution. Written by professional writers, scholars, and nonacademic experts, these books are authoritative, clearly written, up-to-date, and objective. They provide a good starting point for research by high school and college students, scholars, and general readers, as well as by legislators, businesspeople, activists, and others.

Each book, carefully organized and easy to use, contains an overview of the subject; a detailed chronology; biographical sketches; facts and data and/or documents and other primary-source material; a directory of organizations and agencies; annotated lists of print and nonprint resources; a glossary; and an index.

Readers of books in the Contemporary World Issues series will find the information they need in order to understand better the social, political, environmental, and economic issues facing the world today.

VIOLENCE
AND THE MEDIA

A Reference Handbook

David E. Newton

**CONTEMPORARY
WORLD ISSUES**

ABC-CLIO

Santa Barbara, California
Denver, Colorado
Oxford, England

Library of Congress Cataloging-in-Publication Data

Newton, David E.
    Violence and the media : a reference handbook / David E. Newton.
        p.   cm. — (Contemporary world issues)
    Includes bibliographical references and index.
    1. Violence in mass media—Handbooks, manuals, etc.   I. Title.
    II. Series.
    P96.V5N48   1996   303.6—dc20   96-22269

ISBN 0-87436-843-X (alk. paper)

02 01 00 99 98 97 96   10 9 8 7 6 5 4 3 2 1 (cloth)

ABC-CLIO, Inc.
130 Cremona Drive, P.O. Box 1911
Santa Barbara, California 93116-1911

This book is printed on acid-free paper ⊗ .

Manufactured in the United States of America

For Gary Sikkema
with appreciation for a long and true friendship

Contents

Preface

A cartoon figure on a popular Saturday morning children's television program smashes a second cartoon figure with an oversized anvil. Millions of youngsters across the United States burst out in laughter. But is there more to this scene than meets the eye? Does the cartoon episode carry a hidden message that it's okay for one person to strike a second person, in anger or just as a joke? Does the scene help young children relieve frustrations and subdued aggression that they might otherwise act on in real life? Do children know the difference between the fantasy of a cartoon character and the real-life problems they encounter every day? Or is this simply, after all, a funny carton that has no short- or long-term effects at all on viewers?

The question of how violence in the mass media—television, motion pictures, video games, popular music, newspapers, and magazines, for example—affects viewers is one of the critical issues of our society today. It has been an issue about which humans have disagreed from the very first appearance of mass media itself, more than 2,000 years ago.

The purpose of this book is to provide resources with which readers can develop a better understanding of the issue of violence in the mass media. The first chapter of the book is devoted to a general review of the issue, its historical background, and the major questions involved in the debate over violence in the mass media. The second chapter provides a chronology of important events that have taken place over the past two centuries. Chapter 3 contains biographical sketches of some important figures in the long controversy over the place and effects of violence in the mass media. Chapter 4 is composed of important documents such as laws, regulations, court decisions, industry standards, and policy statements relating to the subject of violence in the mass media. Chapter 5 contains a list of organizations interested in and working on the topic of violence in the mass media. Chapters 6 and 7 provide lists, respectively, of print and nonprint resources on the subject of violence in the mass media. Finally, a glossary of important terms used in discussions of this topic follows the last chapter of the book.

Violence and the Media: An Overview

1

On 19 April 1995, a bomb blew apart the Alfred P. Murrah Federal Building in Oklahoma City, Oklahoma. The building was almost totally destroyed, and 168 people were killed. Two weeks later, President Bill Clinton suggested that one factor in the Oklahoma City tragedy may have been "extremist rhetoric from talk show hosts of the radical right." He criticized "loud and angry voices" who "spread hate" on certain talk shows. "They leave the impression," Clinton said, "that violence is acceptable."[1]

One such personality to whom he alluded was G. Gordon Liddy, convicted in the burglary at the Watergate apartment building and office complex in 1972 and now popular talk show host. In a program broadcast shortly before the Oklahoma City incident, Liddy had instructed his listeners as to the best way in which to shoot at federal agents in a gunfight.

At almost the same time that President Clinton was warning about the dangers of inflammatory rhetoric on the radio, Senate Majority Leader Bob Dole (R-Kansas) was launching a broad attack on the quantity of sex and violence in modern movies, television, and popular music. He warned members of these industries that "a line has been crossed—not just of taste, but of human dignity and

1

decency. It is crossed every time sexual violence is given a catchy tune. When teen suicide is set to an appealing beat. When Hollywood's dream factories turn out nightmares of depravity."[2]

The concerns expressed by Clinton and Dole were being repeated almost simultaneously by members of the National Political Congress of Black Women. At a conference of the organization, its chair, DeLores Tucker, claimed that children today "are being exposed to certain music and videos that only offer negative images of human relationships. . . . [Such music] too often teaches Black men how to mistreat Black women—and for our women to accept this—is nothing short of mental contamination."[3]

These incidents were only three of the most noteworthy occasions during which Americans spoke out in the mid-1990s about the problem of violence in the mass media. Almost everywhere one looked during the period, violent scenes and messages abounded. Motion pictures, television, popular music, video games, books, and magazines featured scenes of mayhem, sexual assault, murder, suicide, and other forms of violence. Could the cumulative effect of all these messages, repeated over and over again, *not* have an effect on the way Americans think and behave, especially those who are young?

Violent Themes in History

For all the debate and discussion over violence in the mass media in the 1990s, one element was usually missing: a historical perspective. Most Americans seemed to feel that the portrayal of violence on television and in films, in "gangsta rap," and on video games was a new phenomenon, a symptom perhaps of the moral decay of a once-great nation.

Such an interpretation of events would, however, be very much off target. A number of scholars have clearly shown that violence has always been a part of human society's systems of mass communication. The term *mass communication* or *mass media* is relatively easy to define today. Any form of communication to which large numbers of people have ready access—motion pictures, television, books, magazines, newspapers, and popular music, for example—can be classified as mass media.

But long before the first printing press was invented, people had ways of disseminating news and entertainment to large numbers of the population. In ancient Egypt, for example, hieroglyphics may have been unintelligible to most people, but sculptures, carvings, and other forms of public art could be understood and could be designed to carry a message.

And it was not at all unusual that that message contained a violent theme. In his book *Preposterous Violence*, James B. Twitchell points out the frequency with which violent themes appear in well-known art scenes as diverse as the wall paintings on the caves at Lascaux (15,000–10,000 B.C.), the carvings on the palaces of the Assyrian king Ashurbanipal (650 B.C.), and a broad sample of religious paintings from the Middle Ages.[4]

As an introduction to his historical survey, Twitchell makes a general observation. "The real question about spectacles of symbolic violence," he says, "is not how to do away with them, but why they are there in the first place and in the second place why they won't go away."

> The real question is not whether they cause violent behavior (they may well do so) but why they are so entertaining. Preposterous violence is fun. Whatever inheres in these crude circuses is something that won't be soaped away with rating systems, revisions, or outright censorship. Whatever preposterous violence holds is something that young males will expend great energy to share vicariously. Call it escape, call it wish-fulfillment, call it exploitation, call it junk, call it what you will, scenarios of disorderly conduct have been with us, are with us, and will undoubtedly stay with us.[5]

An important point made by Twitchell's book is that violent themes are by no means restricted to visual presentations. Indeed, tales of horror, gore, and violence in literature can be traced back nearly 200 years, almost to the birth of the novel as a literary form.

One of the most interesting theories developed by Twitchell deals with the place modern horror writer Stephen King holds in the long history of violent fiction. King is, according to Twitchell,

> squarely in the middle of the dominant trend of print media as it has evolved for the last one hundred and fifty years. King's genius is that, as a major portion of the sentimental/Gothic tradition moved to the romance, he was able to corner what remained of that market— the part that had read not for the warm tingles of courtship but for the cold shivers of violence.[6]

New Media as New Menace

One can hardly come away from a reading of Twitchell's book without a clear recognition that violence is as normal and common as any other part of the arts. At the same time, his work shows that public reactions to the displays of violence are at least as common. There is no historical period during which a significant number of critics were not complaining about violence in the popular media, whether it be the newspapers, the dime novels, the earliest "picture shows," television, or gangsta rap.

An especially intriguing analysis of the reaction to violence in the media can be found in Steven Starker's *Evil Influences: Crusades against the Mass Media*. In this book, Starker argues that many critics of violence in the media are reacting not only to the violence itself, but also to the new forms of media in which the violence may be found. To make his case, Starker cites a number of critics who are horrified by the very concept of video games and their wide availability, by the apparently ubiquitous influence of television on Americans, by books and magazines that *anyone can read*, and so on. In fact, he begins his discussion of this phenomenon with a quotation from Plato about the increasing use of the written word over the spoken word. "This discovery of yours," Plato says,

> will create forgetfulness in the learners' souls, because they will not use their memories; they will trust to the external written characters and not remember of themselves. The specific which you have discovered is an aid not to memory, but to reminiscence, and you give your disciples not truth, but only the semblance of truth; they will be hearers of many things and will have learned nothing; they will appear to be omniscient and will generally know nothing; they will be tiresome company having the show of wisdom without the reality.[7]

Many of Starker's historical citations have a familiar ring in the United States of the late twentieth century. Substitute "television" or "gangsta rap" or "video games" in some of these early diatribes, and the commentary could as well have appeared on the editorial page of last week's newspaper.

The spread of inexpensive, widely available newspapers in the last quarter of the nineteenth century, as an example, brought forth this observation from George M. Beard, physician and authority on neurasthenia (nervous exhaustion). Neurasthenia had become an epidemic in American urban centers, Beard wrote in his widely read book *American Nervousness, Its Causes and Consequences*, largely because of the popularity of newspapers.

> The sorrows of any part of the world, many times greater than the old world as known to the ancients, through the medium of the press and the telegraph are made the sorrows of individuals everywhere. . . . With the extension and complexity of populations of the globe, with the rise and growth of many nations and peoples, these local sorrows and local horrors become daily occasions of nervous disorders. Our morning newspaper, that we read with our breakfast, has the history of the sorrows of the whole world for a day; and a nature but moderately sympathetic is robbed thereby, consciously or unconsciously, of more or less nervous strength.[8]

Starker then juxtaposes these observations with similar statements of concern from our own day. He quotes Harvard psychiatrist Alvin Poussaint writing in *Jet Magazine*, for example, about the current problem of violence in video games.

> I think there are strong possibilities that the video games contribute to the problem of violence in society . . . teaching the children that violence is somehow an acceptable thing and is a legitimate way of expressing your anger. . . . There's nothing constructive in the games. Everything is eliminate, kill, destroy, let's get up and do it fast.[9]

The eighteenth century saw the appearance of another form of mass media: the novel. The two predominant themes in the early novel (as they still are today) were romance and violence. In a chapter on violence in prose fiction, Twitchell traces the development of violent action in the Gothic novel in the eighteenth century and shows how it quickly became widely popular among the public in "penny dreadfuls" and "bloody pulps."[10] The appearance of these new book forms made Gothic horrors readily available to the whole of the reading public by the end of the century, according to Twitchell. One historian of the period describes the content of much of the fiction at the time as consisting of "rape, jealous frenzy and murder [as] the staple ingredients of these novels."[11]

It was not long, of course, before critics began ranting about the dangers of popular novels on the public morality. In the United

States, the campaign against violent and immoral literature was led by Anthony Comstock and his New York Society for the Suppression of Vice. Typical of the concerns expressed by such critics were those expressed in an 1808 letter to the *Gentleman's Magazine:*

> How few persons are likely to be contaminated by the performance of an immoral play, compared to those who may be rendered vicious by the publication of an immoral book, which may be circulated throughout the entire kingdom, and may enter every house.[12]

The fierce attacks on violence in television, motion pictures, popular music, and video games in the 1990s has had, therefore, a much longer history than many modern-day critics may recognize.

Violence in a Violent Culture

In the 1960s, black revolutionary leader Stokely Carmichael made what has become a classic commentary on American society. "Violence," he observed, "is as American as cherry pie." Although that comment startled and offended many Americans, there is little doubt that Carmichael was right on target in his assessment. By almost any measure one cares to use, American society is far more violent than that of any developed nation in the world (with the possible exception of South Africa).

It follows, then, that any discussion of violence in the mass media in twentieth-century America must also take into consideration the violent nature of American culture itself. Historians have long been aware of the predominance of violence in American culture and have suggested a number of causes to explain this phenomenon. They have pointed out that the United States was founded as a result of violent revolution and that it then experienced one rebellion after another in the early years of its existence. As settlers moved west, they waged a campaign of genocide against Native Americans and practiced a particularly violent form of personal and social justice within their own pioneer community. Historian Irving J. Sloan has observed that "a certain amount of lawlessness and crime is almost inevitable in the settlement of a new country, but the amount which characterized the American western frontier probably surpasses any measure of reasonableness."[13]

Another observer, Walter M. Gerson, has explored the effect of this tradition on popular attitudes in contemporary American culture. In his essay "Violence as an American Value Theme" he writes that

> Children [in the United States] learn early that it is un-American to be a "chicken." Anti-sissy and anti-pacifist sentiments are quite prevalent in the society. Action is emphasized over non-action. Carry a big stick and speak softly. One should fight for his rights. Possibly the only kind of intellectual who is widely admired by Americans is the one who *demonstrates* power in a tangible manner.[14]

Given this cultural legacy, it is hardly surprising that the mass media that speak about and to this nation do so in terms that are often enveloped in violence.

Violence in the Motion Pictures

The foregoing discussions clearly demonstrate that concerns about the presence of violent themes in the mass media have been around since the time of Plato. It also seems clear, however, that critics today tend to focus more on certain forms of mass communication—motion pictures, television, certain types of music, and video games—than they do on others—radio, books, magazines, and newspapers.

The first complaints about violence in "moving pictures" (whether film or television) can be traced to the very earliest days of the cinema. A popular topic of early films was prizefighting. The Corbett-Fitzsimmons fight of 1897, for example, was one of the first moving picture "hits." A number of observers were distressed, however, at the use of violent themes as a form of general entertainment. A *New York Times* editorialist wrote in 1897, for example, that

> It is not very creditable to our civilization perhaps that an achievement of what is now called the "veriscope" that has attracted and will attract the widest attention should be the representation of the prizefight. Moralists may deplore the fact that the fight in question "sold more extras" than would a presidential election. But they will have to eradicate a great deal of human nature before they can alter it.[15]

A decade later, the controversy had by no means died down, and the police commissioner of New York City recommended to the mayor of the city that all licenses for nickelodeons and penny arcades be canceled on grounds that such houses were "pernicious, demoralizing, and a direct menace to the young."[16]

Concerns like those expressed by the police commissioner highlight the fundamental issues around which debate over violence in the mass media were to rage throughout the century. Clearly the First Amendment of the U.S. Constitution bestows the right of free speech on all American citizens. Does this not mean that film producers have the constitutional right to produce and display any work they choose?

That question, of course, presents a false dilemma. Many constitutionally guaranteed rights have had limitations placed upon them. For example, in a widely quoted comment, Supreme Court Justice Oliver Wendell Holmes pointed out in 1918 that no one has a constitutionally guaranteed right to shout "Fire!" in a crowded theater.

The question really comes down to what kind of limitations can be imposed on a person's right of free speech if the nature of that speech is widely regarded as being harmful to the general public.

The Era of Watchdogs

During the early years of motion pictures, governmental bodies sometimes took a cavalier attitude about the First Amendment rights of filmmakers, producers, and distributors. By 1922, eight states had passed laws requiring some form of license for the distribution and display of motion pictures. A 1911 law in Pennsylvania, for example, established a state board of censors charged with the responsibility of approving every film sold, leased, lent, or exhibited in the state.[17]

For a period of time, state laws censoring the use of motion pictures were on solid ground, laid down by a 1915 U.S. Supreme Court decision in the case *Mutual Film Corporation v. Ohio*. In that case, a film distributor argued that the state of Ohio's censorship laws were unconstitutional since they interfered with the producer's First Amendment rights of free speech. The Court ruled that motion pictures were "a business pure and simple" and, therefore, it was not even necessary to consider the issue of an individual's right of free speech in the case.[18]

It was not until a decade later, in fact, that the Court even took a position as to whether the individual states were required to adhere to the First Amendment provisions of free speech and press. In the 1925 case of *Gitlow v. New York*, the Court laid the foundation that would eventually make censorship boards of any kind increasingly difficult to impose on film producers and distributors.[19]

Long before the *Gitlow v. New York* decision had been announced, however, the film industry had begun to recognize the need for some form of review in order to deal with mounting complaints about violent and sexual themes in movies. In 1909, film producers and distributors formed the Motion Picture Patents Company largely to deal with such problems. One of its first actions was to establish the National Board of Censorship of Motion Pictures, later to be renamed the National Board of Review.

The word *censorship* in the Board's title was included not because anyone really expected to exercise that option, but because, as the early film historian Terry Ramsaye explained, the word was necessary "to satisfy the public and official mind of the day the naughty, naughty motion picture had to be spanked on the wrist."[20]

Although the Board was created originally to review only those films scheduled to open in New York City (with a bow to its police commissioner), its purview rapidly spread to include the whole nation. It relied largely on volunteers and a few paid staff to examine about 95 percent of all films produced in the United States during the period, with considerable success in its early days.

The Board's work never completely silenced the critics of violent and sexual themes in movies, however. A recurring comment was that the industry could hardly be expected to monitor itself with the scrutiny that critics wanted and that could have been achieved with outside observers. In 1919, for example, a resolution by the General Federation of Women's Clubs took aim at the Board's practice of asking women to volunteer to review moving pictures. The Board had, the Federation complained, produced

> a stream of literature [which] is the motion picture's [*sic*] industry's attempt to furnish well-intentioned, reform-bent ladies with "harmless busy work." They persistently and blatantly preach, "promote the good, the beautiful, smother evil with good." Meanwhile the stream of filthy film flows.[21]

In an attempt to quiet such criticisms, motion picture executives, now organized as the Motion Picture Producers and Distributors of America (MPPDA), approached U.S. Postmaster General Will H. Hays in December 1921 and offered him the post of president of the MPPDA.

Hays had been involved in politics at the local, state, and federal levels for more than a decade and had been awarded the post of postmaster general only nine months earlier as a reward for his loyal service. He accepted the MPPDA offer and took over his new position in March 1922. The reason for Hays's selection, according to one biographer, was that the film industry badly needed someone from outside the industry who "could sell the legend of a cleaner Hollywood, who could head off the censorship legislation, who could stop the agitation against movies."[22]

It was not long into Hays's tenure, however, before the MPPDA began to be widely known as "the Hays Office." He quickly established his role as the official arbiter of what was and was not appropriate for motion picture viewing. Hays held his post at MPPDA for 23 years, finally resigning to service as a consultant to the organization in 1945.

The selection of Hays to lead the MPPDA was a step in the right direction by the industry, but in the long run, it did little to halt the avalanche of protests about violent and sexual themes in films. Then, in the early 1930s, a new force entered the debate over the content of motion pictures: the Roman Catholic Church. A group of clerics and laymen established a reform group they called the National Legion of Decency. The original purpose of the group was to review films and warn "good Catholics" which ones to avoid. Within three months of its formation, the Legion claimed a membership of 8 million, all of whom were willing to boycott individual films, theaters, or the whole motion picture industry, if that appeared to be necessary to bring about the reform they sought.[23]

The Legion expressed concern not only about what it saw as an increasingly loose approach to sexual themes in films, but also about an increase in violent action in such films. The early 1930s had seen the release of a number of "gangster" films, which at least some observers saw as giving approval to criminal activities. One of the most interesting observations of the time about these films came from a man with some familiarity with the world of gangsters, Al Capone. "You know," he said, these gang pictures—that's terrible kid stuff. Why, they ought to take them all and throw them into the lake. They're doing nothing but harm to the younger element of this country. I don't blame the censors for trying to bar them . . . these gang movies are making a lot of kids want to be tough guys and they don't serve any useful purpose.[24]

Shaken by the moral and economic threat posed by the Legion, the film industry agreed to reexamine its National Board of Review. In July 1934, the Hays Office announced a new Resolution for Uniform Interpretation and a new Production Code. As one condition of the new code, all U.S.-released films were required to display a "Purity Seal," a stamp of approval from the MPPDA. Administration of the new guidelines was placed under a new MPPDA office to be headed by Joseph Breen, a devout Catholic.[25]

Morality and Science

The Legion of Decency represents an important object lesson in the history of the debate about violence in the mass media. It may well be (as attendance figures for motion pictures have long indicated) that a significant number of Americans—conceivably even a majority of the population—have no objection to the depiction of violent (or sexually oriented) themes in films or in other forms of the media. That fact does not mean, however, that a well-organized, highly motivated group of individuals cannot impose its own moral beliefs on the media, even when those beliefs may run counter to "popular tastes." Such groups are more likely to attain success, of course, if they are able to influence those in positions of power, such as city councillors or state legislators.

A current example of the Legion of Decency lesson is the impact that a group known as American Family Association (AFA) has had on television programming. By convincing advertisers to withhold their financial support from programs that AFA finds morally objectionable, the group has been able to exert an influence over television programming disproportionate to its actual size.

The existence and operation of groups such as the Legion of Decency and American Family Association are by no means evil nor unprincipled. In fact, debates among special interest groups are fundamental in a democracy, and every person and group has a legitimate right, indeed, a responsibility, to shape legislation and public opinion in whatever direction it deems appropriate.

Attempts to censor motion picture content on the basis of individual moral beliefs has long been only one part of the criticism of violence in the mass media. Another vital issue has been the impact that the media are thought to have on the beliefs and actions of viewers, especially of children and teenagers. Although the issue has become somewhat complex, the essential argument appears to be that men and women and boys and girls who see violent acts performed on the movie screen (or on television) are more likely to become aggressive and violent in their own lives.

This viewpoint was expressed early in the history of motion pictures. For example, the head of a mission for "unfortunate women" in New York City pointed out the harmful psychological effects of viewing motion pictures.

> Consequently, what the psychologists call suggestion plays a much larger part in the lives of the border-line class than it is easy for ordinary people to comprehend. As to the effect on the neurasthenic, it is perhaps not best to go into it here. Suffice it to say that any physician with experience among such cases will testify to the immediate and serious mental results of this auto-suggestion.[26]

The point is that the argument about the effects of media on viewers is a very different issue than the question of the moral content of films. The latter issue is really a matter of moral, ethical, and philosophical choice, while the former is a research question that, at least in theory, can be answered by means of appropriate research studies.

It should not be surprising, then, to find educators, sociologists, and psychologists mounting research programs in the 1920s to find out what effects, if any, the viewing of motion pictures had on young people. The most famous of these was a group of studies conceived by the Motion Picture Research Council and financed by the Payne Fund in 1928. W. W. Charters, chairman of the Payne Fund's Committee on Education Research, outlined the rationale for the program of research.

> Motion pictures are not understood by the present generation of adults. They are new; they make an enormous appeal to children; and they present ideas and situa-

tions which parents may not like. Consequently when parents think of the welfare of their children who are exposed to these compelling situations, they wonder about the effect of the pictures upon the ideals and behavior of the children. Do the pictures really influence children in any direction? Are their conduct, ideals, and attitudes affected by the movies? Are the scenes which are objectionable to adults understood by children, or at least by very young children? Do children eventually become more sophisticated and grow superior to pictures? Are the emotions of children harmfully excited? In short, just what effect do motion pictures have upon children of different ages?[27]

The Payne Fund eventually paid for a total of 12 studies carried out between 1928 and 1932. These studies were summarized in nine books published between 1933 and 1935. Some titles of those books give a flavor of the nature of the research reported: *Motion Pictures and the Social Attitudes of Children*; *Motion Pictures and Standards of Morality*; *Movies, Delinquency, and Crime*; and *Boys, Movies, and City Streets*. The overall findings of these studies were summarized by two researchers, Herbert Blumer and Philip Hauser, and foretold with remarkable prescience the kinds of results that would be obtained over and over again from similar studies of motion pictures and television over the next 60 years.

In the first place, it was apparent that no broad, general statement could be made about the effects of violence in films that would apply to all or even most viewers. No one could argue flat out, that is, that scenes of violence in films had any discernible effect on most of the children or adults who viewed the films.

It was possible to say, however, that scenes of violence *sometimes* had *some* effects on *certain* types of viewers in *certain* specific cases. Boys who were predisposed to exhibiting aggressive behavior, for example, might become more aggressive after viewing filmed violence, provided conditions permitted such behaviors.

The ambiguities of the research results they reviewed prompted Blumer and Hauser to take a somewhat vague position on the work sponsored by the Payne Fund. In a 1933 summary that would sound not entirely out of place in one of today's research journals, they concluded:

> It is evident that motion pictures may exert influences
> in diametrically opposite directions. The movies may

> help to dispose or lead persons to delinquency and crime
> or they may fortify conventional behavior. Movies
> shown to inmates may cheer them and help make them
> contented or may make them blue and disconsolate;
> they may be of value in the maintenance of institutional
> discipline or they may create or augment problems of
> institutional misconduct; they may encourage reforma-
> tion of the offender or they may make the inmate bitter
> and resentful against society. Motion pictures may cre-
> ate attitudes favorable to crime and the criminal or un-
> favorable to them.[28]

Perhaps the most intriguing single result of the decades of research
conducted on the effects of filmed and televised violence is that
the pat slogans of critics about the damage done to viewers by
such programming simply cannot be confirmed by carefully controlled studies. On the other hand, there no longer seems any doubt
that the thoughts and actions of *some* viewers under *some* circumstances *may very well be* influenced by such viewing.

Violence in Films Today

For almost two decades, the MPPDA's new system for insuring
the "purity" of films was successful. No picture produced in the
United States was released without the Hays Office's stamp of approval. In many instances, pictures had to be returned to editors
for changes that would earn that stamp for the film.

Then, in 1953, director Otto Preminger decided to release his
film *The Moon Is Blue* even though the MPPDA censors had refused to issue its seal of approval. The film contained prohibited
words such as "virgin" and "mistress" that MPPDA censors said
would have to be removed before the film could be released. Although mild by modern standards, the objectionable passages in
Moon were offensive enough to violate the MPPDA Production
Code standards of the time.

The commercial success of *The Moon Is Blue* (albeit, a modest
success) was sufficient to cause a break in the MPPDA's moral ar-
mor. When Preminger released a second film, *The Man with the
Golden Arm*, in 1956 (dealing with drug addiction), also without
MPPDA approval, the Code's back had been broken.

Within a short time, the MPPDA felt pressured to modify the
Production Code so as to now allow the use of words and actions
that had previously made it impossible for *The Moon Is Blue* and

The Man with the Golden Arm to receive the industry's stamp of approval.

Today, the film industry continues to regulate its own products by means of a rating system, which was first adopted in 1968. According to this system, each film is assigned a letter code describing the "maturity" of its themes. In particular, a film rating is supposed to warn prospective viewers about the amount and nature of violent and sexual themes presented in the picture. A film given an "R" rating, for example, is classified as "restricted." No person under the age of 17 is supposed to be admitted to an R-rated film unless accompanied by a parent or adult guardian.

A number of critics have questioned how effective a self-regulatory system like the film ratings system can be. For example, James B. Twitchell, in his fascinating book *Preposterous Violence: Fables of Aggression in Modern Culture*, points out that one of the current categories, PG-13, is supposed to be assigned to films that contain a single "gratuitous" drug scene or a single "sexually derived word." But what this newest rating actually appears to accomplish, according to Twitchell, is that "the 'soft R' summer slaughter movie will blend in with the PG-13. Thus PG-13 films will have *more* violence [emphasis in original], less sex and drugs."[29]

It is not entirely clear how effective the current MPPDA rating system is in terms of reducing the amount of violent content in films produced in the 1990s. Certainly, critics still find a great deal to complain about in this respect. In a 1993 article in *Mother Jones* magazine, for example, journalist Carl M. Cannon criticizes actors and producers who speak out for a whole host of liberal causes and then shut their eyes to the mayhem produced in their own studios. "In the one area over which they have control—the excessive violence in the entertainment business," Cannon writes, "Hollywood activists remain silent."

After reviewing the massive volume of research done on violence in the mass media and its effects of viewers, Cannon then allows Hollywood producers, directors, and actors to speak for themselves. From Bob Shaye, chief executive officer of New Line Cinema, one of whose products was the series of *Nightmare on Elm Street* horror films:

> We create a product. People buy it or they don't. It pains my aesthetic judgment, but I often feel a good movie is one that makes money. My interest is in entertaining people.

Or from Leslie Moonves, head of Lorimar Studios, which has produced a number of violent films:

> Network presidents don't keep their jobs based on the number of Emmy awards. Let's face it: there is more sensation and violence because it works. The movie of the week has become the killer of the week story.

Or from Richard Donner, director of the *Lethal Weapon* movies:

> If people see gratuitous violence in any of the *Lethal Weapon* movies, I wonder if they've seen the same movie. It's entertainment. That's my obligation.

Or from Sam Hamm, one of the screenwriters on *Batman* and *Batman Returns:*

> I can remember being scared as a kid at horror films and developing a craving for that sort of thing, but that's what may form imagination in a strong way and that's what creates narrative and inner life. It teaches you to look for stuff that's not safe in the art you enjoy later on. . . . Gravitating toward the forbidden is a natural part of growing up.[30]

The issue of violence in motion pictures in the 1990s is further complicated by the fact that the vast majority of films made today are not only being shown in movie theaters, but also end up being offered for sale as videocassettes and rerun on television stations over and over again. The problem of violence in films has become almost inseparable, therefore, from the problem of violence on television, an issue to which we turn later in this chapter.

Trouble in Cartoon-Land

The history of motion pictures and television merged so gradually during the 1950s that one would expect that issues about violent content with regard to the former would naturally reappear with the growth of the latter. And to some extent, as mentioned above, that is true. However, the rather remarkable fact is that the focus of violence in the media shifted during the 1950s to an almost totally unexpected front: comic magazines.

The history of comic magazines goes back nearly a century. Such magazines developed out of newspaper cartoon strips such as "Mutt and Jeff," drawn by H. C. (Bud) Fisher. Fisher's strip first appeared in the *San Francisco Daily Morning Chronicle* in 1907. Fisher's product was soon followed by imitators in newspapers throughout the United States.

The first separate "magazine" devoted to the cartoon-strip concept was probably a publication called *Funnies on Parade*, produced as a promotional giveaway by the Procter and Gamble company in 1933. As with "Mutt and Jeff," the *Funnies on Parade* concept caught on quickly and dozens of comic book publishers had appeared by the beginning of World War II.

Comic books, as their name suggests, were generally considered at first as light entertainment aimed primarily (but not exclusively) at children. They certainly contained violent acts, as did the filmed cartoons of the time—and as would Saturday morning television cartoons later produced for young viewers. But scenes of one character bashing another with a hammer or an anvil seldom produced much of an outcry against "violence in the comics" until after World War II. Then things began to change.

In the first place, criticisms about the depiction and, in some cases, the glorification of crime began to be heard. Without doubt, the most outspoken voice of the period was the psychiatrist Frederic Wertham. A 1922 emigrant to the United States from Austria, Wertham had, by the 1940s, chosen the comics as his field of expertise. He wrote two books, *The Seduction of the Innocent* and *A Sign for Cain: An Exploration of Human Violence*, and a number of articles dealing with violence in comic magazines. Probably his most famous popular work was an article he wrote in 1948 for the *Saturday Review of Literature* entitled "The Comics . . . Very Funny."

In *Seduction of the Innocent*, Wertham prepared his bill of particulars against violence in the comics:

1. The comic book format is an invitation to illiteracy.
2. Crime comic books create an atmosphere of cruelty and deceit.
3. They create a readiness for temptation.
4. They stimulate unwholesome fantasies.
5. They suggest criminal or sexually abnormal ideas.
6. They furnish the rationalization for them, which may be ethically even more harmful than the impulse.
7. They suggest the forms a delinquent impulse may take and supply details of technique.

8. They may tip the scales toward maladjustment or delinquency.[31]

Whatever the scientific basis of Wertham's case (and some critics declared it to be weak), his position was bolstered by a second change in the late 1940s: the appearance of "horror" comics. The first such magazine was published in 1949 by William Gaines, a well-known and widely successful publisher of other forms of comic magazines, including "Picture Stories from the Bible," of which Gaines claimed to have sold more than 5 million copies.

"Horror" comics have been described by Steven Starker as magazines designed for children in which the emphasis is on "particularly gruesome varieties of death, with readers spared no details in the illustrations."[32]

Horror comics appeared on the scene at about the time that public disapproval of comic magazines was becoming more widespread. Nationwide, citizens were banding together to review and report on magazines that they found to be dangerous to young readers. An example of this approach was the Greater Cincinnati Committee on Evaluation of Comic Books, formed in 1948.

The committee consisted of about ten members who met regularly to review the comic magazines then available to children and youth in the Cincinnati area. The job of committee members was to evaluate "every story and picture frame . . . in terms of its cultural, moral, and emotional impact upon children and youths through 15 years of age." Each magazine examined was eventually rated as "no objection," "some objection," "objectionable," or "very objectionable." The results of this rating system were then printed, sent to publishers, released to the public, and used as the basis for public speeches and meetings.[33]

The model on which the Cincinnati group—and dozens like it around the country—was based was the National Organization for Decent Literature (NODL), created in 1938 by a council of bishops of the Roman Catholic Church. NODL was established as a watchdog organization to keep an eye on magazines, pocket books, and comic books that it regarded, for one reason or another, as "objectionable." Women who took part in the "decency crusades" conducted by NODL were given the following instructions:

1. Every establishment which sells comic books, pocket-size books, and magazines within the limit of your parish is to be visited. This includes corner newsstands.

2. It is recommended that your committee work in teams of two women. Each team should be assigned three dealers. It is advisable to make these visits at a time when the storekeeper or manager is not too busy to confer with you.

3. It is suggested that the members of your committee introduce themselves to the owner, manager or clerk in attendance; and, where the purpose of the ACCW [Archdiocesan Council of Catholic Women] Decency Crusade is not already known, a short explanation should be given, stressing the need for the protection of the morality of youth. Next, show the ACCW list of objectionable publications. Courteously request the privilege of examining the display of publications for sale.

4. Where no objectionable titles are found, the committee should commend the owner or manager. Favorable publicity should be given this dealer in your church publication.

5. Where objectionable titles are found, courteously recommend that the manager or owner remove such publications from sale. When the dealer complies, favorable publicity should be given him in your church publication.

6. Instruct your committee workers to leave silently if the owner, manager or clerk refuses cooperation. Little is ever gained by argument, but silence can often be most effective.

7. Report any refusal of cooperation to your pastor or moderator. Future action should be determined by him.[34]

By 1954, horror comics had become a topic of interest for the U.S. Congress. The Senate's Subcommittee to Investigate Juvenile Delinquency of the Committee on the Judiciary held hearings in April and June of that year on the subject of horror comics. William Gaines appeared at one of the subcommittee sessions to defend his creations.

At one point in the hearings, Senator Estes Kefauver (D-Tennessee) displayed a copy of Gaines's *Crime SuspenStories* showing a man with a bloody axe holding a woman's head that had been severed from her body and asked Gaines "Do you think that is in good taste?" Gaines replied, "Yes sir; I do, for the cover of a horror comic. A cover in bad taste, for example, might be defined as holding the head a little higher so that the neck could be seen dripping blood from it and moving the body over a little further so that the neck of the body could be seen to be bloody."[35]

As had the film industry before it, the comic magazine industry decided early on to act on its own before some form of censorship was imposed on it. In 1948, 14 publishers met to establish the Association of Comics Magazine Publishers (ACMP). The primary purpose of the organization was to write a code of ethics dealing with the presentation of crime and violence in comic magazines. Six years later, the ACMP was restructured as the Comics Magazine Association of America (CMAA), which updated and rereleased its code of ethics. The CMAA code provides guidelines for the treatment of crime, violence, obscene and vulgar language, and sexual images and is now updated on a regular basis.

The self-policing actions of the comic magazine industry appear to have satisfied to a large extent the complaints raised by groups such as the NODL and the Cincinnati committee. In any case, concerns about horror comics were very soon superseded by a new and rapidly growing issue, the question of violence in yet another form of mass communication: television.

The Rise of Television

Critics of violence in comic magazines could scarcely have imagined in the 1940s and 1950s that the battle they were fighting would soon be replayed on an even broader screen: that of the television set. The penetration of television in the United States mass communication market occurred so quickly that most people alive today can scarcely remember or imagine a time when television was not a dominant factor in American culture. Yet, in 1950, at the height of the comic magazine debate, only 9 percent of American homes had televisions, a total of 3,880,000 sets.

A year later that number rose to 10,320,000 sets in 23.5 percent of all homes, and by the end of another year, the totals were 15,300,000 sets in 34.2 percent of all American households. A decade later (in 1962), 90 percent of all homes had at least one television set, with the total number of sets in use having reached 48,855,000. By 1978, the number of television sets in homes was continuing to rise by about a million a year, and the percent of homes in which at least one set could be found had leveled off at 98 percent, where it has remained ever since.[36]

If Steven Starker's hypothesis about the tendency of new media to evoke warnings about the dangers of that medium is correct, one would expect to hear such comments about television early on. And such is just the case. In testifying before the Senate Subcommittee on Juvenile Delinquency in 1954, for example, psychiatrist Edward Podolsky warned that

> Seeing constant brutality, viciousness and unsocial acts results in hardness, intense selfishness, even in mercilessness, proportionate to the amount of exposure and its play on the native temperament of the child. Some cease to show resentment to insults, to indignities, and even cruelty toward helpless old people, to women and other children.[37]

Seven years later, Newton Minow, President John F. Kennedy's chairman of the Federal Communications Commission, made one of the most famous of all indictments of television programming. In a speech before the National Association of Broadcasters, he invited listeners to sit down and watch television for a day. His prediction:

> I can assure you that you will observe a vast wasteland. You will see a procession of game shows, violence, audience participation shows, formula comedies about totally unbelievable families, blood and thunder, mayhem, violence, sadism, murder, western badmen, western goodmen, private eyes, gangsters, more violence, and cartoons.[38]

Like Podolsky and Minow, critics of television have often found televised violence to be an easy target. And in many cases, the kind of criticisms that have been offered closely parallel those lodged against motion pictures in the preceding 60 years. But the issue of violence in television differs from that of violence in films for two important reasons, however. In the first place, televised violence has been subjected to far more extensive research analysis than was ever the case with films. Questions as to how much violence can be found on television, what the nature of that violence is, and how televised violence affects people, especially children, have been the subject of more than 1,000 studies in the past

40 years. In fact, Professor Aletha C. Huston, chairwoman of the American Psychological Association's Task Force on Television and Society, told a congressional subcommittee in 1988 that "there is more published research on this topic [the effects of televised violence] than on almost any other social issue of our time."[39]

Secondly, the federal government has become much more involved in the question of televised violence than was ever the case with violence in films. At least part of the reason for that fact has been the growing concern over the place of violence in American society that has been developing since the 1960s. At least four major governmental commissions in the last 30 years have studied the question of violence on television and its impact on the viewing public.

The growth of these two new forces, research and governmental involvement, have fed on each other—with federal funding acting as the driving force behind much of the research on televised violence, and the results of that research acting as the driving force behind the development of federal policy on that topic. Thus, while research and policy making can be separated for purposes of discussion in the pages that follow, the reader should always keep in mind the close connection between the two.

Research on Televised Violence

It is easy enough for critics to berate the spread of violence in television programming and its increasing saturation of the market. But the debate over televised violence can be placed on a more stable foundation if there are data that tell exactly how many violent acts occur during a given period, what kinds of violence are involved, who the perpetrators and the victims of violence are, what the messages of violent acts are, and so on. A variety of research programs have been developed to provide these data.

For example, the Center for Media and Public Affairs in Washington, D.C., has conducted two studies, one in 1992 and one in 1994, known as "A Day of TV Violence." These studies, sponsored by the Harry Frank Guggenheim Foundation, were each conducted over a single 18-hour day on ten television channels. Among the data tabulated were the amount and kinds of violence portrayed, the differences across various types of outlets (network, educational, independent, and cable stations), the context in which violent acts were presented, the presence of violence in commercials and news programs, and the presence of antiviolence public service announcements.[40] The results of these studies showed that the number of violent acts observed increased by 41 percent from 1992 to 1994, and the rate of violent acts per hour increased from an average of 103 in 1992 to 145 in 1994.[41]

A far more detailed and extensive approach to the collection of data about televised violence has been the series of studies conducted by George Gerbner, Dean Emeritus of the Annenberg School of Communication at the University of Pennsylvania, and his colleagues over the past three decades. Gerbner first became involved in the problems of measuring televised violence in the mid-1960s. At the request of the National Commission on the Causes and Prevention of Violence, he was asked to design a research program similar to the "Day of TV Violence" studies described above. In 1967 and 1968, Gerbner and his coworkers counted the number of violent acts in plays, films, and cartoons televised by the three commercial television networks over two representative weeks.

In 1969, Gerbner was awarded a grant by the National Institute of Mental Health to improve and expand his system of observation. That grant and similar awards from other federal agencies continued to support Gerbner's work over the next 25 years. During that time, he and his colleagues invented a number of concrete measures for the quantity and quality of violent acts shown on television.

For example, Gerbner created the Violence Profile, which consists of four parts: (1) the program context in which a violent act occurs, (2) the prevalence, rate, and roles of violent acts observed, (3) the power structure portrayed in the violent act as indicated by the kinds of individuals and groups that make up the perpetrators and victims of those acts, and (4) the extent and ways in which television presents its own views of facts and social realities in its conceptions of its audiences.[42] A short section of a Violence Profile, as taken from a 1977 House Subcommittee on Communications hearing, is reproduced on pages 24–25.

The data needed to construct a Violence Profile, which Gerbner and his associates collect each year, come from a precise system of measuring violent acts known as Message System Analysis (MSA). MSA is a research technique designed to be as scientifically accurate as possible for measuring all the elements of televised acts— number, rate, type, setting, power structures, etc.—observed during a research period.

The kind of data collected and reported by Gerbner is designed for use by governmental and nongovernmental bodies that are

Table 1: All Programs, All Networks

	67–68	69–71	1972	1973	1974	S1975	1975	S1976	1976	TOTAL
SAMPLES: 100% *(Number)*										
Programs (plays) analyzed	183	335	100	99	96	96	111	115	110	1245
Program hours analyzed	120.5	209.2	72.0	75.2	76.0	74.5	77.3	75.7	71.6	852.0
Leading characters analyzed	455	825	300	359	346	282	364	300	291	3522
PREVALENCE *(Percent)*										
(%P) Programs containing violence	81.4	80.6	79.0	72.7	83.3	78.1	78.4	76.5	89.1	80.2
Program hours containing violence	85.1	83.0	84.2	79.7	86.8	81.9	83.0	80.6	89.5	83.7
RATE *(Number)*										
Number of violent episodes	872	611	539	524	522	516	626	559	680	6449
(R/P) Rate per all programs (plays)	4.8	4.8	5.4	5.3	5.4	5.4	5.6	4.9	6.2	5.2
(R/H) Rate per all hours	7.2	7.7	7.5	7.0	6.9	6.9	8.1	7.4	9.5	7.6
Duration of violent episodes (hrs)	—	—	—	3.2	3.8	3.8	3.6	3.1	4.4	21.9
ROLES *(Percent of leading characters)*										
Violents (committing violence)	52.7	48.6	39.3	34.5	40.8	46.5	43.1	44.7	60.8	46.1
Victims (subjected to violence)	60.4	55.9	49.7	48.2	51.2	61.3	53.8	54.3	64.6	55.5
(%V) Any involvement in violence	69.5	64.0	58.3	55.7	60.7	69.5	64.8	63.3	74.9	64.4
Killers (committing fatal violence)	11.6	5.9	7.7	5.8	9.8	10.3	6.3	6.7	6.5	7.7
Killed (victims of lethal violence)	5.5	3.0	4.7	3.3	5.8	5.0	3.6	3.7	3.1	4.1
(%K) Any involvement in killing	15.4	7.6	9.7	7.5	13.6	12.1	9.1	9.3	8.2	10.1
Violents : Victims Ratio	-1.15	-1.15	-1.26	-1.40	-1.26	-1.32	-1.25	-1.22	-1.06	-1.20
Killers : Killed Ratio	+2.12	+1.96	+1.64	+1.75	+1.70	+2.07	+1.64	+1.82	+2.11	+1.88
INDICATORS OF VIOLENCE										
Program Score: PS = (%P) + 2(R/P) + 2(R/H)	105.4	105.6	104.8	97.3	107.9	102.7	105.8	101.0	120.5	105.7
Character V-Score: CS = (%V) + (%K)	84.8	71.6	68.0	63.2	74.3	81.6	73.9	72.7	83.2	74.5
Violence Index: VI = PS + CS	190.3	177.3	172.8	160.5	182.2	184.3	179.7	173.7	203.6	180.2

Table 2: All Family-Hour Programs

	67–68	69–71	1972	1973	1974	S1975	1975	S1976	1976	TOTAL
SAMPLES: 100% (*Number*)										
Programs (plays) analyzed	74	101	27	32	29	25	31	30	25	374
Program hours analyzed	57.0	78.3	23.5	29.0	27.0	23.0	21.5	18.8	20.0	298.1
Leading characters analyzed	205	284	98	110	109	73	105	79	69	1132
PREVALENCE (*Percent*)										
(%P) Programs containing violence	77.0	64.4	74.1	56.3	69.0	56.0	51.6	53.3	72.0	65.2
Program hours containing violence	85.1	75.7	85.1	70.7	77.8	67.4	60.5	60.2	77.5	75.3
RATE (*Number*)										
Number of violent episodes	363	318	122	147	108	85	77	87	94	1401
(R/P) Rate per all programs (plays)	4.9	3.1	4.5	4.6	3.7	3.4	2.5	2.9	3.8	3.7
(R/H) Rate per all hours	6.4	4.1	5.2	5.1	4.0	3.7	3.6	4.6	4.7	4.7
Duration of violent episodes (hrs)	—	—	—	0.9	1.0	0.7	0.5	0.6	0.7	4.4
ROLES (*Percent of leading characters*)										
Violents (committing violence)	48.8	35.6	37.8	29.1	29.4	35.6	16.2	27.8	42.0	35.0
Victims (subjected to violence)	57.6	39.8	40.8	33.6	36.7	42.5	27.6	26.6	43.5	40.5
(%V) Any involvement in violence	66.3	47.2	50.0	40.9	45.0	47.9	36.2	38.0	55.1	48.9
Killers (committing fatal violence)	16.6	6.3	4.1	6.4	12.8	8.2	1.0	1.3	1.4	7.6
Killed (victims of lethal violence)	6.3	2.5	3.1	4.5	7.3	2.7	0.0	0.0	0.0	3.4
(%K) Any involvement in killing	20.5	8.1	5.1	10.0	16.5	9.6	1.0	1.3	1.4	9.6
Violents : Victims Ratio	-1.18	-1.12	-1.08	-1.16	-1.25	-1.19	-1.71	+1.05	-1.03	-1.16
Killers : Killed Ratio	+2.62	+2.57	+1.33	+1.40	+1.75	+3.00	+0.00	+0.00	+0.00	+2.26
INDICATORS OF VIOLENCE										
Program Score: PS = (%P) + 2(R/P) + 2(R/H)	99.6	78.8	93.5	75.6	84.4	70.2	63.7	68.4	88.9	82.1
Character V-Score: CS = (%V) + (%K)	86.8	55.3	55.1	50.9	61.5	57.5	37.1	39.2	56.5	58.6
Violence Index: VI = PS + CS	186.4	134.1	148.6	126.5	145.9	127.7	100.9	107.6	145.4	140.7

interested in tracking the level of violence on television. When television networks say that they are aware of the problem of televised violence and are working to reduce that level (as they generally tend to say), does the Violence Profile show evidence of such changes? If television networks agree to new broadcasting standards committed to the reduction of violence on television (as they have in the past), can actual changes in programming be detected by the Violence Profile?

Members of the television broadcasting community have long taken issue with attempts to measure the amount of violence portrayed on television. Gerbner's research has, of course, been a frequent target of such criticisms. In April 1977, for example, Jack Schneider, president of CBS, wrote Congressman Lionel Van Deerlin, chairman of the House Subcommittee on Communications of the Committee on Interstate and Foreign Commerce, about this issue. He claimed that Gerbner's Violence Profile included "at least four basic—and fatal—flaws." Those flaws, according to Schneider, were:

1. The Gerbner Violence Index is not, and does not claim to be, a measure of the amount of violence on television. Unfortunately, it is so interpreted. Actually, Dr. Gerbner introduces a number of extraneous factors, so that violence can go down while the Violence Index shows an increase. Indeed, that is what happened in his latest study. His own figures show that the number of incidents of violence in the family hour on the CBS Television Network declined from 20 to 11, but his Violence Index claims an increase, apparently because we had the "wrong people" involved in the action.

2. Because of these problems, the Gerbner Index cannot be used as an indicator of whether the trend is up or down in televised violence.

3. Dr. Gerbner only measures one week of television, which can lead to statistical errors of horrendous proportion. There is no longer any "typical" week of television. Our own 13-week monitoring which will be made available to you shortly, shows that the week with the highest amount of violence has from two and a half to three times more incidents of violence than the week with the lowest amount.

4. Finally, the Gerbner definition of violence is highly
   questionable, including, as it does, comedic violence
   and acts of nature. Indeed, you may recall that
   members of your Committee pressed Dr. Gerbner
   on this issue, without satisfactory resolution.[43]

Schneider then provided Representative Van Deerlin with an extensive analysis of televised violence on the CBS television network prepared by its own department of research.

Gerbner's response to the CBS letter came three weeks later.
In addition to a point-by-point refutation of the CBS complaints,
Gerbner argued that

The CBS objections to our Violence Index and Profile
stem from an inadequate conception of the task of scientific research. They reflect a corporate defense mechanism rather than a broad and multi-faceted investigation
into the nature and effects of television violence. As our
accompanying analysis of the CBS report shows, that
basic misconception, coupled with questionable
methods, makes the CBS contentions scientifically
unacceptable.[44]

The contretemps between CBS and Gerbner are described in
some detail here because they reflect the ongoing battle between
television network executives and their critics. In hearing after
hearing, and in other public forums, these two parties and their
allies continually go back and forth at each other with this kind of
"yes, it is"/"no, it isn't" debate. That debate always seems to involve more and more complex data and more and more sophisticated methods of analysis—but these seldom bring the two parties
any closer to an agreement as to whether televised violence is becoming more or less of a problem for the culture.

The Effects of Televised Violence

Hundreds of research studies have been done over the last four
decades in an effort to identify the effects that televised violence
may have on viewers. In general, these studies can be grouped
into one of two large categories: laboratory studies and field, or
"natural," studies.

One of the classic lines of laboratory research has been that
carried out by Albert Bandura and his colleagues. These

experiments involve the use of a Bobo doll, a three-foot tall inflatable plastic toy. Young children are divided into two or more groups, one or more of which is shown violent episodes on television and one of which is not.

Children from each group are then taken individually into a separate room where they are given a variety of toys to play with, including a Bobo doll. Bandura's researchers found that children who had watched scenes of aggression on television were about twice as likely to attack the Bobo doll as were children who saw no televised violence. Bandura drew three conclusions from studies such as these.

1. The experience [of viewing violence on television] tends to reduce the child's inhibitions against acting in a violent, aggressive manner.
2. The experience helps to shape the *form* of the child's aggressive behavior. Most of the children from the first three [experimental] groups sat on the Bobo doll and punched its nose, beat it on the head with a mallet, tossed it into the air and kicked it around the room. . . .
3. Our observations led us to a third, and highly significant, conclusion. We noticed that a person displaying violence on film is as influential as one displaying it in real life.[45]

Representatives of the television industry have not been convinced by the results reported by researchers such as Bandura. At the conclusion of a long paper detailing the "many flaws" of such studies, as viewed by industry scientists, Dr. Joseph T. Klapper summarizes the views of the CBS Office of Social Research, of which he was long head.

It is impossible to predict accurately or even usefully from the results of the laboratory studies reviewed here to everyday viewing situations, partly because individual differences in response to the stimuli used were ignored in the reports. Additionally, the stimuli used were often vastly different from the materials of ordinary exposure in relation to several crucial elements and the behaviors and contexts of behavior used in indices of effect were so contrived as to resemble ordinary life only tenuously. The investigators who have linked the laboratory results with real-life events have done so by the device of using the same generalized label—e.g., "aggression," "violence," "punitiveness"—to bracket quite different behavioral referents. Thus far, the connection between the kinds of behavior thus bracketed remains theoretical and hypothetical.[46]

Another approach to the study of the effects of television viewing may be classified as field or "natural" studies. In such studies, investigators attempt to use children, teenagers, and adults in their own home settings, rather than bringing them into a laboratory (as, for example, with the Bobo experiments). Many variations on this theme are possible. For example, subjects can be subdivided into two groups, those that have television sets at home and those that do not. One can then study evidence of aggressive behavior within the two groups to see if any differences exist. Another approach is to study violent behavior in a community *before* and *after* television has become available to the community.

One of the classical examples of this type of "natural" study is the longitudinal research originally devised by Monroe M. Lefkowitz, Leonard D. Eron, Leopold O. Walder, and L. Rowell Huesmann. That study began in 1960 when researchers worked with 875 third-graders in Columbia County, New York. Using a variety of tests, the researchers looked for correlations between television viewing and aggressive behavior in the subjects. That behavior was measured using four techniques: peer ratings, parent ratings, a personality test, and a self-report questionnaire.

Ten years later, the researchers returned to Columbia County and repeated their studies. They were interested in finding out whether television viewing might have had long-term affects on the boys in their original sample. In the summary of the first decade of their research, investigators concluded that they "have presented compelling evidence that there is a probable causative influence of watching violent television programs in early years on a boy's later aggressiveness."[47]

The Columbia County studies have now been continued into the 1990s with a further finding that "those children who watched the most violent television as youngsters grew up to engage in the most aggressive behavior as adults, from spouse abuse to drunk driving."[48]

After nearly a half century of research in both laboratory and "natural" settings—and approximately 1,000 individual studies—

what can be said about the effects of televised violence on viewers? It has become something of a cottage industry among psychologists, sociologists, and media experts to try answering that question. The bibliography provided in chapter 6 of this book lists a number of publications that try to summarize the results of these studies in greater or lesser detail.

One of the books listed in chapter 6, *Big World, Small Screen* by Aletha C. Huston et al., reports on the results of an extensive review of the literature in psychology dealing with television and society. The conclusion reached by the authors of this book about the relationship between television and violence is as follows:

> The accumulated research clearly demonstrates a correlation between viewing violence and aggressive behavior—that is, heavy viewers behave more aggressively than light viewers. Children and adults who watch a large number of aggressive programs also tend to hold attitudes and values that favor the use of aggression to resolve conflicts. There correlations are solid. They remain even when many other potential influences on viewing and aggression are controlled, including education level, social class, aggressive attitudes, parental behavior, and sex-role identity.

With regard to the causal relationship between television viewing and aggressive behavior, the authors went on to say that

> Both experimental and longitudinal studies support the hypothesis that viewing violence is causally associated with aggression. Studies conducted with preschoolers, school-aged children, college students, and adults confirm that viewing violence on television can lead to increases in aggressive attitudes, values, and behavior.[49]

Government Studies on Violence and Television

Some of the most ambitious efforts to understand the relationship between television viewing and aggressive behavior have been those associated with investigations and committees of the federal government. One of the earliest efforts was a set of hearings held in 1954 by Senator Estes Kefauver's (D-Tennessee) Subcommittee on Juvenile Delinquency. The subcommittee heard a series of comments from critics who felt that the level of violence presented in television programming was too high. In response to these criticisms, executives of the major television networks acknowledged that a modest problem might exist, and that the industry would begin a program of research to find out more about the frequency of violent acts in television programs and the effects that such violence might have on viewers.[50]

Seven years later, in 1961, the issue of televised violence resurfaced before the same Senate subcommittee, now chaired by Senator Thomas Dodd (D-Connecticut). By this time, the exchange between critics of televised violence and network executives was beginning to have a familiar ring. The former charged that the level of violence on television had not decreased since the Kefauver hearings in 1954—and had probably increased—in spite of promises from network executives that "something would be done." In response, those executives assured their critics and the legislators before whom they appeared that they were really serious about investigating this problem now. In fact, they indicated that they were in the initial stages of planning a major research and training center at an important university that would investigate the effects of television on viewers.[51]

At the same hearing, the president of the National Association of Broadcasters (NAB) explained why the research program promised to the Kefauver Subcommittee in 1954 had not yet taken place. The association had since learned, he said, that the CBS television network had planned a massive study of the effects of television on viewers, and the NAB felt that it should wait to see the results of that study.

In fact, the CBS study (finally released in 1963) was one of four such research investigations completed by each of the three major television networks. Such studies, in general, tended not to find any harmful effects of televised violence on viewers. A study conducted by Milavsky, Kessler, Stipp, and Rubens for the NBC television network, for example, reported that there was no evidence to support the hypothesis that viewing violence contributed to aggressive behavior in a sample of boys. Interestingly enough, a committee of media experts who later reviewed these findings came to a different conclusion, arguing that the data *did* support such a relationship.[52]

As evidence of their commitment to learning more about the effects of televised violence, the three major networks agreed to a collaboration in 1962 with the U.S. Department of Health, Education, and Welfare to support a joint Committee for Research on

Television and Children. The purpose of the committee was to solicit and fund research projects dealing with the question of televised violence and its effects on viewers. After two years of operation, the committee had produced only modest results. It had funded only three research studies. Of these, according to one observer, one study

> constituted a criticism and analysis of the inadequacies of research which was detrimental to the industry, not an investigation of the actual effects. The second was conducted by [a researcher] who believed that TV violence was not harmful and might in some cases even help to drain off aggressive impulses. The third study was not even completed.[53]

Network executives and their critics marched to Capitol Hill once again in 1964 to testify before the Senate Subcommittee on Juvenile Delinquency, with little new emanating from either side of the debate. The subcommittee's final report on the hearings made it clear that the senators realized they were hearing the same old story, over and over again. The report noted that the Broadcasting Code for television adopted by the National Association of Broadcasters in 1952 had not been very effective.

> The industry's claim that this Code is an effective vehicle cannot be substantiated in light of the evidence of chronic violation. Network programming policies which deliberately call for the insertion of violence, crime and brutality are hardly conducive to building respect for any central authority within the industry.[54]

While acknowledging that "self-policing" was still the best way to deal with problems of televised violence, the report concluded that "the patience of Congress, though considerable, is not endless. The public's demand for concrete results grows more intense, and indeed it should."

In 1968, the first of three major federal studies focused its attention on the problems of violence in television. This study, the National Commission on the Causes and Prevention of Violence, was created by action of President Lyndon Johnson on 6 June 1968 and was chaired by Dr. Milton Eisenhower. The commission was created largely in response to the outbreak of civil violence that manifested itself in antiwar protests of the late 1960s and domestic violence such as the Watts Riots of 1965 and 1966.

One goal of the commission was to review research on televised violence to see what it could learn about the ways in which such violence might contribute to violent activities by children, youth, and adults. Unlike the surgeon general's study that was to follow shortly in 1973, the Eisenhower commission funded no new studies, but relied on an analysis of existing research for its conclusions on this topic. Those conclusions were as follows:

> We believe it is reasonable to conclude that a constant diet of violent behavior on television has an adverse effect on human character and attitudes. Violence on television encourages violent forms of behavior, and fosters moral and social values about violence in daily life which are unacceptable in a civilized society.
>
> We do not suggest that television is a principal cause of violence in our society. We do suggest that it is a contributing factor. Television, of course, operates in a complex social setting and its effects are undoubtedly mitigated by other social influences. But it is a matter for grave concern that at a time when the values and the influence of traditional institutions such as family, church, and school are in question, television is emphasizing violent, antisocial styles of life.[55]

In one respect, the most important single commission or committee ever to deal with the issue of televised violence was the Surgeon General's Scientific Advisory Committee on Television and Social Behavior, appointed by Secretary of Health, Education, and Welfare (HEW) Robert Finch in 1969. For some time, Senator John Pastore (D-Rhode Island), chairman of the Subcommittee on Communications of the Senate's Commerce Committee, had been concerned about what he saw as the lack of sufficient reliable data on the effects of televised violence. In a 1969 letter Pastore wrote to Finch that he was "troubled by the lack of any definite information which would help resolve the question of whether there is a causal connection between televised crime and violence and antisocial behavior of individuals, especially children." Pastore requested that Finch

> Direct the Surgeon General to appoint a committee comprised of distinguished men and women from whatever professions and disciplines deemed appropriate to devise techniques and to conduct a study under his

supervision using those techniques which will establish scientifically insofar as possible what harmful effects, if any, these programs have on children.[56]

The surgeon general's committee was surrounded by controversy from the moment it began searching for members until the day it published its final report . . . and for years thereafter. At the outset, the television industry apparently exerted considerable influence on the selection of committee members. A list of prospective members was sent to the three national television networks with the request that they indicate the names of any individuals "you would believe would *not* be appropriate for an impartial scientific investigation of this nature." As a result of this request, some highly respected scholars who had studied the problem of televised violence for many years were deleted from the list of prospective members. Among these were Albert Bandura, Otto Larsen, and Percy Tannenbaum.[57]

The surgeon general's committee laid out an ambitious plan for its work. In addition to commissioning an exhaustive review of the existing literature on the effects of televised violence, it funded a number of original research studies on the topic. The committee's final report, issued on 19 January 1972, consisted of seven volumes. The first was the final report itself, consisting of the committee's general conclusions and its recommendations to the secretary of HEW. The other six volumes consisted of reports on research in five general areas and a bibliography on the effects of television viewing on children. The five research areas were "Media Content and Control," "Television and Social Learning," "Television and Adolescent Aggression," "Television in Day-to-Day Life: Patterns of Use," and "Television's Effects: Further Explorations."

The committee's final conclusions were somewhat mixed and confusing, as was apparent from the public reaction it received. Some observers claimed that the committee found essentially no relationship between televised violence and a person's behavior, while others felt that the committee had supported the view that violence on television was likely to increase aggressive behavior among viewers. A detailed and intriguing analysis of the confused response to the committee's report can be found in a book by Douglas Cater and Stephen Strickland, *TV Violence and the Child: The Evolution and Fate of the Surgeon General's Report.*[58]

When Surgeon General Jesse L. Steinfeld, to whom the final report was officially addressed, was asked to explain its fundamental meaning to the Senate Subcommittee on Communications in March 1972, he said, in part

> While the Committee report is carefully phrased and qualified in language acceptable to social scientists, it is clear to me that the causal relationship between televised violence and antisocial behavior is sufficient to warrant appropriate and immediate remedial action. The data on social phenomena such as television and violence and/or aggressive behavior will never be clear enough for all social scientists to agree on the formulation of a succinct statement of causality. But there comes a time when the data are sufficient to justify action. That time has come.[59]

Perhaps a more precise explanation of the committee's final conclusions were provided by Robert Liebert who reviewed five of the major research projects completed for the "Television and Social Learning" section of the project. Liebert's remarks fall into the *some*-effects/*some*-viewers/under-*some*-circumstances rubric. He concluded:

> At least under some circumstances, exposure to televised aggression can lead children to accept what they have seen as a partial guide for their own actions. As a result, the present entertainment offerings of the television medium may be contributing, in some measure, to the aggressive behavior of many normal children. Such an effect has now been shown in a wide variety of situations.[60]

The Network Studies

Television network promises to study the issue of televised violence turned out not to be completely a public relations ploy by the industry. Each of the three major networks did, indeed, commission research studies on the issue and, in the case of CBS, two studies.[61]

Of the four studies eventually completed, three found, in general, no evidence that violence on television causes aggressive behavior by viewers. The fourth study, by William A. Belson, used as its subjects 1,500 male adolescents in London. After eight years of research, Belson came to the conclusion that "high exposure to television violence increases the degree to which boys engage in serious violence." CBS was apparently not particularly impressed by Belson's work since it gave only modest publicity to his findings.[62]

Of the three remaining studies, one (Milgram and Shotland) was an expensive ($500,000) but conceptually modest piece of research in which viewer reactions to three different versions of CBS's *Medical Center* were studied. The authors concluded, "If television is on trial, the judgment of this investigation must be the Scottish verdict: Not proven."[63] This study was later subjected to a reanalysis by communications expert George Comstock, who pointed out a number of methodological flaws in the work.[64]

The ABC research project consisted of a review of research on televised violence and its effects on viewers by psychiatrist Melvin S. Heller and attorney Samuel Polsky. The Heller/Polsky study was never released to the general public in book form, but was of a character to convince network executives, apparently, that "TV violence was not a matter to be concerned about any longer."[65] Again, the network research was reexamined by experts from outside the industry and, like the Milgram and Shotland work, was found to contain a number of methodological problems.[66]

The fourth study was funded by NBC and directed by sociologist J. Ronald Milavsky. It was a three-year longitudinal study of the effect of televised violence on children and teenagers in Minneapolis and Fort Worth. The investigators found a correlation between television viewing and aggressive behavior that was statistically significant, but they made some adjustments in their calculations that they felt were justified—with the result that the correlation was no longer significant.[67]

One More Government Study

The last great federally funded study of violence on television was conducted in the early 1980s. The National Institute of Mental Health (NIMH) selected a prestigious panel of experts to examine the evidence that had been collected about televised violence in the decade since the surgeon general's Scientific Advisory Committee had completed its research.[68]

In its 1982 report, the NIMH panel took a stronger position than had the surgeon general's committee ten years earlier. Violence on television, it concluded does lead to aggressive behavior by children and teenagers who watch the programs. This conclusion is based on laboratory experiments and on field studies. Not all children become aggressive, of course, but the correlations between violence and aggression are positive. In magnitude, television violence is as strongly correlated with aggressive behavior as any other behavioral variable that has been measured. The research question has moved from asking whether or not there is an effect, to seeking explanations for the effect.[69]

As might be expected, television industry executives were still not convinced by what many media experts now saw as the definitive statement on televised violence. One of the objections raised by representatives of the industry was how serious the aggressiveness was that researchers had decided was caused by televised violence. It is quite a different matter, they pointed out, to observe that children are more likely to hit a Bobo doll with a paddle after watching violence on television than to conclude, therefore, that televised violence contributes to the development of criminal personalities.[70]

The debate churned back and forth in congressional hearings and in the public media. The ABC television network, for example, published a detailed critique of the NIMH report entitled *A Research Perspective on Television and Violence*. In it, the network responded point by point to the major conclusions of the NIMH study. For example, it headed one section:

NIMH Conclusion No. 1:
The research findings support the conclusion of a causal relationship between television violence and aggressive behavior.

ABC Response:
The research does not support the conclusion of a causal relationship.[71]

A number of authorities were incensed by the ABC report and by what it saw as stonewalling by the television industry. As part of their response, these authorities polled a large number of experts in the fields of psychology, sociology, and communication. They reported to a congressional hearing that 82 percent of all experts responding to their letter agreed with the principal conclusions of the NIMH report. Interestingly, the level of support for these conclusions ranged from 90 percent of 31 psychologists and 85 percent of 13 communication researchers to 20 percent of 5 sociologists.[72]

Meanwhile, Back in Congress . . .

By the 1990s, there no longer seemed to be much enthusiasm for large government studies of televised violence. Most observers (except for network executives) seemed to have become convinced that televised violence was a problem and that the next question was what to do about it.

One more major study was completed, that by the American Psychological Association (APA) on the effects of television in general.[73] This study devoted relatively little attention (7 out of nearly 200 pages) to the issue of violence in television. Its conclusions were largely similar to those of most preceding studies. It noted that the "accumulated research clearly demonstrates a correlation between viewing violence and aggressive behavior—that is, heavy viewers behave more aggressively than light viewers."

In any case, the action had by now shifted from research laboratories to congressional hearing rooms. Between 1977 and 1993, a variety of subcommittees of the House and Senate conducted at least ten hearings about the issue of violence in television.[74]

Most often, the theme of these hearings was what could be done to protect America's television viewers—especially its younger viewers—from the violence that never seemed to disappear from the screen. The nagging bottom line, of course, was that no one really wanted to talk about censoring offensive shows. Broadcasters' First Amendment rights were just too widely accepted for that possibility to be considered by any but the most radical critics.

Instead, congressional hearings pursued two other possible directions: a self-imposed code of conduct by the industry and a set of technical devices that would allow home viewers to screen out violent programming. The first of these alternatives was the fallback position that media critics and representatives of the industry had long relied on. "Let's hope that media executives *really* care enough about the problems of violence," the argument has always gone, "that they will *voluntarily agree* to a code of conduct that will eliminate the most offensive scenes and programs."

A step in this direction had been attempted once previously. In 1974, Richard E. Wiley, chairman of the Federal Communications Commission, held a number of meetings with the presidents of the three major television networks. Wiley suggested the adoption of a new policy that would keep the evening hours between 7:00 and 9:00 free from programs in which violence and sexual themes were included. In 1975, the National Association of Broadcasters had included these "family viewing hours" within its television broadcasting code.

Polls showed that more than four out of every five viewers agreed with this policy, but an important segment of the population did not: television writers and producers. They saw the policy as an infringement on their First Amendment rights of free expression, and they took the NAB to court to prevent enforcement of that policy. On 4 November 1976, Judge Warren J. Ferguson, of the U.S. District Court for the Central District of California, ruled that the family viewing hour was unconstitutional. The FCC had, Ferguson decided, "jawboned" television executives into adopting a form of censorship that the Constitution prohibited.[75]

Judge Ferguson's decision was overturned by the U.S. Circuit Court of Appeals in 1979, not because the court disagreed with Ferguson's decision, but because it decided the case should be dealt with through the Federal Communications Commission instead of a federal court. As a result of this controversy, the National Association of Broadcasters decided to abandon its family-viewing-time concept and, as Judge Ferguson had recommended, left it up to member stations to determine the suitability of programming during "family viewing hours."[76]

By the time that congressional committees began discussing ways of limiting violence on television in the late 1980s and early 1990s, therefore, they were treading gingerly on a subject thoroughly immersed in issues of First Amendment rights of free speech and expression. For example, one set of congressional hearings was devoted solely to the issue of finding a way of allowing television executives to meet with each other to draw up a code of conduct. Congress was convinced that any effort to hold such meetings would violate federal antitrust laws. They decided that it would be necessary to pass a bill that would specifically grant network executives the right to gather together *for this one purpose only*. Hearings on this bill were held in the spring of 1989 (at which time, those on both sides of the controversy over televised violence continued with their "yes, it is" / "no, it isn't" debate) and the Television Violence Act of 1989 was finally signed by President George Bush the following year.

Having been given permission to meet and discuss televised violence, industry representatives spent the better part of the next two years working on a code of conduct. Finally, in 1992, representatives of the three major networks announced the Standards for the Depiction of Violence in Television Programs.[77]

Some observers were annoyed that the momentous labors of the three great networks had resulted in such a timid product. At yet another congressional hearing in 1993, for example, Representative John Bryant (D-Texas) offered the following comments.

> Here we have the guidelines. They are real whoppers. Number one starts off with this: [Rep. Bryant quotes the first standard: 1) Conflict and strife are the essence of drama and conflict often results in physical or psychological violence. However, all depictions of violence should be relevant and necessary to the development of character, or to the advancement of theme or plot.] Then they get real tough.
>
> Here comes the tough one here. "Gratuitous or excessive depiction of violence are not acceptable" . . .
>
> These are so thoroughly subjective they could be interpreted any way, in a thousand different ways. And I assume, and correct me if I'm wrong, that if you violate these absolutely nothing happens to you. Is that correct?
>
> [Senator Paul Simon responds: "That is correct."]
>
> Well, I think the public ought to be extremely impatient, and the informed public about this topic ought to be angry at us for not being more realistic about this. These guys are not going to do anything unless we hold a club over their head. They are just not going to.
>
> We haven't been talking about this just since 1990 when your [Senator Simon's] bill was passed. This was coming up for years prior to that time. I recall having meetings with industry executives and their lobbyists and bringing up the question of violence and sex on television, and the gratuitous nature of it. Nothing happens unless they are faced with a serious economic threat to them.[78]

It is probably still too soon to tell whether the 1992 network standards will have much effect on the amount of gratuitous violence on television. A 1995 article in *U.S. News & World Report* suggests that there has not been much change in the short term.

> But gratuitous violence is on the rise. "All violence is not equal," says [Director of the UCLA Center for Communication Policy Jeffrey] Cole. "Context is everything, and in some instances, violence is unwarranted and not helpful to the plot. Some movies and made-for-TV movies about crime are just vehicles for violence." Promos for violent shows are especially prone to "condensed violence" with no context.[79]

The second avenue of approach for dealing with violence on television in the 1990s was the use of gimmickry within the television set itself that would allow viewers to block out certain programs carrying unacceptable levels of violence. Of course, as many critics pointed out, such a device already existed: the on/off button. But arguments were presented that a more sophisticated approach was necessary. Some means might be needed, for example, to allow a parent to block certain programs or stations when children were to be alone in the house.

A precedent for this kind of technology already existed. In 1990, the U.S. Congress had passed the Television Decoder Circuitry Act that required the manufacturers of television sets to install a mechanism with the sets they produced that could decode and display closed-captioned messages transmitted with the television picture. Perhaps the development of a similar system for recognizing and blacking out programs that a viewer found objectionable would be a simple and direct solution to the problem of controlling televised violence.

At a hearing of the Subcommittee on Telecommunications and Finance of the House Committee on Energy and Commerce in 1993, a number of proposals were made by experts in the field for television set modifications that would allow the blocking of unwanted television shows. Concepts such as EDS (Extended Data Service), a TeleCommander programmable electronic chip, and a V-chip were all described as ways of blocking programs. Enthusiasm among some members of Congress ran high and at least one bill was later introduced that would require, like the 1990 decoding act, all new televisions to include a V-chip that would allow viewers to block certain programs.[80]

One of the problems with the V-chip concept, however, was that politics was moving faster than technology on this issue. As one observer, Michelle Quinn, wrote in mid-1995: "The chip doesn't exist. No company makes it, nor has any company expressed an interest in doing so."[81]

Engineers testifying at congressional hearings had outlined the way in which V-chip technology could be developed, but this testimony did not take into account the strong objections from TV set manufacturers who claimed that the technology would be too expensive to include in every set manufactured. Broadcasters also objected to the development of a V-chip, claiming that it would be impossible to create a ratings system to which everyone could agree. Quinn completes her review of the V-chip issue as follows:

> The V-chip standards could have been ready by early 1996. But with TV set manufacturers and broadcasters fighting it, the V-chip is years off.
>
> And even then, the V-chip won't be foolproof, [Vice President of the Electronics Industries Association Gary] Shapiro added.
>
> "A smart kid will unplug the television set," he said, "and reset all the ratings."[82]

Some parents and lawmakers were not satisfied even with the V-chip technology, if and when it became available. These critics began talking again about restricting violent television programs to certain evening hours when children were unlikely to be watching. The return to the family-viewing-hour concept indicated how little the debate over televised violence and methods for dealing with the issue had developed in nearly a half century of discussion.[83]

Another turning point in the long battle over violence in television was reached in February 1996. Network executives finally gave up on their long opposition to the use of a rating system for television broadcasts. They agreed to institute a rating system similar to that used by the motion picture industry and, in fact, asked Jack Valenti, chief executive of the Motion Picture Association of America, to head a committee to develop such a system. Executives from all major television networks agreed to a "Statement by All Segments of the Television Industry" that read in part,

> All elements of the TV industry will rise to this challenge, ready to participate in a national voluntary enterprise which we believe will be useful and valuable to the parents of America.[84]

One force driving the executives' decision was the signing into law by President Clinton a few weeks earlier of a telecommunications act that required television manufacturers to begin installing a V-chip in all sets produced in the United States. The V-chip and the ratings system will make it possible for parents to black out programs they don't want their children to watch. Executives indicated that the television rating system should be in operation by January of 1997.

Violent Themes in Popular Music and Video Games: Old Wine in New Bottles

The 1980s and 1990s have seen yet another twist in the continuing debate over violence in the mass media. The newest issues to arise in this controversy involve the use of violent themes in certain types of popular music and video games.

It seems likely that every generation has been at least slightly appalled by the music its children choose to play and listen to. From the Charleston to rock and roll, parents have been bemoaning the fact that "they don't write songs the way they used to." But the post-Vietnam years seem to have spawned new forms of music in which violent and sexual imagery are more pronounced and extreme than had been the case in the past. Perhaps it was no more than a new generation pushing moral boundaries one step beyond the limits their parents had set, but in an era when sexuality and violence had already reached new heights of openness, that next step may have finally been too much for many people.

In any case, many parents had reached the point that they were going to do more than complain; they were going to act. One of the first concrete manifestations of this new determination was the formation in 1985 of the Parents Music Resource Center. The Center was founded in order to educate parents about the sexual and violent themes being presented in much of the popular music then being marketed to children and adolescents. The organization was committed to doing more than simply educate parents, however, and it began an aggressive effort to get the recording industry to "clean up its act" about the kind of music it was producing.

In response to this pressure, the Recording Industry Association of America (RIAA) agreed in 1985 to adopt a parental advisory logo to be affixed to the cover of any recording that contained "explicit lyrics" dealing with sexual or violent themes. The logo itself, shown below, was not actually put into use until five years later. It is one inch by one-half inch in size and is permanently affixed to the CD or cassette cover. Each recording company determines for itself which of its products should have the logo attached.

The impact of the RIAA logo may be difficult to ascertain. One fact is apparent, however. The storm over violent and sexually explicit lyrics in popular music did not diminish to any appreciable extent in the half decade after the logo was put into use. In fact, the furor has probably reached an even higher level, with the major objects of complaint now being a category of music that includes hip-hop and gangsta rap. These musical styles have evolved out of the rhyming sing-song musical form known as rap. They are characterized by a heavy emphasis on violence, sadism, sexual assault, and misogyny. Even to music lovers who enjoy rap music itself, hip-hop and gangsta rap represent a step in the evolution of rap that seems to have gone too far.

On 11 February and 5 May 1994, the Subcommittee on Commerce, Consumer Protection, and Competitiveness of the House Committee on Energy and Commerce held hearings on the problem of violence and sexual content in popular music. Among those who spoke out against some of the themes in hip-hop and gangsta rap was singer Dionne Warwick. In written testimony before the subcommittee, she said:

> I feel the graphic and continued exposure to violence, sexual activities usually reserved and expressed in the privacy of bedrooms, and the appalling abusive use of words in descriptions of women, especially African-American women, via a medium that has long been regarded as the easiest way to get a message across, recordings, and now with the additional help of video used to enhance these recorded messages, I am compelled to ask those who supply these recording and vid-

eos—What and how do you think the mothers, grand-
mothers, sisters, aunts, wives, girlfriends, of the providers of "Gangsta Rap" products feel each time any of
these recordings are played, or videos shown depicting
and expounding the total disrespect and disregard for
the African-American woman specifically, and women
generally?

I can, and will, speak for myself.

I'm hurt, I'm angered, I'm disappointed, and will no
longer sit passively allowing this degradation to be continued by "our children."

In short, I'm tired, and I've had enough.[85]

The response from producers of hip-hop and gangsta rap have been
entirely predictable. A rap artist's style of music is, they say, nothing more than that artist's way of expressing his or her views of
the world around us. They are simply a form of free speech and
free expression guaranteed by the First Amendment. For example,
rap singer Yolanda Whitaker, who performs under the name of Yo
Yo for EastWest Records, told members of the Subcommittee:

Being from the hood, neighborhood, I can tell you that
violence didn't start from a cassette tape that might have
been popped into a home or car stereo system. Whitney
Houston sells more records than any rapper. Why isn't
that man's kids emulating her? Why is it our fault? We
are the product of America your generation created.
Don't shut us down. Hear us out.[86]

At the same hearing, a recording industry executive invoked
the same theme.

These young men and women are passionate about
what they feel. They are poetic. They are very innova-
tive and creative in their expression, but if nothing else,
at this meeting you should be able to come away with
an awareness of the fears and frustrations that they are
so constantly expressing, that is so deeply rooted in their
spirits and their lyrics.

How can rap continually be blamed for the increased
violence in our communities baffles me when the violence was here long before rap music and much longer
than the gangsta rap that has been here. Rap artists ver-
balize their reality. They do not celebrate that reality.[87]

The debate over rap music has foundered—as it has with respect to the other forms of media discussed in this chapter—over the issue of free speech. The basic questions remain the same. Should hip-hop and gangsta rap performers be allowed to say *anything at all* in their lyrics? Is it possible to show a clear connection between their messages of violence and misogyny and the way listeners behave in their lives? What can the general public, the government, or the industry do to provide some control over offensive lyrics without censoring a performer's right of free speech?

The Arts Censorship Project of the American Civil Liberties Union (ACLU) has repeatedly warned about the dangers of censoring speech with which we may not be comfortable, even though it does not present a clear and present danger to the society. A statement of the ACLU policy on this issue was printed in one of its "Briefer" reports.

> The battle over music censorship isn't over. The self-appointed music police will continue to try to impose their personal morality and politics on all of us. The American Civil Liberties Union believes that forcing everyone to conform to the preferences of a few runs counter to our nation's most basic values. Defending the First Amendment rights of all Americans to create, perform and hear music of their own choosing remains one of our highest priorities.[88]

A second set of hearings in 1994, before the Subcommittee on Telecommunications and Finance of the House Committee on Energy and Commerce, tried to deal with this issue with regard to video games. The term *video game* as used here refers to any interactive system in which a player can modify the actions of characters displayed on a video screen by means of some kind of control mechanism such as a joystick. Improvements in technology have made possible highly complex game situations and eye-catching displays that combine to captivate a large number of children and young adults (as well as older adults).

Many of the video games that have been developed involve a high level of violent action. The question that arises again, then, is whether and to what extent the playing of video games that contain violent themes affects the everyday behaviors of players. Is a boy or girl of age ten, for example, who plays video games two hours a day more likely to behave aggressively in his or her own life? So far, only a modest amount of research has been done on this question. In one such study involving the video games Space Invaders and Roadrunners, researchers found that both games tend to raise the level of aggression and lower the level of pro-social play in the sample of five-year-old children who were studied.[89]

The review in which the above research is cited goes on to say, however, that "the effects of video violence are less simple, however, than they at first appeared."[90] Some of the factors involved in determining such effects are the age of children studied, whether games are cooperative or competitive in nature, and whether they are played with another person or alone.

Some authorities have apparently already made up their minds about this issue, however. In testimony before the Subcommittee on Telecommunications and Finance in 1994, a representative of the American Medical Association said that

> While the impact of violent video games is not as clearly established as the impact of violent television programming (which has been substantiated by decades of studies), we are extremely fearful of a potential link between violent video games and aggression. We are concerned that playing violent video games, with their now fully digitalized human images, will promote children becoming more aggressive towards other children and becoming more tolerant of (and more likely to engage in) "real-life" violence.[91]

What can be done to control the level of violence in video games? The answers that have been suggested for that question have a sadly familiar ring. The American Medical Association, for example, has suggested that a written message appear at the beginning of every video game in which a character is killed:

> THIS IS A GAME THAT SHOWS MURDER AND KILLING. IT IS ONLY A VIDEO GAME, BUT IN REAL LIFE, MURDER AND KILLING IS PERMANENT. IT IS VERY WRONG, IT CAUSES A LOT OF PAIN AND SADNESS, AND MURDERERS ARE PUNISHED AND CAN GO TO JAIL FOR A VERY LONG TIME!

In response to recommendations such as these, the interactive video industry has begun to explore a self-policing program like that of the Motion Picture Producers of America (formerly the Motion Picture Producers and Distributors of America) and the TV industry's Standards for the Depiction of Violence in Television Programs. For example, the Sega cable channel system has developed a rating system for the 50 interactive video games it makes available to its subscribers. Sega is a relatively new cable company formed by a consortium comprised of Sega of America, Inc.; Tele-Communications, Inc. (TCI); and Time Warner Entertainment. The three rating categories in the Sega system are as follows:

GA: Appropriate for general audiences.

MA-13: Parental guidance suggested. Appropriate for teenage audiences.

MA-17: Not appropriate for children. For adults only.

Where Do You Draw the Line?

A classical question in issues involving almost any form of freedom in a democracy, "Where do you draw the line?" was used as the title of an important book by Victor Cline on violence in the media.[93] And on that very question hinges much of the current debate about what, if anything, can be done about the overwhelming amount of violence in almost every form of the media today. At what point does a song or a television scene or a video game episode become so offensive that any reasonable person can agree that the song or scene or episode should not be made available to young viewers . . . or, perhaps, viewers of any age.

Another factor to be considered in the issue of violence in the mass media is the rise of new forms of media. As one observer has written:

Looming technological changes, such as interactive multimedia, fiber-optic "information highways," computer bulletin boards, and home satellite services, promise an even more wide-open future. As [Ithiel] de Sol Pool sees it, government should get out of the regulation business altogether—or risk eroding freedom of speech in all media, print included.[94]

The bombing of the Alfred P. Murrah Federal Building in Oklahoma City has prompted a number of Americans to say, "Stop! Enough!" The level of violence in American society has simply reached a point where something must be done. To the extent that violence in the mass media is in any way responsible for this national trend, some restrictions on our hallowed freedoms of speech and expression may be necessary. But a decision as to exactly how an artist can or should be limited in his or her free expression seems to be no easier to make today than it was 200 years ago. The debate over violence in the media is very likely to continue for many years into the future.

Notes

1. As quoted in *Facts on File World News Digest*, 27 April 1995, p. 297A1.

2. As quoted in *Facts on File World News Digest*, 8 June 1995, p. 408C1.

3. "Women Politicos War on Musical 'Garbage,'" *Jet Magazine*, 6 September 1993, p. 59.

4. James B. Twitchell, *Preposterous Violence: Fables of Aggression in Modern Culture* (New York: Oxford University Press, 1989), pp. 8, 17–20, 35.

5. Ibid., pp. 7–8.

6. Ibid., pp. 94–95.

7. Plato, *The Dialogues of Plato* (New York: Random House, 1937), vol. 1, as quoted in Steven Starker, *Evil Influences: Crusades against the Mass Media* (New Brunswick, NJ: Transaction Publishers, 1989), p. 7.

8. George M. Beard, *American Nervousness, Its Causes and Consequences* (New York: G. P. Putnam's Sons, 1881), pp. 133–134, as cited in Starker, p. 8.

9. Alvin Poussaint, *Jet Magazine*, 29 November 1982, p. 12, as cited in Starker, p. 9.

10. Twitchell, chapter 3.

11. Joyce H. S. Tompkins, *The Popular Novel in England 1770–1800* (Lincoln: University of Nebraska Press, 1961), p. 60, as quoted in Twitchell, p. 97.

12. As quoted in Twitchell, p. 96.

13. As quoted in Janelle Rohr, *Violence in America: Opposing Viewpoints* (San Diego: Greenhaven, 1990), p. 33.

14. Walter M. Gerson, "Violence as an American Value Theme," in *Violence and the Mass Media*, ed. Otto N. Larsen (New York: Harper & Row, 1968), p. 157.

15. *New York Times*, 26 May 1897, as cited in Garth Jowett, *Film: The Democratic Art* (Boston: Little, Brown, 1976), pp. 109–110.

16. Starker, p. 95.

17. Jowett, p. 118.

18. 236 U.S. 230.

19. 268 U.S. 652.

20. Terry Ramsaye, *A Million and One Nights* (New York: Simon & Schuster, 1926), pp. 480–481, as quoted in Jowett, p. 126.

21. Jack Schwartz, "The Morality Seekers: A Study of Organized Film Criticism in the United States," in Larsen, p. 192.

22. "Hays, Will H(arrison)," in *Current Biography 1943* (New York: H. W. Wilson, 1943), p. 278.

23. As cited in Richard Maltby, " 'Grief in the Limelight': Al Capone, Howard Hughes, the Hays Code, and the Politics of the Unstable Text," in *Movies and Politics: The Dynamic Relationship*, ed. James Combs (New York: Garland Publishing, 1993), p. 137.

24. As quoted in John Kobler, *Capone: The Life and World of Al Capone* (London: Coronet Books, 1973), p. 313.

25. For a superb review of the politics of film production and distribution during the 1930s, see Maltby, chapter 5.

26. As quoted in Starker, pp. 97–98.

27. In Charters's introduction to Herbert Blumer and Philip M. Hauser, *Movies, Delinquency, and Crime* (New York: The Macmillan Company, 1933), p. vii.

28. Ibid., p. 201.

29. Twitchell, p. 185. Twitchell is actually alluding to comments made by film critic Gene Shalit and others on this issue.

30. All of the above quotations are taken from research done by Michael Krasny for an article by Carl M. Cannon, "Honey, I Warped the Kids," *Mother Jones*, July/August 1993, pp. 17–21.

31. Frederic Wertham, *Seduction of the Innocent* (New York: Rinehart, 1954), p. 118. For an excellent discussion of the comic book controversy, with particular attention to Wertham's role in that debate, see Starker, chapter 5.

32. Starker, p. 83.

33. As described in a memo to the editor, "The Greater Cincinnati Committee on Evaluation of Comic Books," in Larsen, pp. 182–189.

34. As quoted in Larsen, p. 179.

35. *Juvenile Delinquency (Comic Books): Hearing before the Subcommittee To Investigate Juvenile Delinquency of the Committee on the Judiciary*, United States Senate, 83rd Congress, 2nd sess., 21 and 22 April and 4 June 1954, p. 106.

36. Cobbett S. Steinberg, *TV Facts* (New York: Facts on File, 1985), p. 86.

37. As quoted in Walter Goodman, "Bang-Bang! You're Dead!" *New Republic*, 1 November 1954, p. 12.

38. As cited in Starker, p. 130.

39. As quoted in Cannon, p. 18.

40. S. Robert Lichter and Daniel Amundson, *A Day of TV Violence: 1992 vs. 1994* (New York: Center for Media and Public Affairs).

41. Ibid., p. 2.

42. The Gerbner approach to analyzing television violence was described in detail in a presentation made before the U.S. House Subcommittee on Communications of the Committee on Interstate and Foreign Commerce during hearings held on the issue of televised violence and obscenity on 2 March 1977, pp. 21–130.

43. Hearings of the Subcommittee on Communications, p. 467.

44. Ibid., p. 471. For the exchange between CBS and Gerbner, see ibid., pp. 467–479.

45. Albert Bandura, "What TV Violence Can Do to Your Child," *Look*, 22 October 1963, pp. 48–49.

46. Joseph T. Klapper, "The Impact of Viewing 'Aggression': Studies and Problems of Extrapolation" (Summary of a Paper by Dr. Ruth E. Hartley), as reprinted in Larsen, p. 138.

47. Monroe M. Lefkowitz, Leonard D. Eron, Leopold O. Walder, and L. Rowell Huesmann, *Growing Up To Be Violent: A Longitudinal Study of the Development of Aggression* (Elmsford, NY: Pergamon Press, 1977), p. 126.

48. As reported in Marc Silver, "Sex and Violence on TV," *U.S. News & World Report*, 11 September 1995, p. 66.

49. Aletha C. Huston et al., *Big World, Small Screen: The Role of Television in American Society* (Lincoln: University of Nebraska Press, 1992), pp. 54–55.

50. See *Juvenile Delinquency (Television Programs): Hearings before the Subcommittee To Investigate Juvenile Delinquency of the Committee on the Judiciary*, United States Senate, 83rd Congress, 2nd sess., 5 June to 20 October 1954; and *Juvenile Delinquency (Television Programs): Hearings before the Subcommittee To Investigate Juvenile Delinquency of the Committee on the Judiciary*, United States Senate, 84th Congress, 1st sess., 6–7 April 1955.

51. See *Violence and Crime Portrayed on Television: Hearings before the Subcommittee To Investigate Juvenile Delinquency of the Committee on the Judiciary*, United States Senate, 87th Congress, 1st and 2nd sess., 8 June 1961 to 14 May 1962.

52. Huston et al., p. 56.

53. Robert M. Liebert, Joyce N. Sprafkin, and Emily S. Davidson, *The Early Window: Effects of Television on Children and Youth*, 2nd edition (New York: Pergamon Press, 1982), p. 49.

54. As quoted in Liebert, Sprafkin, and Davidson, p. 50. For a discussion

of the history of the NAB radio and television broadcasting codes, see Sydney W. Head, *Broadcasting in America* (Boston: Houghton Mifflin, 1976), chapter 22.

55. *To Establish Justice, To Ensure Domestic Tranquility.* Final Report of the National Commission on the Causes and Prevention of Violence (Washington, DC: Government Printing Office, 1969), p. 199.

56. Quoted in Liebert, Sprafkin, and Davidson, p. 68.

57. Ibid., pp. 68–69.

58. Douglas Cater and Stephen Strickland, *TV Violence and the Child: The Evolution and Fate of the Surgeon General's Report* (New York: Russell Sage Foundation, 1975).

59. Hearings before the Subcommittee on Communications of the U.S. Senate Committee on Commerce, 21–24 March 1972, in Victor Cline, ed., *Where Do You Draw the Line?* (Provo, UT: Brigham Young University Press, 1974), pp. 177–178.

60. Robert M. Liebert, "Television and Social Learning: Some Relationships between Viewing Violence and Behaving Aggressively (Overview)," in *Television and Social Behavior, Reports and Papers, Volume II: Television and Social Learning* (Washington, DC: Government Printing Office, 1971), pp. 29–30.

61. William A. Belson, *Television Violence and the Adolescent Boy* (Farnborough, England: Saxon House, 1978); Melvin S. Heller and Samuel Polsky, *Studies in Violence and Television* (New York: American Broadcasting Company, 1976); J. R. Milavsky, R. C. Kessler, H. Stipp, and W. S. Ruben, *Television and Aggression: A Panel Study* (New York: Academic Press, 1982); Stanley Milgram and R. Lance Shotland, *Television and Antisocial Behavior: A Field Experiment* (New York: Academic Press, 1973).

62. Liebert, Sprafkin, and Davidson, p. 115.

63. Ibid.

64. George Comstock, "Review of Television and Antisocial Behavior: Field Experiments (by S. Milgram and R. L. Shotland)," *Journal of Communication*, Summer 1974, pp. 155–158.

65. Liebert, Sprafkin, and Davidson, p. 116.

66. R. M. Liebert, L. A. Cohen, C. Joyce, S. Murrel, L. Nisonoff, and S. Sonnenschein, "Predisposition Revisited," *Journal of Communication*, Summer 1977, pp. 217–221.

67. Ibid., p. 118.

68. National Institute of Mental Health, *Television and Behavior: Ten Years of Scientific Progress and Implications for the Eighties* (Rockville, MD: U.S. Department of Health and Human Services, Public Health Service, Alco-

hol, Drug Abuse, and Mental Health Administration, National Institute of Mental Health, 1982).

69. Ibid., p. 6.

70. At every congressional hearing on the violence in television, network executives have testified as to their views on the relevance of the research done to date on the effects of televised violence. See the report for any one such hearing for more details about industry positions.

71. The ABC report is reprinted in *Crime and Violence in the Media, Hearing before the Subcommittee on Crime of the Committee on the Judiciary,* House of Representatives, 98th Congress, 1st sess., 13 April 1983, p. 205 et seq.

72. Ibid., p. 261.

73. Huston et al.

74. For a list of those hearings, please see chapter 6.

75. For Ferguson's decision, see 423 F.Supp. 1064.

76. The appeals court decision can be found in 609 F.2d. 355.

77. See chapter 4 for a copy of these Standards.

78. *Violence on Television: Hearings before the Subcommittee on Telecommunications and Finance of the Committee on Energy and Commerce,* House of Representatives, 103rd Congress, 1st sess., 12 May, 25 June, 1 and 29 July, and 15 September 1993, p. 18.

79. Silver, p. 66.

80. The bill referred to here was introduced by Senator Kent Conrad (D-North Dakota) as Senate Bill 322, the "Children's Media Protection Act of 1995."

81. Michelle Quinn, "V-Chip Still Only a Vision," *San Francisco Chronicle,* 28 July 1995, p. B1.

82. Ibid., p. B8.

83. See, for example, the remarks of Shirley Igo, a vice president of the National PTA, as reported in "Demos Want Legal Curb on TV Violence," *San Francisco Chronicle,* 13 July 1995, p. A5.

84. Paul Fahri and John F. Harris, "TV Industry Feels Pressure, Will Develop Ratings System," *The Oregonian,* 29 February 1996, p. A6.

85. *Music Lyrics and Commerce: Hearings before the Subcommittee on Commerce, Consumer Protection, and Competitiveness of the Committee on Energy and Commerce,* House of Representatives, 103rd Congress, 2nd sess., 11 February and 5 May 1994, p. 70.

86. Ibid., p. 41.

87. Ibid., p. 38.

88. "Popular Music under Siege," American Civil Liberties Union Briefer (New York: ACLU, n.d.).

89. S. B. Silvern, P. A. Williamson, and T. A. Countermine, "Video Game Playing and Aggression in Young Children," paper presented to the American Educational Research Association, 1983, as cited in Patricia Marks Greenfield, *Mind and Media: The Effects of Television, Video Games, and Computers,* Cambridge, MA: Harvard University Press, p. 103.

90. S. B. Silvern, P. A. Williamson, and T. A. Countermine, "Video Game Play and Social Behavior: Preliminary Findings," paper presented at the International Conference on Play and Play Environments, 1983, as cited in Greenfield, p. 103.

91. *Violence in Video Games: Hearing before the Subcommittee on Telecommunications and Finance of the Committee on Energy and Commerce,* House of Representatives, 103rd Congress, 2nd sess., 30 June 1994, p. 25.

92. Ibid.

93. Victor B. Cline, ed.

94. Martha Bayles, "Fake Blood: Why Nothing Gets Done about Media Violence," *The Brookings Review,* Fall 1993, p. 22.

Chronology 2

The history of the mass media goes back to the very earliest days of the written word. The chronology provided in this chapter focuses on the development of the major forms of the mass media in the United States, with particular attention to events in which its inclusion of violent material has become an important social and political issue.

1704   Founding of the Boston *News-Letter*, the first newspaper in the United States to be published on a continuous basis. The paper ceases publication in 1776.

1774   The *Royal American Magazine*, the first American magazine containing quality material, begins publication in Boston. The magazine survives slightly more than one year.

1783   The New York *Packet* becomes the first newspaper in the United States to publish on a daily basis. The paper survives until 1792.

1789   William Hill Brown's *The Power of Sympathy*, America's first novel, is published.

1791   The Bill of Rights, the first ten amendments to the United States Constitution, are adopted. Of these, the First Amendment is especially important in the field of media violence since it guarantees to all American citizens the right of free speech. It is that right which so strongly prevents the enactment of censorship codes in the mass media.

1845   Enoch E. Camp and George Wilkes begin publication of *The National Police Gazette* (later, the *Police Gazette*), one of America's most crime- and violence-oriented magazines. The magazine is still published.

1882   Anarchist Leon Czolgosz shoots President William McKinley to death in Buffalo. When a copy of the New York *Morning Journal* is found in Czolgosz's pocket, critics point out that the newspaper has been viciously attacking the president for some time and claim that its editorial stance is at least partially responsible for Czolgosz's act.

1885   Thomas Alva Edison is granted the first radio patent for a system using antennas to transmit radio messages above the earth's curvature.

1887   Edison invents the principle of the motion picture.

1888   The German physicist Heinrich Rudolph Hertz discovers that radio waves can be transmitted through space. The unit for frequency in the metric system (cycles per second) is named in his honor.

1892–
1906   A number of individuals lay claim to having made the first voice broadcast by means of the Hertz principle.

1894   Edison gives his first public demonstration of the motion picture in New York City.

1895   The Italian engineer Guglielmo Marconi invents the wireless radio based on Hertz's original discoveries. He sends the first wireless messages between two locations on his family estate.

1896   The first public showing of a motion picture to a paying
        audience takes place at Koster and Bial's Music Hall in
        New York City. Early films rely heavily on violent themes.
        An 1896 Edison film, for example, depicts the execution
        of Mary, Queen of Scots including a graphic showing of
        her actual decapitation.

1897   The first official court case involving a motion picture is
        held. In *People v. Doris*, the court rules that a scene in the
        movie, pantomiming a wedding night, was "an outrage
        upon public decency."

1903   *The Ladies' Home Journal* becomes the first magazine in
        the United States to have more than 1 million subscribers.

1907   The De Forest Radio Telephone Company, founded by
        Lee de Forest, begins broadcasting in New York City.

        The first regular daily cartoon strip, "Mutt and Jeff,"
        drawn by H. C. (Bud) Fisher, appears in the San Fran-
        cisco *Daily Morning Chronicle*.

1908   In response to growing complaints from politicians and
        the general public about the content of motion pictures,
        the U.S. film industry organizes the National Board of
        Censorship of Motion Pictures, which is given the respon-
        sibility of inspecting motion pictures produced for pub-
        lic exhibition for offensive conduct. The Board's name is
        later changed to the National Board of Review.

        Charles D. Herrold establishes the first radio station with
        a regular schedule of broadcasting in San Francisco. The
        station has survived in one form or another until the
        present day, when it is known as KCBS.

1910   In April, the U.S. Congress passes the Wireless Ship Act
        of 1910, requiring the presence of at least one radio and
        radio operator on all seagoing vessels.

1911   The state of Pennsylvania creates a board of censors that
        is responsible for approving and licensing all films shown
        in the state. Other states that soon adopt similar legislation

1911
cont.
include Ohio (1913), Kansas (1914), Maryland (1916), New York (1922), and Virginia (1922).

1912
The term "radio" (as in "radiotelegraph") is introduced by the U.S. Navy as a substitute for the older term "wireless."

The Second Wireless Ship Act amends the Wireless Ship Act of 1910 to require two radio operators on all ships.

The Radio Act of 1912 becomes the first legislation by which domestic use of radio transmissions are controlled. The three primary sections of the act require that stations be licensed by the Secretary of Commerce, that government stations be given priority over private stations, and that stations choose wavelength and power to allow for the least amount of interference with other stations.

1915
The National Board of Censorship's name is changed to the National Board of Review.

Representative D. M. Hughes of Georgia introduces a bill that would create a federal motion picture commission whose responsibility it would be to examine, censor, and license movies. The bill was defeated.

In *Mutual Film Corporation v. Ohio*, the U.S. Supreme Court rules that motion pictures are not protected by the First Amendment as a form of free speech. Films are, the Court rules, "a business pure and simple . . . not to be regarded, nor intended to be regarded as part of the press of the country or as organs of public opinion."

1919
The U.S. Supreme Court announces the "clear and present danger" rule in *Schenck v. United States*. According to this rule, speech can be regulated by the government only if the content of that speech contributes immediately and proximately to the occurrence of an activity that is itself subject to government regulation.

1921
The Department of Commerce grants the first radio broadcasting license in the United States to station WBZ

in Springfield, Massachusetts. WBZ later moved to Boston, where it is still in existence.

1922   The first experimental radio network, consisting of stations WJZ in New York City and WGY in Schenectady, broadcasts the World Series of that year.

The first National Radio Conference is held. The conference adopts a number of recommendations to the Department of Commerce for regulation of radio transmissions.

Then-Postmaster General Will Hays is chosen to become president of the Motion Picture Producers and Distributors of America (MPPDA). This organization, supported and financed by all major film producing companies in the United States, is responsible for ensuring that motion pictures do not offend community moral standards. For the next 25 years, the MPPDA is commonly referred to as "the Hays Office."

The first of four annual radio conferences is held in Washington, D.C. The first conference is called by Secretary of Commerce Herbert Hoover who is seeking advice as to the regulatory powers he should be allowed to exercise in the supervision of radio broadcasting.

1923   Russian-American engineer Vladimir Zworykin invents the iconoscope, a primitive instrument for transmitting pictures without the use of electrical wires. Zworykin's discovery is often credited as marking the birth of modern television.

The National Association of Broadcasters is formed. It is created as a trade organization with the purpose of representing and protecting the interests of radio broadcasters.

1924   Two sensationalistic tabloids are founded in New York City, Bernard Macfadden's *Evening Graphic* and William Randolph Hearst's *Daily Mirror*. Both papers rely on sexual and violent themes to attract subscribers.

1925   In *Gitlow v. New York*, the U.S. Supreme Court publishes for the first time the doctrine that First Amendment rights of free speech apply to individual states as well as to the federal government.

1926   The National Broadcasting Company, consisting of 24 radio stations, is created. NBC is created as a joint effort of three industrial giants, General Electric, Radio Corporation of America (RCA), and Westinghouse.

1927   The Columbia Phonograph Broadcasting System (later, the Columbia Broadcasting System) is established.

The U.S. Congress passes the Radio Act of 1927, which, among other things, creates the Federal Radio Commission (FRC). The FRC's responsibilities include the assigning of radio broadcast wavelengths and the determination of the location and power of transmitters.

Warner Bros. pictures introduces the first "talking" picture, *The Jazz Singer*.

Scientists at Bell Telephone Laboratories transmit an experimental television program (over a telephone line between New York City and Washington) featuring Secretary of Commerce Herbert Hoover.

1928   Station WGY in Schenectady broadcasts the first television dramatic production.

The Lights of New York, the first talking gangster movie, is released.

1929   The motion picture industry adopts a Production Code that specifies the "do nots and be carefuls" of film production. For the next few years, the Code proves to be singularly ineffective in controlling the use of sexual and violent themes in films.

The National Association of Broadcasters announces a "Code of Ethics and Standards of Commercial Practice," the first set of self-imposed regulations adopted by the industry.

Archibald Maddock Crossley founds the first broadcast rating service, Crossley's Cooperative Analysis of Broadcasting. One of the most important findings in his early studies was that the majority of people listened to their radios during the period between 7:00 and 11:00 P.M. This finding leads to the concept of a "prime time" for radio, and later television, broadcasting.

1930s   A flood of motion pictures dealing with gangster themes hits the market. Among these are *Little Caesar*, *Scarface*, *Public Enemy*, *Johnny Eager*, and *Manhattan Melodrama*. Such films often glamorized the life of mobsters.

1930   Disturbed by the film industry's apparent inability to regulate itself and to carry out the provisions of its own Production Code, two Roman Catholics, layman Martin Quigley and Jesuit Daniel Lord, draft a revised version of the film code, the Hollywood Production Code. The Code is officially adopted by film producers in 1934.

1931   The first court decision prohibiting prior-restraint legislation is announced. In the case of *Near v. Minnesota ex rel. Olson*, the U.S. Supreme Court rules that the state of Minnesota cannot prevent publication of a Minneapolis "scandal sheet" known as the *Saturday Press* that had been critical of public officials.

1933   Members of the Roman Catholic Church create the Legion of Decency, an organization committed to improving the moral tone of motion pictures. The Legion is successful in convincing the Hays Office to take a more aggressive stance in the enforcement of its own Production Code and to obtain the appointment of Catholic layman Joseph I. Breen as head of the MPPDA's Production Code Administration.

The first modern American comic book, *Funnies on Parade*, is published as a promotional giveaway by the Procter and Gamble company.

1934   The sweeping Communications Act of 1934 is adopted. The Act includes most of the provisions of the Radio Act of 1927 and creates the Federal Communications Commission (FCC). The FCC is prohibited from censoring programs, but is allowed to decide if a station's policies and programs serve the best interests of the public.

1939   The FCC publishes a list of 14 kinds of programs that it deems to be "not in the public interest." These include depiction of torture and excessive suspense on children's programs as the closest items to prohibitions on violence.

1941   The FCC authorizes the operation of commercial television stations. The first ten stations begin operation on 1 July 1942.

1943   The American Broadcasting Company is created from the former "Blue Network" of the National Broadcasting Company.

1945   The Motion Picture Producers and Distributors of America changes its name to the Motion Picture Association of America.

1946   The Federal Communications Commission publishes a report entitled "Public Service Responsibility of Broadcast Licensees," more commonly known as "The Blue Book." The report claims not to set forth new standards, but simply to codify existing FCC policy on licensee responsibilities. Broadcasters complain that the FCC is subtly attempting to censor radio programming, which it is specifically prohibited from doing by the Communications Act of 1934.

1947   A commission headed by University of Chicago president Robert Maynard Hutchins issues a report entitled "A Free and Responsible Press" on the social and ethical responsibilities of America's mass communications, including newspapers, radio, motion pictures, magazines, and books. The commission suggests that the government should intervene in cases in which the media do not exercise social responsibility.

The Council of Bishops of the Roman Catholic Church in the United States creates the National Organization for Decent Literature. Its purpose is to develop standards for print media and to enforce that code among publishers and retailers of books, magazines, and newspapers.

1948   Fourteen publishers of comic books join together to form the Association of Comics Magazine Publishers (ACMP). The organization adopts a code of ethics that prohibits the publication of magazines that glorify crime, describe crime in detail, use obscene or vulgar language, or contain sexual images. ACMP is superseded in 1954 by the Comics Magazine Association of America.

1949   The FCC announces the "fairness doctrine," which requires broadcasters to "afford reasonable opportunity for the discussion of conflicting views of public importance." The rule is opposed by many as an invasion of the First Amendment rights of broadcasters.

1950s   In an effort to improve weak sales of comic books, William Gaines introduces a new line of books under the title of E. C. (for "entertaining comics") Comics. Among the titles included in this new series are *Crypt of Terror, The Vault of Horror*, and *The Haunt of Fear*. Critics soon begin to attack these very successful books because of the harmful effect they are thought to have on young readers.

1951   The first transcontinental television broadcast carries President Harry Truman's address to the opening session of the United Nations.

1952   The U.S. Supreme Court rules in *Joseph Burstyn, Inc. v. Wilson* that motion pictures are protected by the First Amendment. The case involves the distribution of a film, *The Miracle*, that the New York State Board of Regents had denied a license on the grounds that it is sacrilegious. The case is the first since 1915 to deal with First Amendment rights of motion pictures.

The first congressional hearings devoted to the subject of television are conducted before the House Committee on Interstate and Foreign Commerce.

1952   The National Association of Broadcasters announces its
cont.   first television code. The code eventually undergoes a
         number of modifications until it is declared unconstitu-
         tional by the U.S. Supreme Court in 1982.

1953   The nation's first educational television station, KUHT
         in Houston, begins operation.

         Director Otto Preminger decides to release his film *The
         Moon Is Blue* without a seal of approval from the Hays
         Office. The film is the first major motion picture in more
         than 20 years to have challenged the industry code.

1954   The Subcommittee on Juvenile Delinquency of the U.S.
         Senate Committee on the Judiciary, under the chairman-
         ship of Senator Estes Kefauver (D-Tennessee), holds hear-
         ings on the issue of violence on television. Additional
         hearings are held again the following year.

         In response to criticisms about the level of violence in
         comic magazines, the Comics Magazine Association of
         America (CMAA) is created. The CMAA develops and
         publishes a "Comics Code," to which magazines must
         subscribe if they are to receive the association's seal of
         approval.

         The first content-analysis research on television program-
         ming is reported by D. Smythe and S. W. Head.

1956   Otto Preminger releases his film *The Man with the Golden
         Arm* without the MPPDA code of approval. Approval is
         withheld because the film deals with the subject of drug
         abuse. In the same year, the code is revised to permit the
         mention of drugs.

1958   The FCC rules that it does not have the legal authority to
         regulate cable television.

1959   In *Kingsley International Pictures Corp. v. Regents of
         University of State of New York*, the U.S. Supreme Court
         rules that motion pictures are protected by the First
         Amendment.

1961   Senator Thomas Dodd (D-Connecticut), chair of the Sub-
        committee on Juvenile Delinquency of the Committee on
        the Judiciary, conducts hearings on the question of vio-
        lence on television. He holds similar meetings again in
        1961 and 1964.

1962   The U.S. Department of Health, Education, and Welfare
        and representatives of the television industry join to-
        gether to cosponsor the Joint Committee for Research on
        Television and Children. Only three research projects ever
        develop as a result of this effort, one of which is never
        completed.

1963   A research report sponsored by CBS called *The People Look
        at Television* is released. The report provides a summary
        of the attitudes of parents and other viewers as to the
        effects of television on children, but does not offer any
        new experimental results.

        The FCC announces plans to establish broadcasting stan-
        dards (including those dealing with violence) based on
        the National Association of Broadcasters (NAB) Code.
        The NAB *opposes* this proposal and, a year later, the U.S.
        Congress adopts a bill that prohibits the FCC from so
        acting.

1965   The FCC makes its first regulations regarding the opera-
        tion of community antenna television (CATV), later to
        become cable television. Over the next few years, the FCC
        continued to expand its regulation of this form of televi-
        sion transmission. The FCC's right to regulate cable TV
        is affirmed in a 1968 decision by the U.S. Supreme Court
        in *United States v. Southwestern Cable Co.*

        Intelstat I, the first commercial satellite, is placed into
        orbit.

1966   The MPAA code is liberalized to permit mention of
        abortion and suicide and to allow the use of common
        profanity.

1966   In *Office of Communication of United Church of Christ v. FCC,*
cont.   the U.S. Court of Appeals for the District of Columbia
           rules that citizens' groups have a legal right to partici-
           pate in hearings held by the FCC.

1967   The Corporation for Public Broadcasting is created by
           the Public Broadcasting Act of 1967. A major provision
           of the act is to provide federal funding for noncommer-
           cial television. The Public Broadcasting Service (PBS) ac-
           tually begins operation four years later.

1968   In an attempt to stop the commercial exploitation of chil-
           dren in television and improve the general quality of
           children's television, three mothers from Newtonville,
           Massachusetts—Peggy Charren, Judith Chalfen, and
           Evelyn Sarson—found Action for Children's Television
           (ACT). For nearly three decades, ACT remains one of the
           most persuasive groups arguing for a reduction in the
           level of violence in television programming aimed at
           children.

           President Lyndon Johnson appoints Dr. Milton
           Eisenhower as chairman of the National Commission on
           the Causes and Prevention of Violence. The Commission's
           report is originally expected in one year, but its life is
           extended a year by action of President Richard Nixon in
           June 1969.

           The motion picture industry abandons the old "Hays
           Office" Production Code and adopts a new and more lib-
           eral ratings system. The system introduces ratings such
           as G (films for general audiences), PG (parental guidance),
           R (restricted), and X (prohibited to persons under the age
           of 17).

1969   Senator John Pastore, of Rhode Island, writes Secretary
           of Health, Education, and Welfare Robert Finch asking
           for a study of the effects of television violence on chil-
           dren. He suggests that the surgeon general appoint a com-
           mittee of experts to analyze the scientific data on the ques-
           tion and report to the Congress on its findings.

ACT petitions the Federal Communications Commission to publish three rules governing children's television: (1) no commercials to be allowed on programs designed for children, (2) no mention of products by brand name on such programs, and (3) 14 hours of commercial-free television for children each week. Five years later, the FCC declines to enact any of these rules.

1970   The FCC publishes the Prime Time Access Rule, which states that stations can show no more than three hours of network programming per night. One motivation for this rule was to get local stations to develop original programming which, presumably, would contain less violence than did network programming. There is little evidence that this effect actually occurred.

1972   The surgeon general issues the report of his Scientific Advisory Committee on *Television and Growing Up: The Impact of Televised Violence*. The report includes 23 independent research projects and more than 40 technical papers on the subject. The advisory committee concludes that there may be a "preliminary and tentative indication of a causal relationship" between television and violent behavior in children.

The FCC begins to deregulate cable television programming. That process is completed in 1984 with the Cable Communications Policy Act of 1984 (see also 1984).

1974   Senator Pastore holds a second round of hearings on televised violence at which government and industry officials testify about the surgeon general's report of 1972. Television executives assure Pastore that significant progress is being made in reducing the level of violence in televised programs.

1975   The National Association of Broadcasters adopts a Family Viewing Hour (8:00 P.M. to 9:00 P.M.), during which programs are to be free from themes that would be objectionable for child viewers. Such themes are primarily those involving sexual and violent content.

1975   Time, Inc. introduces Home Box Office, a pay-television
cont.   system that almost immediately proves the value of sat-
       ellite transmission of commercial television program-
       ming.

1976   Judge Warren J. Ferguson of the U.S. District Court, Cen-
       tral District, Los Angeles, rules that the Family Viewing
       Hour concept is unconstitutional because it violates the
       right of free speech guaranteed in the First Amendment.
       This decision is overturned in 1979, but on jurisdictional
       and not substantive grounds. As a result, the National
       Association of Broadcasters abandons its family-viewing-
       time concept and leaves it up to member stations to de-
       termine the suitability of programming during "family
       viewing hours."

1977   The Subcommittee on Communications of the U.S. House
       Committee on Interstate and Foreign Commerce, chaired
       by Lionel Van Deerlin (D-California), holds hearings on
       the issue of sex and violence on television.

1978   The U.S. Supreme Court rules that the FCC has the au-
       thority to take action against stations that broadcast in-
       decent programs during times when children are likely
       to be watching. The FCC does not begin enforcing this
       decision until 1987.

1981   Warner Cable Corporation establishes the first television
       station dedicated entirely to the showing of music vid-
       eos, the Music Television (MTV) station. Within three
       years, MTV claims that it is reaching 24.2 million view-
       ers daily.

1982   The National Institute of Mental Health (NIMH) pub-
       lishes a review of studies done on television and violence
       in the ten-year period following the surgeon general's
       report of 1972. NIMH reports a much stronger relation-
       ship between television violence and violent behavior by
       children, but the report is later criticized by a special com-
       mittee of the National Academy of Sciences as drawing
       conclusions that were not warranted by the evidence.

A survey by the Gallup Poll organization finds that nearly two-thirds of adults questioned agree with the statement that there is a relationship "between violence on television and the rising crime rate in the United States."

The National Association of Broadcasters (NAB) Code for television is declared unconstitutional. The decision results from an antitrust suit filed by the Justice Department against the NAB on an issue unrelated to that of program content, but on the basis of inflated costs for commercials because of limitations imposed by the code.

1983   The Subcommittee on Crime of the U.S. House Committee on the Judiciary, chaired by William J. Hughes (D-New Jersey), conducts hearings on the subject of crime and violence in the media. The hearing is motivated by strong opposition to a report by the National Institute of Mental Health issued a year earlier in which a strong association between television viewing and aggressive behavior is affirmed.

1984   The Cable Communications Policy Act of 1984 removes essentially all of the remaining regulations on cable television systems originated by the FCC in 1972 (see also 1992).

MPPDA adds the category of PG-13 (parental discretion for children under the age of 14) to its system of rating motion pictures.

1985   The Recording Industry Association of America reaches an agreement with the National Parent Teachers Association and the Parents Music Resource Center on the development of a ratings system that will alert consumers to offensive lyrics and explicit depictions of violence in future recordings.

1987   The FCC decides to revoke the "fairness doctrine" that it had originally adopted in 1949.

1988   The U.S. Congress passes legislation prohibiting the broadcast of indecent programming at any time during

1988   the day or night. The courts rule that this law infringes
cont.   on the First Amendment rights of broadcasters.

1989   Senator Paul Simon (D-Illinois) in the U.S. Senate and
          Representatives Dan Glickman (D-Texas) and Edward F.
          Feighan (D-Ohio) introduce legislation to exempt repre-
          sentatives of the three national broadcasting companies
          from antitrust legislation in order to allow them to work
          together on the development of policies dealing with vio-
          lence on television. The bills pass both houses of Con-
          gress and are signed into law the following year.

1990   The U.S. Congress adopts the Children's Television Act,
          which sets limits on advertising during children's pro-
          grams and requires stations to provide at least some edu-
          cational programming for young viewers.

1992   A committee of the American Psychological Association
          (APA) issues a very detailed report on the role of televi-
          sion in American society. In its report, the APA commit-
          tee states that the harmful effects of televised violence
          have now been proved beyond doubt.

          Congress attempts once more to limit the broadcast of
          indecent programming (see 1988) by declaring the pe-
          riod from midnight to 6:00 A.M. as a "safe harbor" for such
          broadcasts. The courts once again strike down this law.

          Congress passes, over President George Bush's veto, the
          Cable Television Consumer Protection and Competition
          Act that once more introduces regulation of the cable tele-
          vision business.

1993   The Subcommittee on Telecommunications and Finance
          of the U.S. House Committee on Energy and Commerce,
          chaired by Edward J. Markey (D-Massachusetts), holds
          a series of five hearings on the issue of violence on tele-
          vision.

1994   The House Subcommittee on Telecommunications and
          Finance holds hearings on the problem of violence in
          video games.

Satisfied that the 1990 Children's Television Act will accomplish the goals for which it was established, Action for Children's Television disbands.

1995   The Catholic Communications Campaign, successor to the Roman Catholic Church's National Legion of Decency, announces a new program for giving motion pictures a "moral rating." The rating system contains levels such as A-1 (general audience), A-2 (adults and adolescents), A-3 (adults), A-4 (adults, with reservations), and O (morally offensive). The Campaign also sets up a toll-free number that people can call to find out the moral rating for any picture on which a decision has been made.

1996   President Bill Clinton signs into law an omnibus telecommunications act that requires television set manufacturers to include a V-chip in all sets made in the United States.

Executives of all major television networks agree to adopt a ratings system for television programs similar to that of the motion picture industry.

Biographical Sketches 3

M any individuals in the fields of communication, psychology, sociology, and other disciplines have made important contributions to our understanding of the way in which the media influence the way people think and behave. Those listed below are only a few of the many who have focused their attention in particular on the issue of violence in the media and the ways it affects humans.

Albert Bandura (1925–)

One of the most honored names in the field of research on the effects of televised violence is that of Albert Bandura. Some of his studies on the use of a Bobo doll in the early 1960s to study aggression in young children exposed to televised violence are among the most widely quoted in the field. In addition, an article in a 1963 issue of *Look* magazine by Bandura entitled "What TV Violence Can Do to Your Child" has been credited by some observers as placing the issue of televised violence in front of the American public.

But Bandura's work has not been limited to studies of violence and aggression. Indeed, one of his biographers has pointed out that Bandura's "interests range widely, [and he] is in the habit of pursuing several lines of research concurrently." Indeed, a review of the titles of a few of his nine books reflect this fact. Those titles include *Adolescent Aggression* (1959), *Social Learning and Personality Development* (1963), *Principles of Behavior Modification* (1969), *Social Learning Theory* (1977), and *Self-Efficacy: The Exercise of Control* (1995). Bandura's books have been internationally popular and have been translated into Polish, Spanish, Portuguese, German, Japanese, Chinese, and French.

Albert Bandura was born on 4 December 1925 in the tiny town of Mundare, in northern Alberta. After completing his precollegiate education in Mundare, he entered the University of British Columbia, from which he received his bachelor of arts degree in 1949. He then moved on to the University of Iowa, where he earned his M.A. (1951) and Ph.D. (1952) degrees.

Upon his graduation from Iowa, Bandura accepted an appointment as instructor of psychology at Stanford University. Over the next four decades, he worked his way up through the ranks at Stanford to become professor of psychology and, for one year, chairman of that department. During this long and active career, Bandura has held numerous offices in scientific societies, including president of the American Psychological Association (1974), member of the U.S. National Committee for the International Union of Psychological Sciences (1985–1993), and member of the Committee on International Affairs of the Society for Research in Child Development (1991–present). Bandura has also served on the editorial boards of more than 30 journals and serial volumes, including *Child Development*, *Behavior Therapy*, *Journal of Anxiety Disorders*, *Psychological Inquiry*, *Social Behavior and Personality*, and *Annual Review of Psychology*.

Among his many honors and awards, Bandura has been awarded honorary doctorates from the universities of Lethbridge, Waterloo, New Brunswick, Salamanca, New York (Stony Brook), and Rome. In 1989, he was elected a member of the Institute of Medicine of the National Academy of Sciences.

Brandon S. Centerwall (1954–)

In 1981, Brandon Centerwall was asked to help establish the violence research program at the Centers for Disease Control (now the Centers for Disease Control and Prevention) in Atlanta. He was invited to take this position because he possessed the unusual qualification of having a background in both psychiatry and epidemiology. One of the most important tasks undertaken by the new violence research program was the question of why the rate of violent crime in the United States had doubled in the previous three decades.

Centerwall attacked this question by looking at a vast number of factors that might have been related to the staggering increase of violence in the United States—factors such as trends in alcohol abuse, civil unrest, availability of firearms, urbanization, and television viewing. Seven years later, he had come to the conclusion that the only factor that consistently correlated with the increase in violence in the United States was television viewing. In 1989, he published his first paper on this topic, "Exposure to Television as a Cause of Violence" in the *American Journal of Epidemiology*. By comparing television viewing patterns in the United States, Canada, and South Africa with violent crimes in those countries, Centerwall came to the conclusion that increased exposure to televised violence caused an increase in violent behavior among viewers.

Brandon S. Centerwall was born on 15 February 1954 in Los Angeles, California. He received his B.S. degree in molecular biophysics and biochemistry from Yale University in 1975 and his M.D. from the University of California at San Diego in 1979. A year later he was awarded his master of public health degree from Tulane University.

In addition to his work at the Centers for Disease Control, Centerwall has served as assistant professor in the department of psychiatry and behavioral sciences (1987–1990) and the department of epidemiology (1992–present) at the University of Washington. He also has a private practice in psychiatry in Seattle. In 1987, Centerwall was awarded the Sandoz Award for Superior Academic Achievement and Contribution to Health Care.

Peggy Charren (1928–)

In a 20 January 1992 article on Peggy Charren, *Time* magazine commented that "few people in any field have demonstrated the power of a single impassioned voice as well as Peggy Charren." Charren was accorded this high praise because of her role in the founding of Action for Children's Television (ACT) in 1969. Along with two neighbors in Newtonville, Massachusetts, Charren created ACT because of her concerns about the commercialism of children's television during the 1960s. For more than two decades, the members of ACT were the primary spokespeople for reducing the amount of violence and commercialism in television aimed at younger viewers.

Charren decided to disband ACT in 1992 primarily because of Congress's adoption of the 1990 Children's Television Act. The act put into law a number of the regulations for which ACT had fought for more than two decades, although some observers were (and are) dubious about the long-term effectiveness of the 1990 act. For example, the limitations placed on commercial advertising on children's programs—12 minutes an hour on weekdays and 10 $^1/_2$ minutes per hour on weekends—were higher than network averages at the time.

Charren was born on 9 March 1928 in New York City. She graduated with a bachelor of arts degree from Connecticut College in 1949 before opening her own art shop, Art Prints, Inc., in Providence, Rhode Island, in 1951. In addition to her work with ACT, Charren has served on a number of educational boards and panels, including the Carnegie Commission on the Future of Public Broadcasting and the President's Commission on Mental Health. Among her many awards have been honorary doctorates from Regis College (1978), Emerson College (1984), Bank Street College (1985), Tufts University (1988), and Wheelock College (1990). She has also been awarded the Distinguished Public Information Service Award of the American Academy of Pediatrics, a Distinguished Service Award of the Massachusetts Radio and Television Association, and the Helen Homans Gilbert Award from Radcliffe College.

George Comstock (?–)

George Comstock has been one of the most astute observers and most prolific writers on the subject of violence in the media for more than two decades. He is author or coauthor of 16 books on the subject of mass communication and social behavior and of more than 100 articles, reports, papers, book chapters, and reviews on the subject. He has been guest speaker and panel member at more than three dozen conferences, meetings, and other sessions dealing with the effects of mass communications, especially television, on human behavior. Comstock has served as guest professor in the field of communication at the University of Michigan (1981 and 1988), the University of Wyoming (1983), and the University of California at Los Angeles (1987). He has also served on the Social Science Advisory Panel for the National Broadcasting System.

Many of Comstock's professional activities have focused on review and editorial responsibilities for journals dealing with mass communication. He has served on the editorial board of the *Journal of Visual/Verbal Languaging* and of *Public Opinion Quarterly*, as consulting editor to *Journal of Communication*, as associate editor of the *Journal of Applied Communication Research*, and as a referee for the *Journal of Broadcasting*.

After receiving his bachelor of arts degree from the University of Washington in 1954, Comstock entered the U.S. Air Force for two years. He then returned to Stanford University, where he earned his master of arts in communications in 1958. That year he took a job as a reporter for the *San Francisco Examiner*. From 1964 to 1967, Comstock served as research director for the Peace Corps and Stanford at the Institute for Communication Research in Bogota, Colombia. At the end of that stint, he was awarded his Ph.D. in communications by Stanford.

Comstock's first academic position was with New York University, where he served as assistant professor from 1967 to 1968. He then accepted a position as science advisor and senior research coordinator with the Surgeon General's Scientific Advisory Committee on Television and Social Behavior. When that assignment concluded in 1972, Comstock was appointed senior social psychologist with the Rand Corporation in Santa Monica, California. At Rand, Comstock was author of a number of booklets, articles, and other publications describing and discussing the work and findings of the surgeon general's committee.

In 1977, Comstock was appointed professor at the S. I. Newhouse School of Public Communications at Syracuse University. Two years later, he became Samuel I. Newhouse Professor of Public Communications at Syracuse, a post he continues to hold.

Kent Conrad (1948–)

In June 1993, Senator Kent Conrad announced the formation of a group of 28 national organizations representing medical professions, parents, educators, law enforcement groups, and churches for the purpose of studying televised violence, with particular attention to its effect on children. Six months later, the group sent Attorney General Janet Reno a set of seven recommendations for dealing with the problem of violence on television. Shortly thereafter, Senator Conrad incorporated most of those recommendations into Senate Bill 322, the Children's Media Protection Act of 1995.

Among the provisions of that act were a call for the establishment of a television rating code, a requirement for the inclusion of modifications in all television sets for the blocking of specific programs, and the elimination of violent programming during certain hours of the day. The act was passed and signed into law by President Bill Clinton in early 1996.

Kent Conrad was born in Bismarck, North Dakota, on 12 March 1948. In 1972, he was awarded a bachelor's degree in government from Stanford University and in 1975 a master's of business administration from George Washington University. In 1980, he was elected tax commissioner for the state of North Dakota and was reelected to the same post four years later. In 1986, Conrad was elected to the U.S. Senate from North Dakota as a Democrat, and at the end of that turn, was reelected in a special election to fill the remaining two years of the late Senator Quentin Burdick's term. In addition to his interest in televised violence, Conrad has been a strong spokesperson for rural states and an advocate for reducing the national budget deficit.

Leonard D. Eron (1920–)

For more than 40 years, Leonard Eron has been involved in research on the ways in which children learn aggressive behavior. His long-term studies of the effects of televised violence on aggressive behavior are among the most widely cited and most influential in the field.

He has served on two important commissions investigating the effects of violence in the media on children, the National Research Council Panel on Understanding and Control of Violence and the American Psychological Association Commission on Violence and Youth, of which he was also chair.

Leonard David Eron was born in Newark, New Jersey, on 22 April 1920. He received his B.S. degree from the City College of New York in 1941, his M.A. from Columbia University in 1946, and his Ph.D. from the University of Wisconsin in 1949. His first teaching position was at Yale University, where he served as assistant professor of psychology and psychiatry from 1948 to 1955. He then became director of research at the Rip Van Winkle Foundation (1955–1962), professor of psychology at the University of Iowa (1962–1969), and research professor at the University of Illinois at Chicago (1969–present), where he is now research professor emeritus.

In 1992, Eron was invited to become professor of psychology and research scientist at the Research Center for Group Dynamics of the Institute for Social Research at the University of Michigan, a post he continues to hold. In addition to his academic appointments, Eron has served as editor of the *Journal of Abnormal Psychology* and as associate editor of the *American Psychologist*. In 1980, he received an award for Distinguished Professional Contribution to Psychology in the Public Interest from the American Psychological Association and in 1995 was awarded the Gold Medal Award for Life Contribution to Psychology in the Public Interest.

George Gerbner (1919–)

For the better part of three decades, George Gerbner has been involved in studies of the incidence and nature of violence on television. He is the founder of a major research project called Cultural Indicators that provided a significant portion of data for the surgeon general's report on violence in television in 1969. Gerbner's research in this field had its beginnings in another major study on violence, the National Commission on the Causes and Prevention of Violence in 1967. Continued support for his research has been provided over the years by the National Science Foundation, the U.S. Office of Education, the National Institute of Mental Health, the Administration on Aging, and the Center for Substance Abuse Prevention.

George Gerbner was born in Budapest, Hungary, in August 1919. He graduated from the Joseph Eotvos Realgymnasium in 1937 and then enrolled at the University of Budapest. Two years later, faced with the possibility of having to serve in the Hungarian army as an ally of Nazi Germany, Gerbner chose instead to migrate to the United States. His first job in this country was with the *San Francisco Chronicle*, a post he held until he enlisted in the U.S. Army in 1943. Gerbner became a naturalized citizen of the United States in the same year.

After the war, Gerbner continued his education at the University of California, where he received his B.A., and at the University of Southern California, from which he earned his M.S. degree in 1951 and his Ph.D. in 1955. Over the next decade, Gerbner held a series of teaching jobs at John Muir College in Pasadena, California, at the University of Southern California, at El Camino College in Torrance, California, and at the University of Illinois Institution of Communications Research.

In 1964, Gerbner was named dean of the Annenberg School of Communications at the University of Pennsylvania. In addition to his research with Cultural Indicators, Gerbner has served as executive editor of the quarterly *Journal of Communications* and as chair of the editorial board of the *International Encyclopedia of Communication*. He is author, editor, or coeditor of a number of books and papers, including *The Analysis of Communication Content: Developments in Scientific Theories* (1969), *Communications Technology and Social Policy* (1973), *Mass Media Policies in Changing Cultures* (1977), *The Global Media Debate: Its Rise, Fall and Renewal* (1993), and "Television Violence: The Power and the Peril," in *Gender, Race, and Class in Media: A Critical Text-Reader* (1995).

Will H. Hays (1879–1954)

During the early 1930s, the United States motion picture industry was under heavy attack from religious and other organizations because of its portrayal of sexual themes and violence. Contrary to common belief, it was probably the horrors of gangster movies, rather than the sexuality portrayed in films, that inspired the most widespread complaints.

In an effort to establish some form of self-regulation, leaders of the motion picture industry created an organization called the Motion Picture Producers and Distributors of America, Inc. (MPPDA) and asked then–Postmaster General of the United States Will H. Hays to become its first president. At the time, Hays had been in political life for more than two decades and had earned a reputation as a man of high moral standards. Hays led the MPPDA and administered its code of ethical standards until 1945, and then remained with the group as an advisor until 1950.

Will Harrison Hays was born in Sullivan, Indiana, on 5 November 1879. He earned his bachelor of arts degree from Wabash College in 1900 and his master of arts from Lincoln Memorial University in 1904. He was admitted to practice in the Indiana Bar in 1900. Hays practiced law from 1900 until 1910, and was then elected city attorney for Sullivan County. He held that post until 1914.

Hays' political career began the year he graduated from Wabash College when he was elected to the Republican precinct committee at the age of 21. He then went on to become chairman of that committee, of the Republican State Central Committee, and the Republican National Committee. In 1921, he was appointed postmaster general by President Warren G. Harding.

Hays served as a member and trustee of many corporate, charitable, and philanthropic organizations, including the Continental Banking Company, the Chicago and Eastern Illinois Railroad, the American Red Cross, the Institute for Crippled and Disabled Men, the Boy Scouts of America, and the Citizens Committee of the Salvation Army. Hays died in New York City on 7 March 1954.

Marjorie Heins (1946–)

Most discussions about the problem of violence in the media eventually get to the question of broadcasters' "First Amendment rights." That is, the question arises as to whether or at what point the programs sent out over television, radio, motion pictures, and other forms of media become so harmful that the government finds it necessary to place limitations on broadcasters. Perhaps the most outspoken group supporting virtually no limitations on broadcasting is the American Civil Liberties Union's Arts Censorship Project. A founder and director of that project since its formation in the spring of 1991 is Marjorie Heins.

Marjorie Heins was born in New York City on 9 October 1946. She received her bachelor's degree from Cornell University in 1967 and then her J.D. in 1978, magna cum laude, from Harvard Law School. At Harvard, she was articles editor of the Harvard Civil Rights Civil Liberties Law Review.

After leaving Harvard, Heins served as staff counsel for the Civil Liberties Union of Massachusetts, chief of the Civil Rights Division in the Office of the Attorney General of Massachusetts, and visiting professor at Boston College Law School. In 1991, she received the Luther McNair award of the Massachusetts Civil Liberties Union for significant contributions to civil rights and in both 1992 and 1993 was recognized as a "First Amendment Hero" by the Boston Coalition for Freedom of Expression.

Heins is the author of many articles in legal journals and general interest magazines and of three books, *Strictly Ghetto Property: The Story of Los Siete de la Raza* (1975), *Cutting the Mustard: Affirmative Action and the Nature of Excellence* (1987), and *Sex, Sin, and Blasphemy: A Guide to America's Censorship Wars* (1993).

Joseph Klapper (1917–1984)

The three original television broadcasting systems—ABC, CBS, and NBC—have long maintained their own departments in which research has been conducted on the effects of television on children and adults. From 1962 to 1984, Joseph Klapper was the director of the Office of Social Research at the Columbia Broadcasting System (CBS). In that role, he was long a thoughtful and respected respondent to criticisms of the effects of televised violence. He testified for CBS and the television industry at most of the congressional hearings held to study this problem.

Joseph Thomas Klapper was born in New York City on 11 January 1917. He received his bachelor of science degree from Harvard University in 1936, his master of arts from the University of Chicago in 1938, and his Ph.D. in sociology from Columbia University in 1960. Prior to completing his doctoral degree, Klapper had worked in the Bureau of Applied Social Research at Columbia, had taught at the University of Washington, and had served in the National Broadcasting Division of the U.S. Information Agency.

In addition to his work at CBS, Klapper served on a number of national committees dealing with the mass media in American society. He was a member of the Presidential Commission on Obscenity and Pornography from 1958 to 1970, a member of the Surgeon General's Scientific Advisory Committee on Television and Social Behavior from 1969 to 1971, and a research consultant to the National Council of Churches from 1957 to 1963 and the American Jewish Committee from 1957 to 1964. He served as president, vice-president, and secretary-treasurer of the American Association of Public Opinion Research.

Klapper died in New York City on 14 May 1984.

John Pastore (1907–)

One of the most outspoken critics of violence in the media during the late 1960s and early 1970s was Senator John Pastore, Democrat of Rhode Island. As chairman of the Subcommittee on Communications of the Senate Commerce Committee, Pastore was a constant irritant to television network executives who were reluctant to admit to the widespread existence of violence on television or to take any kind of action that would have dealt with that problem. Finally, in 1969, Pastore was able to convince then–Secretary of Health, Education, and Welfare Robert Finch to instigate a study on the predominance and effects of televised violence. That study resulted in the surgeon general's report on this topic three years later, a report that is one of the most important in the long history of televised violence in U.S. history.

John Orlando Pastore was born in Providence, Rhode Island, on 17 March 1907, the son of an immigrant tailor and his wife. He earned his law degree from Northeastern University in Boston in 1931 and then entered private practice. A decade later, he became interested in politics and was elected lieutenant governor of Rhode Island in 1944. A year later, he ran for the office of governor of the state and won again.

In 1950, Pastore was elected to the U.S. Senate from Rhode Island, the first American of Italian heritage to have achieved that honor. He served in the Senate until 1976 when he resigned to allow his successor, Republican John Chafee, to benefit from the body's seniority rules. In addition to his work on televised violence, Pastore is best remembered for his role in the creation of the Energy Research and Development Administration, successor to the old Atomic Energy Commission in the early 1970s. He was also instrumental in the passage of the Federal Election Campaign Act of 1971, which produced the first significant reform in campaign financing in half a century.

Deborah Prothrow-Stith (1954–)

Deborah Prothrow-Stith received her bachelor of arts degree in mathematics from Spelman College in Atlanta in 1975 and her M.D. from Harvard Medical School in 1979. Over the past two decades, she has been an active spokesperson and writer on issues of violence in American society. In the three-year period from 1992 through 1994, for example, she delivered nearly a hundred lectures on violence-related issues to colleges, professional organizations, public interest groups, and conferences. She is the coauthor of a highly influential book on violence and adolescents, *Deadly Consequences: How Violence Is Destroying Our Teenage Population and a Plan To Begin Solving the Problem*, as well as the *Violence Prevention Curriculum for Adolescents*, developed in association with the Education Development Center in Newton, Massachusetts.

Prothrow-Stith completed her residency in internal medicine at Boston City Hospital between 1979 and 1982 and later served as consulting physician at the Libre Methadone Detoxification Clinic in Boston (1983–1986), as codirector of the Health Promotion Center for Urban Youth for the Boston Department of Health and Hospitals (1985–1987), as clinical chief at the Adolescent Clinic of the Harvard Street Neighborhood Health Center (1986–1987), and as staff physician at Boston City Hospital (1982–1987).

In 1987, Prothrow-Stith was appointed commissioner of public health for the Commonwealth of Massachusetts and then, in 1990, assistant dean for government and community programs at the Harvard School of Public Health, a position she currently holds.

Among her honors and awards are honorary doctorates from North Adams State College, Wheelock College, Springfield College, and Morehouse Medical School. She has also been named one of the Outstanding Young Women of America (1983) and been given the Amelia Earhart Award (1987), the Humanitarian of the Year Award of the Metro-Boston Alive (Association of Recovering Addicts, 1988), Women of Achievement Award of the Big Sisters Association (1988), the Rebecca Lee Award of the Massachusetts Department of Public Health (1990), the World Health Day Award of the American Association for World Health of the World Health Organization (1993), the Peace Award of the Physicians for Social Responsibility (1995), and the Tribute to Outstanding Black Women Educators of the Black Educator's Alliance of Massachusetts (1995).

Eli Rubinstein (1919–)

The somewhat unenviable task of chairing the surgeon general's study on televised violence in 1969 fell to then–assistant director for behavioral sciences of the National Institute of Mental Health, Eli Rubinstein. Rubinstein was confronted with the challenge of bringing together critics and defenders of television programming policies to deal with one of the most controversial issues of the day. In spite of the forces operating against him—and against the work of the surgeon general's committee—Rubinstein managed to organize and oversee a substantial research effort on televised violence and to hammer out a final report that all members of the commission were able to sign.

Eli Abraham Rubinstein was born in New York City on 27 April 1919. He received his B.S. degree from the City College of New York in 1939, his M.A. from the Catholic University of America in 1948, and his Ph.D. from the same institution three years later. After serving as a clinic associate at Catholic University, Rubinstein accepted an appointment at the National Institute of Mental Health (NIMH), first as an analyst in mental health, then as assistant chief and then chief of the training branch, then as associate director of extramural programs and director of mental health manpower.

In 1971, Rubinstein left NIMH to take a position as professor of psychiatry at the State University of New York at Stony Brook.

In addition to his academic work, he has served as consulting editor for the *Journal of Communications* and the *Journal of Women Quarterly*. In 1966, Rubinstein was awarded the Superior Service Award of the Department of Health, Education, and Welfare.

Paul Simon (1928–)

Paul Simon was the successor of Estes Kefauver, Thomas Dodd, and John Pastore as the U.S. Senate's watchdog on violence in the media. In 1989, he introduced legislation granting an exemption from antitrust regulations to the three television networks in order to allow them to develop a code for the treatment of violence in that medium. That legislation was passed the following year and became known as the Television Program Improvement Act of 1990.

Paul Martin Simon was born on 29 November 1928 in Eugene, Oregon. His parents were Lutheran missionaries who had returned from China in order that their child be born in the United States. After graduating from Eugene High School, Simon enrolled at the University of Oregon. When his family moved to Illinois, however, Simon transferred to Dana College, a small Lutheran college in Blair, Nebraska. His college studies were interrupted two years later, however, when he learned of an opportunity to purchase a struggling weekly newspaper, the *Tribune* of Troy, Illinois. At the age of 19, he became the youngest newspaper editor and publisher in the United States.

After a tour of duty with the U.S. Army, Simon became interested in a political career and ran for a seat in the Illinois House of Representatives. He was elected in 1954 and then reelected three more times to the House and twice to the state senate. After a failed run for the state governorship, Simon left politics briefly to teach at Sangamon State University, in Springfield, and at Harvard's Kennedy School of Government.

In 1974, Simon returned to politics as a candidate for the U.S. House of Representatives from Illinois's 24th congressional district. He won that seat and then was reelected four more times before deciding to run for the Senate in 1984. After serving two terms in the U.S. Senate, Simon announced his intention to retire and return to private life. In 1987, Simon made a brief and unsuccessful run for the Democratic nomination for the U.S. presidency.

In addition to his political career, Simon has managed to maintain an active writing career. He is the author of 11 books, including *Lovejoy, Martyr to Freedom* (1964), *Lincoln's Preparation for Greatness: The Illinois Legislative Years* (1965), *A Hungry World* (cowritten with his wife, 1966), *The Glass House: Politics and Morality in the Nation's Capital* (1984), and *Let's Put America Back to Work* (1987).

Included among Simon's many awards and honors are 39 honorary doctorates and his selection as Best Legislator in Illinois (seven times).

Jerome L. Singer (1924–)

Jerome L. Singer was born in New York City on 6 February 1924. He earned his B.A. from the College of the City of New York in 1943 at the age of 19. After serving in the U.S. Army from 1943 to 1946, he then entered the University of Pennsylvania, from which he received his Ph.D. in psychology in 1950. His work experience has included appointments at the Philadelphia Veterans Administration Medical Hygiene Clinic (1946–1950), the Franklin D. Roosevelt Veterans Administration Hospital in Montrose, New York (1950–1955), the William Alanson White Institute of Psychiatry, Psychoanalysis, and Psychology (1954–1959), the Teachers College at Columbia University (1957–1963), and the City University of New York (1963–1972). In 1972, Dr. Singer was appointed professor of psychology and director of the Graduate Program in Clinical Psychology at Yale University. Since 1976, he and his wife, Dorothy—who is also a prolific writer in the field of televised violence and its effects on children—have been codirectors of the Yale University Family Television Research and Consultation Center.

C. DeLores Tucker (1927–)

One of the most persistent and outspoken critics of the form of music known as gangsta rap is C. DeLores Tucker, one of the founding members of the National Political Congress of Black Women and former secretary of state for the Commonwealth of Pennsylvania. In testimony before the House Subcommittee on Commerce, Consumer Protection, and Competitiveness of the Committee on Energy and Commerce, in 1994, Ms. Tucker remarked:

> Images that degrade our dignity and insult our children and families concern us too, as any other self-respecting member of society. Even if it comes out of our own

mouths, the gangsta rap and misogynist lyrics that glorify violence and denigrate women is nothing more than pornographic smut.

Because this pornographic smut is in the hands of our children, it coerces, influences, encourages, and motivates our youth to commit violent behavior, to use drugs and abuse women through demeaning sex acts. The reality of the 1990s is that the greatest fear in the African-American community does not come from earthquake, floods or fires, but from violence, the kind of violence that has already transformed our communities and schools into war zones where children are dodging bullets, instead of balls, and planning their own funerals.

Tucker has written and spoken and, with her supporters, protested against the message of gangsta rap. In the process, she has been arrested on a number of occasions.

In recognition of her work in this and other fields, Tucker has been given more than 300 awards and honors, including the Philadelphia Urban League Whitney Young Award (1990), the NAACP Thurgood Marshall Award (1982), the National Association of T.V. and Radio Artists Woman of the Year award (1972), the National NAACP Freedom Fund Award (1961), and the Dr. Martin Luther King, Jr. Award of the Philadelphia Trade Unions Council.

C. DeLores Tucker was born in Philadelphia on 4 October 1927, the tenth of 11 children to Reverend Whitfield and Captilda Gardiner Nottage. She attended the Philadelphia High School for Girls and then Temple University, where she majored in finance and real estate. With her husband of two years, William Tucker, she established the Tucker and Tucker Real Estate company in July 1951.

During the 1960s, Tucker became active in the civil rights movement, serving as vice president of the Philadelphia chapter of the National Association for the Advancement of Colored People (NAACP) and delegate to President John F. Kennedy's White House Conference on Civil Rights in 1968. In the same year, she became chairperson of the Pennsylvania Black Democratic Committee.

In January 1971, Governor Milton Shapp appointed Tucker as secretary of state of the Commonwealth of Pennsylvania, a post she held until 1977. She is currently chair of the National Political Congress of Black Women, an organization that she founded with

Shirley Chisholm to assist African-American women who are interested in running for public office.

Jack Valenti (1921–)

Few names have been so closely associated with the motion picture industry in the United States as that of Jack Valenti. Valenti was appointed president and chief executive officer of the Motion Picture Association of America (MPAA) in 1966, a post he has now held for three decades. During that time, he has been an articulate spokesperson for the industry and the individual most responsible for enforcing the industry's production code. Valenti has testified for the motion picture industry at virtually every congressional hearing held on violence in the media.

Jack Joseph Valenti was born in Houston, Texas, on 5 September 1921. He graduated from Sam Houston High School in 1936 at the age of 15, the youngest graduate in the school's history to that time. He then went to work as an office boy at the Humble Oil and Refining Company in Houston, where he was soon promoted to the advertising department. In 1938, he enrolled in night classes at the University of Houston.

After serving in World War II from 1942 to 1945, Valenti returned to the University of Houston, from which he received his bachelor of arts degree in business in 1946. He then continued his education at Harvard Business School, which granted him his master's degree in 1948. After another two-year stint at Humble Oil, Valenti opened the advertising firm of Weeky and Valenti, Inc. with a former classmate of his from the University of Houston.

Valenti first became interested in national politics in 1956 when he met then U.S. Senator Lyndon Johnson. After Johnson's accession to the U.S. presidency in 1963 following John F. Kennedy's assassination, Valenti was appointed special assistant to the president with the somewhat ambiguous assignment of "trouble-shooter and expediter." Valenti resigned from his post in the Johnson administration in April of 1966 to assume the post of president of the MPAA.

In addition to his work at the MPAA, Valenti has found the time to write four books, *Bitter Taste of Glory* (1971), *A Very Human President* (1976), *Speak Up with Confidence: How To Prepare, Learn and Deliver an Effective Speech* (1982), and *Protect and Defend* (1992).

Frederic Wertham (1895–1981)

Trained as a psychiatrist, Wertham's name was long associated with a number of controversial social causes. During the 1930s and 1940s, for example, he was widely known among criminal defense lawyers as the only psychiatrist who was willing to appear in court cases involving Black defendants.

Wertham's interest in the mass media and violence arose in the late 1940s when he became convinced that comic magazines were having a harmful effect on their young readers. At one point he expressed the view that "comic books represent systematic poisoning of the well of childhood spontaneity."

A 1948 article that Wertham wrote for the *Saturday Review of Books* on comic magazines entitled "The Comics . . . Very Funny!" was later reprinted and quoted widely. His 1953 book, *Seduction of the Innocent*, summarized in exhaustive detail his arguments about the effects of violence in comic magazines on children. In a late chapter of the book, Wertham also introduces a discussion of the potential effects of television, then a young industry, on children.

Frederic Wertham was born in Germany in 1895 and received his medical education at King's College, London. He continued his medical studies in Germany at the universities of Munich, Erlangen, and Würzburg, receiving his M.D. in 1921 from the last of these. His postgraduate work in psychiatry took place in Vienna, Paris, London, and Munich.

In 1922, Wertham was invited to join the Phipps Psychiatric Clinic at Johns Hopkins University Hospital in Baltimore. A decade later, he moved to New York City, where he established a psychiatric clinic in connection with the city's Court of General Sessions. The clinic was the first of its kind in the United States at which convicted felons were able to receive a psychiatric evaluation.

Wertham was also named senior psychiatrist of the New York City Department of Hospitals in 1932, a post he held until his death in 1981. Perhaps his greatest contribution to the field of psychiatry was his view that violent crime often has very specific and very clear warning signs that can be detected. His arguments for this position were presented in what may have been his most famous book, *The Show of Violence*, published in 1949.

Donald E. Wildmon (1938–)

One of the most effective ways that ordinary citizens have to influence the content of programs produced by the media is to influence advertisers that pay for those programs. This premise is a crucial operating principle of the American Family Association (AFA), founded by Donald Wildmon in 1977. Wildmon has argued that the entertainment business presents one of the most serious threats to the survival of Christian America in this century. To counteract that threat, Wildmon and his organization monitor programs presented on television, movies, and other forms of media presentations to assess their morality. Those presentations that do not meet AFA standards then become the target of boycotts and letter-writing campaigns to companies that advertise or support those presentations.

Donald E. Wildmon was born on 18 January 1938 and attended Millsaps College in Jackson, Mississippi, from which he received his bachelor of arts degree in 1960. He then earned a master of divinity degree from Emory University in Atlanta in 1965. He has also been awarded an honorary doctor of law degree by Asbury College (1990) and an honorary doctor of divinity degree by Wesley Biblical Seminary (1994).

After serving in the Special Services section of the U.S. Army from 1961 to 1963, Wildmon accepted an appointment as minister of the Iuka United Methodist Church in Iuka, Mississippi. He then moved on to the Lee Acres Methodist Church in Tupelo, Mississippi, and the First United Methodist Church in Southaven, Mississippi before founding the AFA.

Wildmon is the author of 22 books with more than 1 million copies in print. He is also a frequent guest of television programs such as *Meet the Press*, *Good Morning America*, the *Tomorrow Show*, the *Today Show*, *Nightline*, and the *700 Club*. He has also been featured in articles in *TV Guide*, *Time*, *Newsweek*, *People*, *Saturday Evening Post*, and the *Wall Street Journal*.

Documents and Opinions

4

F ive types of documents and a section of opinions about violence and the media make up this chapter. The first consists of laws and regulations that have been adopted and proposed to regulate the mass media, in general, and to deal with violence in the media, in particular. The second section presents various standards that have been set by the mass media industry itself for monitoring violence in presentations. An example of the documents included in this section is the code of the Comics Magazine Association of America.

Section 3 presents some important court cases that have dealt with issues of free speech in the media and with the depiction of violence by the media. Section 4 includes a number of policy statements and recommendations that have been made by those interested in this issue. Section 5 includes brief summaries of reports presented by three important national commissions concerned with the depiction of violence in the media, and a final section offers some sample opinions on the topic.

Every effort has been made to reproduce the texts of the laws and policy statements faithfully from the originals, both in terms of content (wherein readers may notice a few minor typographical errors) and general format.

Laws and Regulations

The number of legal documents dealing with violence in the media is relatively small. The United States Constitution appears to restrict legislation that limits free speech, even if that speech appears to encourage or contribute to violent behavior in readers and listeners. The first document listed below, for example, specifically prohibits the Congress from passing any laws that would be construed as limiting a person's free speech.

Communications Act of 1934

The fundamental law dealing with the nonprint mass media in the United States is the Communications Act of 1934. Following are the introduction to that act, in which the Federal Communications Commission is created, and section 326, to which reference is often made in the debate over violence in the media, and in which the government is prevented from abridging the free speech rights of radio and television stations and networks.

AN ACT

To provide for the regulation of interstate and foreign communication by wire or radio, and for other purposes.

Be it enacted by the Senate and House of Representatives of the United States of America in Congress assembled,

TITLE I—GENERAL PROVISIONS
PURPOSES OF ACT;
CREATION OF FEDERAL COMMUNICATIONS COMMISSION

SECTION 1. For the purpose of regulating interstate and foreign commerce in communication by wire and radio so as to make available, so far as possible, to all the people of the United States a rapid, efficient, nation-wide, and world-wide wire and radio communication service with adequate facilities at reasonable charges, for the purpose of the national defense, and for the purpose of securing a more effective execution of this policy by centralizing authority heretofore granted by law to several agencies and by granting additional authority with respect to interstate and foreign commerce and wire and radio communication, there is hereby crated a commission to be known as the "Federal Communications Commission," which shall be constituted as hereinafter provided, and which shall execute and enforce the provisions of this Act. . . .

CENSORSHIP; INDECENT LANGUAGE

SEC. 326. Nothing in this Act shall be understood or construed to give the Commission the power of censorship over the radio communications or signals transmitted by any radio station, and no regulation or condition shall be promulgated or fixed by the Commission which shall interfere with the right of free speech by means of radio communication. No person within the jurisdiction of the United States shall utter any obscene, indecent, or profane language by means of radio communication.

Source: 73rd Congress, 2nd Sess., Ch. 652, 19 June 1934, pp. 1064, 1091.

Public Law 101-650

One of the very few acts of Congress that deals directly with the question of violence in the mass media is Title V of the Judicial Improvements Act of 1990. This legislation specifically granted immunity to the three television networks in order to allow them to "develop voluntary industry standards to alleviate the negative impact of televised violence." The legislation was attached as an amendment to a somewhat unrelated law dealing with the appointment of federal circuit and district judges.

TITLE V—TELEVISION PROGRAM IMPROVEMENT

SEC. 501. TELEVISION PROGRAM IMPROVEMENT

(a) SHORT TITLE.—This section may be cited as the "Television Program Improvement Act of 1990."

(b) DEFINITIONS.—For purposes of this section—

    (1) the term "antitrust laws" has the meaning given it in subsection (a) of the first section of the Clayton Act (15 U.S.C. 12(a)), except that such term includes section 5 of the Federal Trade Commission Act (15 U.S.C. 45) to the extent that such section 5 applies to unfair methods of competition;

    (2) the term "person in the television industry" means a television network, any entity which produces programming (including theatrical motion pictures) for telecasting or telecasts programming, the National Cable Television Association, the Association of Independent Television Stations, Incorporated, the National Association of Broadcasters, the Motion Picture Association of America, the Community Antenna Television Association, and each of the networks' affiliate organizations, and shall include any individual acting on behalf of such person; and

    (3) the term "telecast" means—
        (A) to broadcast by means of a television broadcast station; or
        (B) to transmit by a cable television system or a satellite televi-
           sion distribution service.
(c) EXEMPTION.—The antitrust laws shall not apply to any joint
    discussion, consideration, review, action, or agreement by or among
    persons in the television industry for the purpose of, and limited to,
    developing and disseminating voluntary guidelines designed to
    alleviate the negative impact of violence in telecast material.
(d) LIMITATIONS—
    (1) The exemption provided in subsection (c) shall not apply to any
        joint discussion, consideration, review, action, or agreement
        which results in a boycott of any person.
    (2) The exemption provided in subsection (c) shall apply only to any
        joint discussion, consideration, review, action, or agreement
        engaged in only during the 3-year period beginning on the date
        of the enactment of this section.

Source: Public Law 101-650, 1 December 1990, 1044 Stat. 5089, 5127-5128. Cited as 47 U.S.C. 303c.

Public Law 101-431

Critics of violence in television programming have suggested that one partial solution to this problem might be to provide the technology within television sets that would allow parents to black out programs they do not want shown in their homes. A model for legislation along these lines is the "Television Decoder Circuitry Act of 1990," which requires that certain television sets built after 1 July 1993 be equipped with a device that permits close-captioned programming for hearing-impaired individuals. The provisions of that act are as follows:

AN ACT

To require new televisions to have built in decoder circuitry.
    Be it enacted by the Senate and House of Representatives of the United States of America in Congress assembled,

SHORT TITLE

SECTION 1. This Act may be cited as the "Television Decoder Circuitry Act of 1990."

FINDINGS

Sec. 2. The Congress finds that—

(1) to the fullest extent made possible by technology, deaf and hearing-impaired people should have equal access to the television medium;

(2) closed-caption television transmissions have made it possible for thousands of deaf and hearing-impaired people to gain access to the television medium, thus significantly improving the quality of their lives;

(3) closed-captioned television will provide access to information, entertainment, and a greater understanding of our Nation and the world to over 24,000,000 people in the United States who are deaf or hearing-impaired;

(4) closed-captioned television will provide benefits for the nearly 38 percent of older Americans who have some loss of hearing;

(5) closed-captioned television can assist both hearing and hearing-impaired children with reading and other learning skills, and improve literacy skills among adults;

(6) closed-captioned television can assist those among our Nation's large immigrant population who are learning English as a second language with language comprehension;

(7) currently, a consumer must buy a TeleCaption decoder and connect the decoder to a television set in order to display the closed-captioned television transmissions;

(8) technology is now available to enable that closed-caption decoding capability to be built into new television sets during manufacture at nominal cost by 1991; and

(9) the availability of decoder-equipped television sets will significantly increase the audience that can be served by closed-captioned television, and such increased market will be an incentive to the television medium to provide more captioned programming.

REQUIREMENT FOR CLOSED-CAPTIONED EQUIPMENT

SEC. 3. Section 303 of the Communications Act of 1934 (47 U.S.C. 303) is amended by adding at the end thereof the following: "(u) Require that apparatus designed to receive television pictures broadcast simultaneously with sound be quipped with built-in decoder circuitry designed to display close-captioned television transmissions when such apparatus is manufactured in the United States or imported for use in the United States, and its television picture screen is 13 inches or greater in size."

PERFORMANCE AND DISPLAY STANDARDS

SEC. 4.

(a) Section 330 of the Communications Act of 1934 (47 U.S.S. 330) is amended by redesignating subsection (b) as subsection (c), and by inserting immediately after subsection (a) the following new subsection: "(b) No person shall ship in interstate commerce, manufacture, assemble, or import from any foreign country into the United States, any apparatus described in section 303(u) of this Act except in accordance with rules prescribed by the [Federal Communications] Commission pursuant to the authority granted by that section. Such rules shall provide performance and display standards for such built-in decoder circuitry. Such rules shall further require that all such apparatus be able to receive and display closed captioning which have been transmitted by way of line 21 of the vertical blanking interval and which conform to the signal and display specifications set forth in the Public Broadcasting System engineering report numbered E-7709-C dated May 1980, as amended by the Telecaption II Decoder Module Performance Specification published by the National Captioning Institute, November 1985. As new video technology is developed, the Commission shall take such action as the Commission determines appropriate to ensure that closed-captioning service continues to be available to consumers. This subsection shall not apply to carriers transporting such apparatus without trading it."

(b) Section 330(c) of such Act, as redesignated by subsection (a) of this section, is amended by deleting "and section 303(s)" and inserting in lieu thereof, "section 303(s), and section 303(us)."

EFFECTIVE DATE

SEC. 5. Sections 3 and 4 of this Act shall take effect on July 1, 1993.

Source: Public Law 101-431, 15 October 1990, 104 Stat. 960-961. Cited as 47 U.S.C. 303 note.

Senate Bill 332 (104th Congress, First Session)

On 2 February 1995, Senator Kent Conrad (D-North Dakota) introduced a bill into the U.S. Senate dealing with the problem of televised violence. After reviewing the scientific evidence that had been elucidated on this subject, Senator Conrad argued that the most appropriate way of dealing with the problem in the 1990s was to establish a television violence rating code and then to require manufacturers of television sets to install electronic circuitry that would make it possible for viewers to block out programs with certain ratings. The text of Senator Conrad's bill follows:

S. 332

Be it enacted by the Senate and House of Representatives of the United States of America in Congress assembled,

SECTION 1. SHORT TITLE.

This Act may be cited as the "Childrens' Media Protection Act of 1995."

SEC. 2. FINDINGS.

Congress makes the following findings:

(1) On average, a child in the United States is exposed to 27 hours of television each week, and some children are exposed to as much as 11 hours of television each day.

(2) The average American child watches 8,000 murders and 100,000 acts of other violence on television by the time the child completes elementary school.

(3) By the age of 18 years, the average American teenager has watched 200,000 acts of violence on television, including 40,000 murders.

(4) The Times Mirror Center reports that a recent poll of Americans indicates that 72 percent of the American people believe that there is too much violence on television, and according to a survey by *U.S. News and World Report* dated May 1994, 91 percent of American voters believe that mayhem in the media contributes to violence in real life.

(5) On several occasions since 1975, the *Journal of the American Medical Association* has alerted the medical community to the adverse effects of televised violence on child development, including an increase in the level of aggressive behavior and violent behavior among children who view it.

(6) The National Commission on Children recommended in 1991 that producers of television programs exercise greater restraint in the content of programming for children.

(7) A report of the Harry Frank Guggenheim Foundation, dated May 1993, indicates that there is an irrefutable connection between the amount of violence depicted in the television programs watched by children and increased aggressive behavior among children.

(8) It is in the National interest that parents be empowered with the technology to block the viewing of television programs whose content is overly violent or objectionable for other reasons.

(9) Technology currently exists to permit the manufacture of television receivers that are capable of permitting parents to block television programs having violent or otherwise objectionable content.

SEC. 3. ESTABLISHMENT OF TELEVISION VIOLENCE RATING CODE.

Section 303 of the Communications Act of 1934 (47 U.S.C. 303) is amended by adding at the end the following: "(v) Prescribe, in consultation with television broadcasters, cable operators, appropriate public interest groups, and interested individuals from the private sector, rules for rating the level of violence in television programming, including rules for the transmission by television broadcast systems and cable systems of signals containing specifications for blocking violent programming."

SEC. 4. REQUIREMENT FOR MANUFACTURE OF TELEVISIONS THAT BLOCK PROGRAMS.

Section 303 of the Communications Act of 1934 (47 U.S.C. 303), as amended by section 3, is further amended by adding at the end the following: "(w) Require, in the case of apparatus designed to receive television signals that are manufactured in the United States or imported for use in the United States and that have a picture screen 13 inches or greater in size (measured diagonally), that such apparatus—
"(1) be equipped with circuitry designed to enable viewers to block the display of channels, programs, and time slots;["] and "(2) enable viewers to block display of all programs with a common rating."

SEC. 5. SHIPPING OR IMPORTING OF TELEVISIONS THAT BLOCK PROGRAMS.

(a) Regulations.—Section 330 of the Communications Act of 1934 (47 U.S.C. 330) is amended—
   (1) by redesignating subsection (c) as subsection (d); and
   (2) by adding after subsection (b) the following new subsection (c):
      "(c)(1) Except as provided in paragraph (2), no person shall ship in interstate commerce, manufacture, assemble, or import from any foreign country into the United States any apparatus described in section 303(w) of this Act except in accordance with rules prescribed by the Commission pursuant to the authority granted by that section. "(2) this subsection shall not apply to carriers transporting apparatus referred to in paragraph (1) without trading it."
   (3) The rules prescribed by the Commission under this subsection shall provide performance standards for blocking technology. Such rules shall require that all such apparatus be able to receive the rating signals which have been transmitted by way of line 21 of the vertical blanking interval and which conform to the signal and blocking specifications established by the Commission."
   (4) As new video technology is developed, the Commission shall take such action as the Commission determines appropriate to ensure that blocking service continues to be available to consumers."
(b) Conforming Amendment.—Section 330(d) of such Act, as redesignated by subsection (a)(1), is amended by striking "section 303(s), and section 303(u)" and inserting in lieu thereof "and sections 303(s), 303(u), and 303(w)."

SEC. 6. ELIMINATION OF VIOLENT PROGRAMMING ON TELEVISION DURING CERTAIN HOURS.

Title I of the Children's Television Act of 1990 (47 U.S.C. 303a et seq.) is amended by adding at the end the following: "PROHIBITION ON VIOLENT PROGRAMMING" Sec. 105. (a) The Commission shall, within 30 days of the date of the enactment of this Act, initiate a rule-making proceeding to prescribe a prohibition on the broadcast on commercial television and by public telecommunications entity, including the broadcast by cable operators, from the hours of 6 A.M. to 10 P.M., inclusive, of programming that contains gratuitous violence. "(b) As used in this section: "(1) The term 'cable operator' has the meaning given such term in section 602 of the Communications Act of 1934 (47 U.S.C. 522). "(2) the term 'programming'; includes advertisements but does not include bona fide newscasts, bona fide news interviews, bona fide news documentaries, and on-the-spot coverage of bone [*sic*] fide news events."(3) The term 'public telecommunications entity' has the meaning given such term in section 397(12) of the Communications Act of 1934 (47 U.S.C. 397(12))."

SEC. 7. BROADCAST ON TELEVISION AND CABLE OF EDUCATIONAL AND INFORMATIONAL PROGRAMMING FOR CHILDREN.

(a) Broadcast Television.—Section 309 of the Communications Act of 1934 (47 U.S.C. 309) is amended by adding at the end the following: "(k) Educational and Information Programming for Children.—In granting an application for a license for a television broadcasting station (including an application for renewal of such a license), the Commission shall impose such conditions upon the applicant as the Commission requires in order to ensure that the applicant complies under the license with the standards for children's television programming established under section 102 of the Children's Television Act of 1990 (47 U.S.C. 303a) and otherwise serves the educational and informational needs of children through its overall programming."

(b) Cable Service.—Part III of title VI of the Communications Act of 1934 (47 U.S.C. 541 et seq.) is amended by adding at the end the following: "EDUCATIONAL AND INFORMATION PROGRAM-MING FOR CHILDREN "Sec. 629. A franchise, including the renewal of a franchise, may not be awarded under this part unless the cable operator to be awarded the franchise agrees to comply with the standards for children's television programming estab-lished under section 102 of the Children's Television Act of 1990 (47 U.S.C. 303a) and to otherwise serve the educational and informa-tional needs of children in the provision of cable service under the franchise."

Standards

Given the inability of Congress and other legislative bodies to pass laws dealing with violence in the mass media, about the only method for limiting such depictions is through self-imposed voluntary codes adopted by professional organizations. In this section, samples of such codes are presented. At least one of these codes, the National Association of Broadcasters Television Code, is now obsolete, having been declared unconstitutional by the courts. It is presented here, therefore, for its historical interest.

Motion Picture Association of America (MPAA) Rating System

The Rating System was first adopted in 1974 and has undergone a number of changes since that time. The general purposes of the system are as follows:

> From the outset, the purpose of the rating system was to provide *advance information to enable parents* to make judgments on movies they wanted their children to see or not to see. Basic to the program was and is the *responsibility of the parent to make that decision.*
>
> The Rating Board does not rate for quality or the lack of it. That role is left to the movie critic and the audience. . . .
>
> The only objective of the ratings is to advise the parent in advance so he may determine the possible suitability or unsuitability of viewing by his children. But, to repeat, the rating would not even make a final judgment on that; except for the X rating, the parent's decision remained the key to children's attendance.
>
> Inherent in the rating system is the fact that to those 17 and over, and/or married without children, the ratings have little if any meaning.
>
> Among the Rating Board's criteria are: theme, language, nudity and sex, and violence, and part of the rating comes from the assessment of how each of these elements is treated in each individual film.

Source: Motion Picture Association of America, "The Movie Rating System of 1978," as reprinted in William L. Rivers, Wilbur Schramm, and Clifford G. Christians, *Responsibility in Mass Communication* (New York: Harper & Row, 1980), p. 301.

The Current Rating System

The current rating system, with the meaning of each of the designated abbreviations, is as follows:

> **G**: For general audiences; in practice, the rating is usually given to cartoons and children's films.
> **PG**: Parental guidance is suggested, and some material may be unsuitable for younger children.
> **PG-13:** Parents are strongly cautioned, and some material may be inappropriate for children under the age of 13.
> **R**: Restricted to adults and to children under the age of 17, provided that they are accompanied by a parent or adult guardian.
> **NC-17**: No person under the age of 17 is to be admitted.

Source: As summarized in Bernard Weinraub, "Film Ratings under Attack from More than One Angle," *New York Times*, 6 September 1994, p. C13. The symbols G, PG, PG-13, R, and NC-17 are registered trademarks of the Motion Picture Association of America.

Showtime Networks' Guidelines

One of the problems associated with the MPAA rating system is what effect such ratings will have when motion pictures are shown on television. The decision a consumer makes about viewing a film might be quite different depending on whether that film is shown in a motion picture theater or on the screen of one's own television set at home. This problem was addressed at a hearing of the House Subcommittee on Telecommunications and Finance of the Committee on Energy and Commerce in 1993.

Winston H. Cox is chairman and chief executive officer of Showtime Networks, Inc., which owns and operates three subscription television networks: Showtime, The Movie Channel, and FLIX. He is also chairman of the National Cable Television Association's Satellite Network Programmers Committee. In the following remarks, he outlines the guidelines followed by Showtime Networks as well as "other premium services such as HBO" with regard to the use of violence in programming.

> Under Showtime's guidelines, we do not exhibit any program that we believe to be outside socially accepted standards of entertainment, or any program that is gratuitous or excessive in either violent or sexual content. It is also our policy not to exhibit any picture rated "X" or "NC-17" by the MPAA, or any unrated picture that we believe would qualify for either of those ratings.

To provide our subscribers with information about a program, so that they may wisely exercise their election to view or not view a particular program, we precede each exhibition of a motion picture with an on-screen visual stating the picture's MPAA rating. . . . For original programs, which generally are not rated by the MPAA, we have developed our own form of advisory and we precede each exhibition of these programs with an on-screen viewer-advisory when we feel that parental discretion is warranted.

In addition, in the program guides that we produce and in the program schedules we furnish to other television listing publications and services, we include MPAA ratings for motion pictures . . . and our own advisory for original programs, where warranted. We also inform the cable customer sales representatives who sell our program services at local cable systems about our program selection and scheduling policies, and these sales reps communicate our policies to potential subscribers.

Our efforts to minimize children's exposure to violence on television do not stop at on-screen and printed ratings and advisories. Every month various programming, acquisition, scheduling and other executives, including myself, meet to decide (among other things) the time of day most appropriate for each program's exhibition. We know that children are more likely to watch television during the day and early evening, so we are sensitive to programs exhibited before 8:00 P.M. Because the viewing public generally understands "R"-rated motion pictures to be adult in content, we do not exhibit any "R"-rated motion pictures before this hour (in the Eastern and Pacific time zones) on Showtime, our "flagship" service. In fact, our evaluation of a program may lead us to decide that it should not be schedule [sic] until after 9 P.M., 10 P.M., or even later.

Similarly, we are sensitive in scheduling promotional information about our movies and original programs. For example, when promoting some programs with violent or otherwise mature subject matter, we have occasionally created two versions of a promo—one for daytime use, another more suitable for exhibition at night. Some programs are deemed unsuitable to be promoted during the day, regardless of the content of the promo itself. Finally, we do not promote "R"-rated motion pictures (or comparable original programs) adjacent to or near any program designed for children's viewing—not even with a promo otherwise suitable for daytime viewing.

Source: *Violence on Television: Hearings before the Subcommittee on Telecommunications and Finance of the Committee on Energy and Commerce,* House of Representatives, 103rd Congress, 1st sess., 12 May, 25 June, 1 and 29 July, and 15 September 1993, pp. 225–227.

Film Advisory Board System

Some critics are dissatisfied with the MPAA Rating System described above. One organization, the Film Advisory Board, has developed an alternative method of rating films. The Board claims that its system is more useful since it includes descriptive phrases for films that it rates. The categories used by the Board are as follows:

      C: Children (ages 10 and under): Exclusively for young children.

      F: Family (all ages): Suitable for viewing by all family members. Content description, in some cases, as in historical pieces, may state "violence in battle scenes" or "frightening for younger children." Compares to MPAA's "G" rating.

    PD: Parental discretion (content description implies age suitability): Subject matter may not be suitable for or of interest to young children. Content description may state "sexual innuendos/mild language/violence/substance abuse." Compares to MPAA's "PG" rating.

  PD-M: Parental discretion-mature (ages 13 and over): Subject matter may be too mature for pre-teens. Content description may state "brief nudity/sexual situations/strong language/violence." Compares to MPAA's PG-13 rating.

    EM: Extremely mature (ages 17 and over): Subject matter may be too "extreme" for children under the age of 17. Content description may state "frontal nudity/sex/strong language/graphic violence." Compares to MPAA's "R" rating.

    AO: Adults only (ages 18 and over): Not suitable for children. Contains sexually explicit material beyond what the EXTREMELY MATURE category might represent. Contents may state "explicit sex and language/erotica/extreme nudity." Compares to MPAA's "NC-17" rating.

Source: ©1993 Film Advisory Board, Inc.

Radio Code of the National Association of Broadcasters

The first Radio Code of the National Association of Broadcasters was adopted in 1937. It was revised for the first time in 1945, and then periodically in subsequent years, as it seemed appropriate to the organization. Sections of the twenty-first edition of the code (June 1978) that deal with programming violence are summarized below:

G. RESPONSIBILITY TOWARD CHILDREN

Broadcasters have a special responsibility to children. Programming which might reasonably be expected to hold the attention of children should be presented with due regard for its effect on children. . . .

5. Programming should be consistent with integrity of realistic production, but should avoid material of extreme nature which might create undesirable emotional reaction in children. . . .

7. Programming should present such subjects as violence and sex without undue emphasis and only as required by plot development or character delineation.
   Violence, physical or psychological, should only be projected in responsibly handled contexts, not used to excess or exploitatively. Programs involving violence should present the consequences of it to its victims and perpetrators. . . .

8. The treatment of criminal activities should always convey their social and human effects. . . .

H. DRAMATIC PROGRAMMING

5. In determining the acceptability of any dramatic program, especially those containing elements of crime, mystery, or horror, consideration should be given to the possible effect on all members of the listening audience.
   In addition, without sacrificing integrity of presentation, dramatic programs on radio shall avoid:
   (a) the presentation of techniques of crime in such detail as to be instructional or invite imitation;
   (b) presentation of the details of violence involving the excessive, the gratuitous, and the instructional;
   (c) sound effects calculated to mislead, shock, or unduly alarm the listener;
   (d) portrayals of law enforcement in a manner which does not contribute to its proper role in our society.

Source: Motion Picture Association of America, "The Radio Code of the National Association of Broadcasters," as reprinted in William

L. Rivers, Wilbur Schramm, and Clifford G. Christians, *Responsibility in Mass Communication* (New York: Harper & Row, 1980), pp. 311–312.

Television Code of the National Association of Broadcasters

A ruling of the U.S. Supreme Court in 1982 made the Television Code of the National Association of Broadcasters (NAB) moot. For historical interest, however, the portions of that code that deal with violence are summarized below.

IV. SPECIAL PROGRAM STANDARDS

1. **Violence; conflict.**
   A. Violence, physical or psychological, may only be projected in responsibly handled contexts, not used exploitatively. Programs involving violence should present the consequences of it to its victims and perpetrators.

      Presentation of the details of violence should avoid the excessive, the gratuitous and the instructional.

      The use of violence for its own sake and the detailed dwelling upon brutality or physical agony, by sight or by sound, are not permissible.
   B. **Conflict and children.** The depiction of conflict, when presented in programs designed primarily for children, should be handled with sensitivity.
2. **Anti-social behavior; crime.** The treatment of criminal activities should always convey their social and human effects.

   The presentation of techniques of crime in such detail as to be instructional or incite imitation shall be avoided.
3. **Self-destructive behavior: drugs; gambling; alcohol.**
   A. Narcotic addiction shall not be presented except as a destructive habit. The use of illegal drugs or the abuse of legal drugs shall not be encouraged or shown as socially acceptable.
   B. The use of gambling devices or scenes necessary to the development of plot or as appropriate background is acceptable only when presented with discretion and in moderation, and in a manner which would not excite interest in, or foster, betting nor be instructional in nature.
   C. The use of liquor and the depiction of smoking in program content shall be deemphasized. When shown, they should be consistent with plot and character development.

Source: Motion Picture Association of America, "The Television Code of the National Association of Broadcasters," as reprinted in William L. Rivers, Wilbur Schramm, and Clifford G. Christians, *Responsibility in Mass Communication* (New York: Harper & Row, 1980), p. 325.

Standards for the Depiction of Violence in Television Programs

In December 1992, the three major television networks, ABC, CBS, and NBC, issued the following standards for the depiction of violence on network programs.

PREFACE

The following Standards for the Depiction of Violence in Television Programs are issued jointly by the ABC, CBS, and NBC Television Networks under the Antitrust exemption granted by the Television Violence Act of 1990.

Each Network has long been committed to presenting television viewers with a broad spectrum of entertainment and information programming. Each Network maintains its own extensive published broadcast standards governing acceptability of both program (including on-air promotion) and commercial materials.

These new joint standards are consistent with each of the Network's long-standing preexisting policies on violence. At the same time they are set forth in a more detailed an [sic] explanatory manner to reflect the experience gained under the preexisting policies. While adopting and subscribing to these joint Standards, each Network will continue the tradition of individual review of material, which will necessitate independent judgments on a program-by-program basis.

The standards are not intended to inhibit the work of producers, directors or writers or to impede the creative process. They are intended to proscribe gratuitous or excessive portrayals of violence.

In principle, each of the ABC, CBS, and NBC Television Networks is committed to presenting programs which portray the human condition, which may include the depiction of violence as a component. The following Standards for the Depiction of Violence in Television Programs will provide the framework within which the acceptability of content will be determined by each Network in the exercise of its own judgment.

STANDARDS FOR THE DEPICTION OF VIOLENCE IN TELEVISION PROGRAMS

These written standards cannot cover every situation and must, therefore, be worded broadly. Moreover, the Standards must be considered against the creative context, character and tone of each individual program. Each scene should be evaluated on its own merits with due consideration for its creative integrity.

1) Conflict and strife are the essence of drama and conflict often results in physical or psychological violence. However, all depictions of violence should be relevant and necessary to the development of character, or to the advancement of theme or plot.

2) Gratuitous or excessive depictions of violence, (or redundant violence shown solely for its own sake), are not acceptable.

3) Programs should not depict violence as glamorous, nor as an acceptable solution to human conflict.

4) Depictions of violence may not be used to shock or stimulate the audience.

5) Scenes showing excessive gore, pain or physical suffering are not acceptable.

6) The intensity and frequency of the use of force, and other factors relating to the manner of its portrayal, should be measured under a standard of reasonableness so that the program, on the whole, is appropriate for a home viewing medium.

7) Scenes which may be instructive in nature, e.g., which depict in an imitable manner, the use of harmful devices or weapons, describe readily usable techniques for the commission of crimes, or show replicable methods for the evasion of detection or apprehension, should be avoided. Similarly, ingenious, unique or otherwise unfamiliar methods of inflicting pain or injury are unacceptable if easily capable of imitation.

8) Realistic depictions of violence should also portray, in human terms, the consequences of that violence to its victims and its perpetrators. Callousness or indifference to suffering experienced by victims of violence should be avoided.

9) Exceptional care must be taken in stories or scenes where children are victims of, or are threatened by acts of violence (physical, psychological or verbal).

10) The portrayal of dangerous behavior which would invite imitation by children, including portrayals of the use of weapons or implements readily accessible to this impressionable group, should be avoided.

11) Realistic portrayals of violence as well as scenes, images or events which are unduly frightening or distressing to children should not be included in any program specifically designed for that audience.

12) The use of real animals shall conform to accepted standards of humane treatment. Fictionalized portrayals of abusive treatment should be strictly limited to the legitimate requirements of plot development.

13) Extreme caution must be exercised in any themes, plots or scenes which mix sex and violence. Rape and other sexual assaults are violent, not erotic, behavior.

14) The scheduling of any program, commercial or promotional material, including those containing violent depictions, should take into consideration the nature of the program, its content and the likely composition of the intended audience.

15) Certain exceptions to the foregoing may be acceptable, as in the presentation of material whose overall theme is clearly and unambiguously anti-violent.

Source: *Violence on Television: Hearings before the Subcommittee on Crime and Criminal Justice of the Committee on the Judiciary,* House of Representatives, 102nd Congress, 2nd sess., 15 December 1992, pp. 167–169.

Statement of R. E. Turner, Chairman and President of Turner Broadcasting System, Inc.

Some networks other than the "Big Three" soon subscribed to the standards outlined above. A sample of the kind of statements made by such networks is the one that follows.

> We have subscribed to the Broadcast Network's Violence Code, at the same time maintaining our own standards and practices, which in operation are stricter than the network standards.
>
> We have banned promotions for action films and other motion pictures that contain violence from children's programming, and we will assure that promotions appearing in family programming are appropriate for family audiences.
>
> We will apply the same test to promotional materials contained in paid advertising for theatrical motion pictures. I will note for the record, Mr. Chairman, that for several years in the early 1980s, I personally made the decision not to run ads at all for any motion pictures rated R for violence. . . .
>
> We are reviewing our selecting and editing policies for theatrical movies and we will label motion pictures containing violence where parental discretion or guidance would particularly be promote [*sic*].

Source: *Violence on Television: Hearings before the Subcommittee on Telecommunications and Finance of the Committee on Energy and Com-*

merce, House of Representatives, 103rd Congress, 1st sess., 12 May, 25 June, 1 and 29 July, and 15 September 1993, pp. 106–107.

General Policy, Association of Independent Television Stations

The Association of Independent Television Stations, Inc. (INTV) is a nonprofit trade association that represents local television stations that are not affiliated with any one of the major television networks. INTV has developed a policy regarding the depiction of violence in programs that it carries. That policy is as follows:

GENERAL POLICY OUTLINE

1. These policies apply to programs and to promotional material, are directed solely at entertainment programming, and in no way are designed to inhibit journalistic or editorial discretion in the coverage and reporting of news or sports events.
2. Violence should be depicted only when necessary, and to no greater extent than necessary, to the development of the story line, plot, context, or theme of, or character in, a television program.
3. Depiction of violence in such way as to glamorize violent behavior or to ignore or trivialize its consequences to either the victim, the perpetrator, or society should be avoided.
4. Depiction of violence in such way as might be instructive or as might suggest imitative behavior should be avoided.
5. Presentation of programs depicting violence and the depiction of violence should not be undertaken solely as a means of exploiting or shocking the audience.
6. The depiction of violence in a sexual context requires special sensitivity with respect to its potential to exploit, debase, demean, shock, or stimulate. Violence never should be depicted so as to appeal to the prurient interests of the audience.
7. Graphic or detailed depictions of violence or dwelling on gore, pain, or physical suffering should be avoided.
8. The special needs of children should be considered, and special care should be taken, in the scheduling and editing of programs and promotional materials which include the depiction or description of violent behavior.
9. Depiction of violent acts in a manner which might distress or frighten children should be avoided in programming intended primarily for children.
10. In appropriate circumstances, the station may determine to inform viewers through appropriate on-air advisories that specific

programs contain depictions of violent behavior so that individual viewers may make informed viewing decisions and avoid unexpected depictions of violence which are unsuited to their particular tastes. Such advisories might state:

"The following program depicts violent acts or behavior."

"The following program depicts violent acts or behavior. Viewer discretion is advised."

"The following program depicts violent acts or behavior which may be unsuitable for children. Parental discretion is advised."

"The following program involves realistic portrayals of human behavior, including acts of violence, which may be disturbing to some viewers."

"The following program involves realistic portrayals of human behavior, including acts of violence, which may be disturbing to children. Parental discretion is advised."

Code of the Comics Magazine Association of America

The 1950s saw a growing concern about the presentation of sex and violence in comic magazines. A number of critics pointed out that young readers were being exposed to a heavy diet of very violent episodes. The comic magazine industry rather quickly recognized the problem it was facing and adopted a code governing the way comics should be presented. The code consists of nine sections: Preamble, Institutions, Language, Violence, Characterizations, Substance Abuse, Crime, Attire and Sexuality, and Administrative Procedure. The following sections are those dealing most directly with the question of violence in the media.

PREAMBLE

The Comics Magazine Association of America was formed in 1954 by a group of publishers committed to the principle that the public deserved decent and wholesome comic books as entertainment for children. To that end, those publishers set content guidelines, created a reviewing authority and established the Comics Code Seal. This seal was to appear on covers of CMAA member comics as a way of communicating to the public their shared commitment to uphold thee [sic] standards.

While the comic book industry has changed over the intervening three decades, as has almost every other facet of American life, the publisher members of the CMAA remain committed to providing decent and wholesome comic books for children. This new updated

version of the Comics Code is a reaffirmation of that commitment.
The member publishers of the Comics Magazine Association of
America hereby affirm our joint commitment to our shared principle:
that comics carrying the Comics Code Seal be ones that a parent can
purchase with confidence that the contents uphold basic American
moral and cultural values. . . .

VIOLENCE

Violent actions or scenes are acceptable within the context of a comic
book story when dramatically appropriate. Violent behavior will not be
shown as acceptable. If it is presented in a realistic manner, care should
be taken to present the natural repercussions of such actions. Publishers
should avoid excessive levels of violence, excessively graphic depictions
of violence, and excessive bloodshed or gore. Publishers will not present
detailed information instructing readers how to engage in imitable
violent actions. . . .

CRIME

While crimes and criminals may be portrayed for dramatic purposes,
crimes will never be presented in such a way as to inspire readers with a
desire to imitate them nor will criminals be portrayed in such a manner
as to inspire readers to emulate them. Stories will not present unique
imitable techniques or methods of committing crimes. . . .

Source: "Code of the Comics Magazine Association of America"
(New York: Comics Magazine Association of America, n.d.).

Lyrics Labeling Program of the Recording Industry Association of America

Beginning in about 1985, pressures were brought to bear on the
recording industry for its production of certain music that contained lyrics that offended a number of adult listeners. In order to
deal with this problem, the Recording Industry Association of
America (RIAA) adopted the Voluntary Lyrics Labeling Program,
described in the following statement.

> Since 1985, the recording industry has responsibly addressed
> the concerns of the public, and parents in particular, regard-
> ing the explicit nature of certain sound recordings. In that year,
> the RIAA reached an agreement with the National Parent
> Teacher Association and the Parents Music Resource Center
> under which record companies would voluntarily identify and

label newly released sound recordings with lyrics that reflect explicit violence, explicit sex or explicit substance abuse.

In 1990, the RIAA greatly enhanced the effectiveness of this voluntary program as a tool for parents and guardians who wish to monitor what their children purchase and listen to by implementing a uniform parental advisory logo that continues in use today. The Parental Advisory program allows record companies and their artists to exercise their artistic rights and, at the same time, exercise their social responsibilities to the community as well.

The black-and-white logo, shown here, is made part of the each [sic] record's permanent packaging, beneath the shrink-wrap, and is now widely used not only by RIAA members, which represent approximately 90 percent of the music industry, but also by most non-member companies as well, particularly those releasing rap and heavy metal music.

While the decision to label a particular sound recording is properly left to each company, in conjunction with the artist, there is little question that the industry has taken this program seriously. Indeed, virtually every recording that has been the target of public controversy, either because of its sexually-explicit or violently-explicit nature, has a voluntary Parental Advisory on its cover. And the Parental Advisory also has served as an important tool for radio stations and record retailers when considering whether specific explicit recordings should be broadcast or made available for sale to minors.

Given the increased public attention to violence in America, and the desire of all Americans to eliminate it, the recording industry may well hear calls for a government censorship system or for a voluntary ratings system similar to the one currently in use by the motion picture industry and those now being considered for the video game industry as well.

While a voluntary ratings system may be appropriate for motion pictures, its application to sound recordings would be both inappropriate and impractical. First, the lyrical content of musical recordings is far more subjective than the explicit visual images of motions pictures. In the context of violence for example, what some may perceive as a "call to arms" may in fact be a cry for help to address the hard realities of the artist's social environment. Second, given the vast number of songs (over 10,000) released each year, compared with the 577 films rated in 1993, developing a ratings board to review and rate each and every recording would be a near impossible task.

And of course, a government mandated censorship system would run afoul of the full and unimpeded protection of artistic expression given by the First Amendment.

Accepting a difference of values among people is part of living in a free society. Simply put, the voluntary Parental Advisory Program balances the rights of free expression with the desires for social responsibility. The recording industry has made great strides implementing its voluntary Parental Advisory Program and educating the public about its intended use. It vows to continue to do so in the future.

Court Cases

Courts at all levels of the state and federal judiciary have considered the question of free speech in the United States for more than 200 years. The most important of the decisions made in these cases are those emanating from the United States Supreme Court and its district courts. A sample of those cases is given below. It appears that in only one of these cases has the Supreme Court dealt specifically with the issue of violence, that being *Winters v. New York*, in 1948.

Mutual Film Corporation v. Ohio (1915) (236 U.S. 230)

This case involved an important early ruling about the nature of the motion picture industry and whatever constitutional rights its producers, directors, and distributors might have. Mutual Film was a company in the business of purchasing, selling, and leasing films in a number of states and foreign countries. The point is clearly made early on in the decision that "Nothing [in the films] is depicted of a harmful or immoral character."

In an effort to transact business in the state of Ohio, Mutual was confronted with a state law requiring that all films be submitted to a state censor who had the authority to determine in advance of any sale or showing whether a film could be released. The case was originally brought in the U.S. District Court for Northern Ohio by Mutual claiming that Ohio's censorship law constituted a case of prior restraint that violated the company's rights of free speech and expression under the First and Fourteenth Amendments.

The district court refused to restrain the enforcement of the state censorship law, and Mutual appealed to the U.S. Supreme Court. In its consideration of this case, the Supreme Court focused on what rights of free speech and expression, if any, could be claimed by an abstract concept such as "moving pictures," in contrast to those of individual humans. In the first part of his decision, speaking for the Court, Justice Joseph McKenna muses on the possible dangers that the new form of the media may pose to the general public and what government can do about such dangers:

The next contention is that the [Ohio] statute violates the freedom of speech and publication guaranteed by the Ohio Constitution. In its discussion counsel have gone into a very elaborate description of moving picture exhibitions and their many useful purposes as graphic expressions of opinion and sentiments, as exponents of policies, as teachers of science and history, as useful, interesting, amusing, educational, and moral. And a list of the "campaigns," as counsel call them, which may be carried on, is given. We may concede the praise. It is not questioned by the Ohio statute, and under its comprehensive description, "campaigns" of an infinite variety may be conducted. Films of a "moral, educational, or amusing and harmless character shall be passed and approved," are the words of the statute. No exhibition, therefore, or "campaign" of complainant will be prevented if its pictures have those qualities. Therefore, however missionary of opinion films are or may become, however educational or entertaining, there is no impediment to their value or effect in the Ohio statute. But they may be used for evil, and against that possibility the statute was enacted. Their power of amusement, and, it may be, education, the audiences they assemble, not of women alone, nor of men alone, but together, not of adults only, but of children, make them the more insidious in corruption by a pretense of worthy purpose or if they should degenerate from worthy purpose. Indeed, we may go beyond that possibility. They take their attraction from the general interest, eager and wholesome it may be, in their subjects, but a prurient interest may be excited and appealed to. Besides, there are some things which should not have pictorial representation in public places and to all audiences. And not only the state of Ohio, but other states, have considered it to be in the interest of the public morals and welfare to supervise moving picture exhibitions. We would have to shut our eyes to the facts of the world to regard the precaution unreasonable or the legislation to effect it a mere wanton interference with personal liberty.

Justice McKenna then outlines the Court's reasoning in its final decision to uphold the ruling of the district court:

Are moving pictures within the principle [of free speech and expression] as it is contended they are? They, indeed, may be mediums of thought, but so are many things. So is the theater, the circus, and all other shows and spectacles, and their performances may be thus brought by the like reasoning under the same immunity from repression or supervision as the public press,—made the same agencies of civil liberty.

Counsel have not shrunk from this extension of their contention, and cite a case in this court where the title of drama was accorded to pantomime; and such and other spectacles are said by counsel to be publications of ideas, satisfying the definition of the dictionaries,—that is, and we quote counsel, a means of making or announcing publicly something that otherwise might have remained private or unknown,—and this being peculiarly the purpose and effect of moving pictures, they come directly, it is contended, under the protection of the Ohio constitution.

The first impulse of the mind is to reject the contention. We immediately feel that the argument is wrong or strained which extends the guaranties of free opinion and speech to the multitudinous shows which are advertised on the billboards of our cities and towns. . . .

Justice McKenna then makes the key point on which the Court's decision was based and for which the case is best known. In referring to a number of precedents raised in arguing this case, he says:

It seems not to have occurred to anybody in the cited cases that freedom of opinion was repressed in the exertion of the power which was illustrated. The rights of property were only considered as involved. It cannot be put out of view that the exhibition of moving pictures is a business, pure and simple, originated and conducted for profit, like other spectacles, not to be regarded, nor intended to be regarded by the Ohio Constitution, we think, as part of the press of the country, or as organs of public opinion. They are mere representations of events, of ideas and sentiments published and known; vivid, useful, and entertaining, no doubt, but, as we have said, capable of evil, having power for it, the greater because of their attractiveness and manner of exhibition. It was this capability and power, and it may be in experience of them, that induced the state of Ohio, in addition to prescribing penalties for immoral exhibitions, as it does in its Criminal Code, to require censorship before exhibition, as it does by the act under review. We cannot regard this as beyond the power of government.

Schenck v. United States (1918)
(249 U.S. 47)

Those who work within the media (as well as many of those who do not) frequently point to the First Amendment of the U.S. Constitution as giving all Americans "freedom of speech and expression." While that is certainly true, it is also true that these freedoms are not given without restraint. Congress and the courts have always made it clear that a person's freedom of speech, of expression, and of the press can be abridged under certain circumstances. One of the landmark rulings in this regard is the one quoted here. Schenck was general secretary of the Socialist Party when he was charged with conspiracy to violate the Espionage Act as a result of his role in the printing and distribution of pamphlets encouraging young American men to refuse to be drafted into the U.S. Army during World War I. After outlining the facts of this case, Justice Oliver Wendell Holmes went on to explain the Court's decision in upholding Schenck's conviction:

We admit that in many places and in ordinary times the defendants, in saying all that was said in the circular, would have been within their constitutional rights. But the character of every act depends upon the circumstances in which it is done [citations omitted]. . . . The most stringent protection of free speech would not protect a man in falsely shouting fire in a theater, and causing a panic. It does not even protect a man from an injunction against uttering words that may have all the effect of force [citations omitted]. . . . The question in every case is whether the words used are used in such circumstances and are of such a nature as to create a clear and present danger that they will bring about the substantive evils that Congress has a right to prevent. It is a question of proximity and degree. When a nation is at war many things that might be said in time of peace are such a hindrance to its effort that their utterance will not be endured so long as men fight, and that no court could regard them as protected by an [*sic*] constitutional right.

The issue is then addressed as to whether there is a difference between Schenck's advocating the avoidance of the draft by young men and their actually taking such actions. The Court ruled that:

It seems to be admitted that if an actual obstruction of the recruiting service were proved, liability for words that produced that effect might be enforced. The Statute of 1917, in §4, punishes conspiracies to obstruct as well as actual obstruction. If the act (speaking, or circulating a paper), its tendency and the intent with which it is done, are the same, we perceive no ground for saying that success alone warrants making the act a crime. . . .

Gitlow v. New York (1925)
(268 U.S. 652)

This case is of significance for discussions of violence in the media because it clearly states for the first time that the rights of free speech and expression guaranteed in the First Amendment to the U.S. Constitution apply to state law as well as to legislation passed by the U.S. Congress. The part of the Fourteenth Amendment that is relevant to this discussion reads as follows:

No State shall make or enforce any law which shall abridge the privileges or immunities of citizens of the United States; nor shall any State deprive any person of life, liberty, or property, without due process of law; nor deny to any person within its jurisdiction the equal protection of the laws.

Benjamin Gitlow was business manager and a member of the board of directors of *Revolutionary Age*, the official newspaper of the Left Wing section of the Socialist Party. Following a conference in New York City in June 1919, the newspaper carried a statement of policy, "The Left Wing Manifesto," advocating strikes and other actions against the government. The Court begins its analysis in the present case with a review of the lower court's decision:

Benjamin Gitlow was indicted in the supreme court of New York, with three others, for the statutory crime of criminal anarchy [citations omitted]. . . . He was separately tried, convicted, and sentenced to imprisonment. The judgment was affirmed by the appellate division and by the court of appeals [citations omitted]. . . . The case is here on writ of error to the supreme court, to which the record was remitted [citations omitted]. . . .

The contention here is that the statute, by its terms and as applied in this case, is repugnant to the due process clause of the Fourteenth Amendment.

The Court then cites sections 160 and 161 of the New York law that are at question in this case and reviews the evidence that was presented at earlier trials. The Court next states specifically what the issue is that it has been asked to decide:

> The precise question presented, and the only question which we can consider under this writ of error, then, is whether this statute, as construed and applied in this case by the state courts, deprived the defendant of his liberty of expression, in violation of the due process clause of the 14th Amendment.

The Court next specifically states the principle for which this case is so important in the issue of free speech, namely that states are under the same First Amendment obligations as is the federal government:

> For present purposes we may and do assume that freedom of speech and of the press—which are protected by the 1st Amendment from abridgment by Congress—are among the fundamental personal rights and "liberties" protected by the due process clause of the 14th Amendment from impairment by the states. We do not regard the incidental statement in *Prudential Ins. Co. v. Cheek* [citations omitted] . . . that the 14th Amendment imposes no restrictions on the states concerning freedom of speech, as determinative of this question.

This basic principle having been stated, the Court then returns to the question of the state's right to pass laws against speech advocating violent overthrow of the government. Briefly, it makes the following points:

> It is a fundamental principle, long established, that the freedom of speech and of the press which is secured by the Constitution does not confer an absolute right to speak or publish, without responsibility, whatever one may choose, or an unrestricted and unbridled license that gives immunity for every possible use of language, and prevents the punishment of those who abuse this freedom [citations omitted]. . . . Reasonably limited, it was said by Story in the passage cited, this freedom is an inestimable privilege in a free government; without such limitations, it might become the scourge of the Republic.
> That a state, in the exercise of its police power, may punish those who abuse this freedom by utterances inimical to the public welfare, tending to corrupt public welfare, incite to crime, or disturb the public peace is not open to question.

The Court further strengthens its argument that a state has the right to protect itself against the kind of speech advocating uprisings against itself and concludes that

We cannot hold that the present statute is an arbitrary or unreasonable exercise of the police power of the state, unwarrantably infringing the freedom of speech or press; and we must and do sustain its constitutionality. . . .

And finding, for the reasons stated, that the statute is not in itself unconstitutional, and that it has not been applied in the present case in derogation of any constitutional right, the judgment of the Court of Appeals is affirmed.

That is, Gitlow's conviction and sentence are affirmed.

Near v. Minnesota ex rel. Olson (1931) (283 U.S. 697)

This case was appealed to the U.S. Supreme Court by the defendant Near after he had been found guilty of publishing a newspaper that contained "malicious, scandalous and defamatory articles" against public officials of the city of Minneapolis. A local court found Near guilty of being a nuisance under a state law that prohibited the publication of such articles. Further, and far more importantly, the court prohibited Near from publishing future issues of his newspaper, *The Saturday Press*. Near's conviction was upheld by the Supreme Court of the state of Minnesota. The key issue in his appeal to the U.S. Supreme Court was the constitutionality of the Minnesota law that provided for prior restraint, that is, the prohibition on a publication that had not yet appeared in print. It is to this issue that the judges addressed themselves and for which the case described here is most important. In his decision, Chief Justice Charles E. Hughes begins:

This statute, for the suppression as a public nuisance of a newspaper or periodical, is unusual, if not unique, and raises questions of grave importance transcending the local interests involved in the particular action. It is no longer open to doubt that the liberty of the press and of speech is within the liberty safeguarded by the due process clause of the 14th Amendment from invasion by state action. . . .

The appellee insists that the questions of the application of the statute to appellant's periodical, and of the construction of the judgment of the trial court, are not presented for review; that appellant's sole attack was upon the constitutionality of the statute, however it might be applied. The appellee contends that no question either of motive in the publication, or whether the decree goes beyond the direction of the statute, is before us. The appellant replies that, in his view, the plain terms of the statue were not departed from in this case and that, even if they were, the statute is nevertheless unconstitutional under any reasonable construction of its terms. The appellant states that he has not argued that the temporary and permanent injunctions were broader than were warranted by the statute; he insists that what was done was properly done if the statute is valid, and that the action taken under the statute is a fair indication of its scope.

The Court then examines a number of features of the Minnesota law on which it has to make decisions.

First. The statute is not aimed at the redress of individual or private wrongs. Remedies for libel remain available and unaffected. . . .

Second. The statute is directed not simply at the circulation of scandalous and defamatory statements with regard to private citizens, but at the continued publication by newspapers and periodicals of charges against public officers of corruption, malfeasance in office, or serious neglect of duty. . . .

Third. The object of the statute is not punishment, in the ordinary sense, but suppression of the offending newspaper or periodical. . . .

Fourth. The statute not only operates to suppress the offending newspaper or periodical but to put the publisher under an effective censorship. . . .

If we cut through mere details of procedure, the operation and effect of the statute in substance is that public authorities may bring the owner or publisher of a newspaper or periodical before a judge upon a charge of conducting a business of publishing scandalous and defamatory matter—in particular that the matter consists of charges against public officers of official dereliction—and unless the owner or publisher is able and disposed to bring competent evidence to satisfy the judge that the charges are true and are published with good motives and for justifiable ends, his newspaper or periodical is suppressed and further publication is made punishable as a contempt. This is of the essence of censorship.

The question is whether a statute authorizing such proceedings in restraint of publication is consistent with the conception of the liberty of the press as historically conceived and guaranteed.

The Court then conducts an extensive review of the history of freedom of press and freedom of speech discussions in England and the early Colonies before concluding that:

The fact that for approximately one hundred and fifty years there has been almost an entire absence of attempts to impose previous restraints upon publications relating to the malfeasance of public officers is significant of the deep-seated conviction that such restraints would violate constitutional right. Public officers whose character and conduct remain open to debate and free discussion in the press, find their remedies for false accusations in actions under libel laws providing for redress and punishment, and not in proceedings to restrain the publication of newspapers and periodicals.

The Court's final decision, then, is that:

For these reasons we hold the statute, so far as it authorized the proceedings in this action under clause (b) of section one, to be an infringement of the liberty of the press guaranteed by the 14th Amendment. We should add that this decision rests upon the operation and effect of the statute, without regard to the question of the truth of the charges contained in the particular periodical. The fact that the public officers named in this case, and those associated with the charges of official dereliction, may be deemed to be impeccable, cannot affect the conclusion that the statute imposes an unconstitutional restraint upon publication.
   Judgment reversed.

Joseph Burstyn, Inc. v. Wilson (1952) (343 U.S. 495)

The plaintiff in this case had been granted a license by the state of New York in 1950 to show the film *The Miracle*. After the film had been showing for a period of weeks, however, the State Board of Regents received so many letters complaining about its "sacrilegious" content that it canceled the company's license. Shortly thereafter, the company brought suit against the state on the basis of three claims. To quote the Court's decision:

Among the claims advanced by appellant were (1) that the [New York State licensing] statute violates the Fourteenth Amendment as a prior restraint upon freedom of speech and of the press; (2) that it is invalid under the same Amendment as a violation of the guaranty of separate church and state and as a prohibition of the free exercise of religion; and, (3) that the term "sacrilegious" is so vague and indefinite as to offend due process.

The Court began its decision with a recognition that the precedent in cases such as this one for many years had been *Mutual Film Corp. v. Industrial Commission* (236 U.S. 230), in which the Court had ruled that moving pictures were "a business, pure and simple, originated and conducted for profit, like other spectacles, not to be regarded, nor intended to be regarded by the Ohio Constitution, we think, as part of the press of the country, or as organs of public opinion." In this decision, however, the Court breaks with that precedent, as it explains here:

It cannot be doubted that motion pictures are a significant medium for the communication of ideas. They may affect public attitudes and behavior in a variety of ways, ranging from direct espousal of a political or social doctrine to the subtle shaping of thought which characterizes all artistic expression. The importance of motion pictures as an organ of public opinions is not lessened by the fact that they are designed to entertain as well as to inform [citations omitted]. . . .

It is urged that motion pictures do not fall within the First Amendment's aegis because their production, distribution, and exhibition is a large-scale business conducted for private profit. We cannot agree. That books, newspapers, and magazines are published and sold for profit does not prevent them from being a form of expression whose liberty is safeguarded by the First Amendment. We fail to see why operation for profit should have any different effect in the case of motion pictures.

It is further urged that motion pictures possess a greater capacity for evil, particularly among the youth of a community, than other modes of expression. Even if one were to accept this hypothesis, it does not follow that motion pictures should be disqualified from First Amendment protection. If there be capacity for evil it may be relevant in determining the permissible scope of community control, but it does not authorize substantially unbridled censorship such as we have here.

For the foregoing reasons, we conclude that expression by means of motion pictures is included within the free speech and free press guaranty of the First and Fourteenth Amendments. To the extent that language in the opinion in *Mutual Film Corp. v. Industrial Commission* [citations omitted] . . . is out of harmony with the views here set forth, we no longer adhere to it.

The Court then goes on to consider the fact that having made the previous ruling, it "does not follow that the Constitution require absolute freedom to exhibit every motion picture of every kind at all times and all places." It turns, therefore, to the question as to whether New York State can prohibit the showing of *The Miracle* because it is regarded by state censors as "sacrilegious."

However, from the standpoint of freedom of speech and the press, it is enough to point out that the state has no legitimate interest in protecting any or all religions from views distasteful to them which is sufficient to justify prior restraints upon the expression of those views. It is not the business of government in our nation to suppress real or imagined attacks upon a particular religious doctrine, whether they appear in publications, speeches, or motion pictures.

Since the term "sacrilegious" is the sole standard under attack here, it is not necessary for us to decide, for example, whether a state may censor motion pictures under a clearly drawn statute designed and applied to prevent the showing of obscene films. That is a very different question from the one now before us. We hold only that under the First and Fourteenth Amendments a state may not ban a film on the basis of a censor's conclusion that it is "sacrilegious."

Reversed.

Kingsley International Pictures Corp. v. Regents of University of State of New York (1959) (360 U.S. 684)

As of 1959, the New York Education Law still made it illegal to "exhibit, or to sell, lease or lend for exhibition at any place of amusement for pay or in connection with any business the state of New York, any motion picture film or reel, unless there is at the time in full force and effect a valid license or permit therefore of the education department." The department was required to withhold such a license, however, if it found that any part of the film was obscene, indecent, immoral, inhuman, sacrilegious, or "of such character that its exhibition would tend to corrupt morals or incite to crime." When the Kingsley International Pictures Corporation applied for a license to distribute the film *Lady Chatterley's Lover*, it was denied the license on the grounds that three isolated scenes in the film were "immoral" and that the film as a whole tended to present adultery as a "desirable, acceptable and proper pattern of behavior." After proceeding through the lower courts, the case finally reached the U.S. Supreme Court, where it was argued on 23 April 1959 and decided on 29 June 1959. The Court agreed with the characterization of the film as described above, but then went on to rule that

What New York has done, therefore, is to prevent the exhibition of a motion picture because that picture advocates an idea—that adultery under certain circumstances may be proper behavior. Yet the First Amendment's basic guarantee is of freedom to advocate ideas. The State, quite simply, has thus struck at the very heart of constitutionally protected liberty.

It is contended that the State's action was justified because the motion picture attractively portrays a relationship which is contrary to the moral standards, the religious precepts, and the legal code of its citizenry. This argument misconceives what it is that the Constitution protects. Its guarantee is not confined to the expression of ideas that are conventional or shared by a majority. It protects advocacy of the opinion that adultery may sometimes be proper, no less than advocacy of socialism or the single tax. And in the realm of ideas it protects expression which is eloquent no less than that which is unconvincing.

The Court reversed the lower court's decision and found that the New York law violated the First and Fourteenth Amendments. Although this case deals with a matter of sexual morality, the principles it laid down have been taken to apply as well to the portrayal of violent episodes in the media.

Office of Communication of United Church of Christ v. FCC (1966) (359 F.2d 994)

This case is of importance to the issue of violence in the media because it is the first occasion on which the courts have acknowledged that members of the general public have a right to present their opinions before government agencies, such as the Federal Communications Commission. The Court's decision itself begins with a review of the two questions it was being asked to adjudicate (only the first of which is of significance here):

This is an appeal from a decision of the Federal Communications Commission granting to the Intervenor a one-year renewal of its license to operate television station WLBT in Jackson, Mississippi. Appellants filed with the Commission a timely petition to intervene to present evidence and arguments opposing the renewal application. The Commission dismissed Appellants' petition and, without a hearing, took the unusual step of granting a restricted and conditional renewal of the license. Instead of granting the usual three-year renewal, it limited the license of one year from June 1, 1965, and imposed what it characterizes here as "strict conditions" on WLBT's operations in that one-year probationary period.

The questions presented are (a) whether Appellants, or any of them, have standing before the Federal Communications Commission as parties in interest under Section 309(d) of the Federal Communications Act to contest the renewal of a broadcast license; and (b) whether the Commission was required by Section 309(e) to conduct an evidentiary hearing on the claims of the Appellants prior to acting on renewal of the license.

Because the question whether representatives of the listening public have standing to intervene in a license renewal proceeding is one of first impression, we have given particularly close attention to the background of these issues and to the Commission's reasons for denying standing to Appellants.

The United Church of Christ was interested in the renewal of the WLBT license because it claimed that the station had consistently maintained racist policies that "did not give a fair and balanced presentation of controversial issues, especially those concerning Negroes, who comprise almost forty-five per cent of the total population within its prime service area."

In the next portion of its decision, the Court outlines the reasons that the church believes it should have standing before the FCC:

(1) They are individuals and organizations who were denied a reasonable opportunity to answer their critics, a violation of the Fairness Doctrine.
(2) These individuals and organizations represent the nearly one half of WLBT's potential listening audience who were denied an opportunity to have their side of controversial issues presented, equally a violation of the Fairness Doctrine, and who were more generally ignored and discriminated against in WLBT's programs.
(3) These individuals and organizations represent the total audience, not merely one part of it, and they assert the right of all listeners, regardless of race or religion, to hear and see balanced programming on significant public questions as required by the Fairness Doctrine and also their broad interest that the station be operated in the public interest in all respects.

Among the many points made next by the Court is a representation of the FCC's position on this issue, namely that it speaks for the general public and, therefore, does not require any additional input other than letters and other written evidence to know how the public feels about an issue. Besides, if it were to give "standing" to everyone who wanted to appear before it, argued the Commission, it would spend all its time listening to testimony and never be able to make a decision. The Court's answers to these arguments are as follows:

The theory that the Commission can always effectively represent the listener interests in a renewal proceeding without the aid and participation of legitimate listener representatives fulfilling the role of private attorneys general is one of those assumptions we collectively try to work with so long as they are reasonably adequate. When it becomes clear, as it does to us now, that it is no longer a valid assumption which stands up under the realities of actual experience, neither we nor the Commission can continue to rely on it. The gradual expansion and evolution of concepts of standing in administrative law attests that experience rather than logic or fixed rules has been accepted as the guide.

The Commission's attitude in this case is ambivalent in the precise sense of that term. While attracted by the potential contribution of widespread public interest and participation in improving the quality of broadcasting, the Commission rejects effective public participation by invoking the oft-expressed fear that a "host of parties" will descend upon it and render its dockets "clogged" and "unworkable." The Commission resolves this ambivalence for itself by contending that in this renewal proceeding the viewpoint of the public was adequately represented since it fully considered the claims presented by Appellants even though denying them standing. It also points to the general procedures for public participation that are already available, such as the filing of complaints with the Commission, the practice of having local hearings, and the ability of people who are not parties in interest to appear at hearings as witnesses. In light of the Commission's procedure in this case and its stated willingness to hear witnesses having complaints, it is difficult to see how a grant of formal standing would pose undue or insoluble problems for the Commission.

Thus we are brought around by analogy to the Supreme Court's reasoning in *Sanders;* unless the listeners—the broadcast consumers—can be heard, there may be no one to bring programming deficiencies or offensive overcommercialization to the attention of the Commission in an effective manner. By process of elimination those "consumers" willing to shoulder the burdensome and costly processes of intervention in a Commission proceeding are likely to be the only ones "having a sufficient interest" to challenge a renewal application. . . .

In order to safeguard the public interest in broadcasting, therefore, we hold that some "audience participation" must be allowed in license renewal proceedings. We recognize this will create problems for the Commission but it does not necessarily follow that "hosts" of protestors must be granted standing to challenge a renewal application or that the Commission need allow the administrative processes to be obstructed or overwhelmed by captious or purely obstructive protests. The Commission can avoid such results by developing appropriate regulations by statutory rulemaking. . . .

The responsible and representative groups eligible to intervene cannot here be enumerated or categorized specifically; such community organizations as civic associations, professional societies, unions, churches, and educational institutions or associations might well be helpful to the Commission. These groups are found in every community; they usually concern themselves with a wide range of community problems and tend to be representative of broad as distinguished from narrow interests, public as distinguished from private or commercial interests. . . .

We hold that the grant of a renewal of WBLT's [sic] license for one year was erroneous. The Commission is directed to conduct hearings on WLBT's renewal application, allowing public intervention pursuant to this holding. Since the Commission has already decided that Appellants are responsible representatives of the listening public of the Jackson area, we see no obstacle to a prompt determination granting standing to Appellants or some of them.

Consistent with the Court ruling, the FCC did hold a hearing on renewing WLBT's license and decided to approve renewal for a three-year period.

United States v. Southwestern Cable Co. (1967) (392 U.S. 157)

As new forms of the electronic media have been developed over the past four decades, the Federal Communications Commission has sometimes been uncertain as to what its authority is with regard to these new systems. After all, it was originally empowered by the Communications Act of 1934 to regulate radio broadcasting only. To a large extent, this indecision was resolved in the case of the *United States v. Southwestern Cable Co.*

In 1959, the FCC announced that it did not intend to regulate community antenna television (CATV), but that it would suggest legislation to deal with this growing arm of television. When that legislation was never adopted, the FCC announced in 1965 that CATV systems would not be allowed to broadcast into areas making up the 100 largest television markets in the nation. In 1966, Midwest Television asked for an order from the FCC banning the broadcast of Southwestern Cable (originating in Los Angeles) into Midwest's San Diego region. The Ninth Circuit Court of Appeals ruled that the FCC lacked authority to impose such a restriction, and the case was referred to the Supreme Court. The Court's decision, as written by Justice John Marshall Harlan, said in part:

The [Federal Communications] Commission has been charged with broad responsibilities for the orderly development of an appropriate system of local television broadcasting. The significance of its efforts can scarcely be exaggerated, for broadcasting is demonstrably a principal source of information and entertainment for a great part of the Nation's population. The Commission has reasonably found that the successful performance of these duties demands prompt and efficacious regulation of community antenna television systems. We have elsewhere held that we may not, "in the absence of compelling evidence that such was Congress' intention . . . prohibit administration action imperative for the achievement of an agency's ultimate purposes [citation omitted]. . . ." There is no such evidence here, and we therefore hold that the Commission's authority over "all interstate . . . communication by wire or radio" permits the regulation of CATV systems.

There is no need here to determine in detail the limits of the Commission's authority to regulate CATV. It is enough to emphasize that the authority which we recognize today under §152 (a) is restricted to that reasonably ancillary to the effective performance of the Commission's various responsibilities for the regulation of television broadcasting. The Commission may, for these purposes, issue "such rules and regulations and prescribe such restrictions and conditions, not inconsistent with law," as "public convenience, interest, or necessity requires [citation omitted]. . . ." We express no views as to the Commission's authority, if any, to regulate CATV under any other circumstances or for any other purposes.

Writers Guild v. Federal Communications Commission (1979)
(609 F.2d 355)

This decision was made by the United States Court of Appeals, Ninth Circuit, on 14 November 1979. The court had heard an appeal to a decision made by the U.S. District Court for the Central

District of California, by Warren J. Ferguson (423 F.Supp 1064). In the first section of the court's decision, it outlines the case brought before Justice Ferguson and outlines the judge's decision in the case.

Plaintiffs Writers Guild of America, West, Inc. (Writers Guild) and Tandem Productions, Inc. (Tandem) instituted these consolidated actions against the Federal Communications Commission (FCC) and its Commissioners Wiley, Hooks, Lee, Quello, Redi, Robinson, and Washburn, the three major television networks (ABC, CBS, and NBC), and the National Association of Broadcasters (NAB) to challenge the adoption of the so-called "family viewing policy" as an amendment to the NAB Television Code. The Writers Guild plaintiffs sought declaratory and injunctive relief against the government defendants for violations of the First Amendment, the Administrative Procedure Act, and section 326 of the Federal Communications Act, and against the private defendants on both First Amendment and antitrust grounds. Tandem sought damages in addition to declaratory and injunctive relief against the government defendants for violations of the First Amendment and section 326 of the Federal Communications Act, and against the private defendants on First Amendment and antitrust grounds. The actions were consolidated and tried before the district court. The court, in a lengthy and closely reasoned published opinion, concluded that: (1) threats, influence, and pressure by the Chairman of the FCC caused the networks and the NAB to adopt the family viewing policy; (2) the FCC committed a per se violation of the First Amendment by exerting improper pressure on the networks; (3) the FCC violated the Administrative Procedure Act (APA) by implementing public policy by informal pressure instead of by complying with the Act's procedural requirements; (4) the action of the networks and the NAB constituted "government action" for purposes of the First Amendment both because adoption of the family viewing policy had been caused substantially by FCC pressure and because the networks, the NAB, and the FCC participated in an "unprecedented joint venture" in an effort to compromise the independent judgments of other broadcast licensees; and (5) the networks and the NAB violated the First Amendment by "fail[ing] to exercise independent program judgments and instead becom[ing] surrogates in the enforcement of government policy" and by agreeing to compromise the independent programming judgments of individual broadcast licensees [citation omitted]. . . . All parties have appealed.

The appeals court then outlines six primary issues involved in the appeal to it. Five of those six issues are substantive, dealing with issues such as whether the actions of the networks and the NAB amounted to "governmental action" for purposes of the First

Amendment and whether the conduct of the FCC, the networks, and the NAB violated the First Amendment. The court decides, however, not to act on any of these issues, but on the one procedural issue involved, namely,

(1) Whether the district court erred in concluding that the district court was proper forum for this litigation and that neither the doctrine of exhaustion of administrative remedies nor the doctrine of primary jurisdiction required FCC consideration of plaintiff's claims prior to district court action.

The court then goes on to review a number of reasons that it feels that the district court was not the proper place for this case to have been tried, but that it should have been heard first before the Federal Communications Commission. It concludes its decision as follows:

[5] While we agree that the use of these techniques by the FCC [in pressuring the networks and the NAB to accept a family viewing policy] presents serious issues involving the Constitution, the Communications Act, and the APA, we nevertheless believe that the district court should not have thrust itself so hastily into the delicately balanced system of broadcast regulation. Because the "line between permissible regulatory activity and impermissible 'raised eyebrow' harassment of vulnerable licensees" is so exceedingly vague [citation omitted], it is important that judicial attempts to control these techniques be sensitive to "the particular regulatory context in which it occurs, the interests affected by it, and the potential for abuse [citation omitted]." The development of standards governing the agency's use of informal methods to influence broadcast industry policy is an issue "that should be dealt with in the first instance by those especially familiar with the customs and practices of the industry [citations omitted]. . . ." Deferral to the FCC is, we believe, essential to further the purposes of the delicately balanced system of broadcast regulation [citation omitted]. Hence, primary jurisdiction over plaintiffs' challenges to the official agency action complained of in this case as a violation of the APA rests with the FCC.
     In conclusion, we think it appropriate to note our support for the following views expressed by the District of Columbia Circuit Court in ACT another case in which FCC jawboning activities were involved: The Commission, as the expert agency entrusted by Congress with the administration and regulation of the crucial, dynamic communications field, required and deserves some latitude in carrying out its substantial responsibilities. It may not be the sole guardian of the public's interest in broadcasting—licensees, the courts and the general public in varying

ways share responsibility with it for defining and advancing that interest—but, in the formulation of broadcast policy, the Commission nevertheless must continue to play a leading role. . . .

Accordingly, we vacate the judgment of the district court and remand with instructions to refer plaintiffs' claims against the government defendants to the FCC, and to hold in abeyance plaintiffs' claims against the private defendants pending resolution and judicial review of the administrative proceedings before the FCC.

Thus, the substantive issues concerning the Family Viewing Policy were not even discussed, let alone resolved, by the appeals court. As it happens, the issue of the Family Viewing Policy never went any further in the judicial system since the NAB and the three major networks decided to discontinue the policy. Although the district court's ruling was overturned, the effect it would have achieved occurred nonetheless.

Winters v. New York (1948)
(333 U.S. 507)

This case is the only occasion on which the U.S. Supreme Court has dealt specifically with the issue of violence in the media. The dispute involves the arrest of a New York City bookseller, Winters, on a charge that he violated subsection 2 of section 1141 of the New York Penal Law. That subsection made it a misdemeanor to print, utter, publish, sell, lend, give away, distribute or show "any book, pamphlet, magazine, newspaper or other printed paper devoted to the publication, and principally made up of criminal news, police reports, or accounts of criminal deeds, or pictures, or stories of deeds of bloodshed, lust or crime." Winters appealed his conviction, and its subsequent affirmation by the New York State Supreme Court, to the U.S. Supreme Court. His attorney argued that the New York statute violated his right of free speech and press because it was "so vague and indefinite, in form and as interpreted, as to permit within the scope of its language the punishment of incidents fairly within the protection of the guarantee of free speech. . . ." The Court agreed and reversed Winters's conviction. Its line of reasoning was as follows:

We recognize the importance of the exercise of a state's police power to minimize all incentives to crime, particularly in the field of sanguinary or salacious publications with their stimulation of juvenile delinquency. Although we are dealing with an aspect of a free press in its relation to public morals, the principles of unrestricted distribution of publications admonish us of the particular importance of a maintenance of standards of certainty in the field of criminal prosecution for violation of statutory prohibitions against distribution. We do not accede to appellee's suggestion that the constitutional protection for a free press applies only to the exposition of ideas. The line between the informing and the entertaining is too elusive for the protection of that basic right. Everyone is familiar with instances of propaganda through fiction. What is one man's amusement, teaches another's doctrine. Though we can see nothing of any possible value to society in these magazines, they are as much entitled to the protection of free speech as the best of literature.

The Court then reviews the history of New York State Penal Law §1141 (2), noting that it was first designed to protect children, but then expanded to include the total state population, regardless of age. The Court explains why it thinks the New York law is too broad and vague to pass the test of constitutionality under the Fourteenth Amendment. It says:

The subsection of the New York Penal Law, as now interpreted by the Court of Appeals prohibits distribution of a magazine principally made up of criminal news or stories of deeds of bloodshed, or lust, so massed as to become vehicles for inciting violent and depraved crimes against the person. But even considering the glass put upon the literal meaning by the Court of Appeals' restriction of the statute to collections of stories "so massed as to become vehicles for inciting violent and depraved crimes against the person . . . not necessarily . . . sexual passion," we find the specification of publications, prohibited from distribution, too uncertain and indefinite to justify the conviction of this petitioner. Even though all detective tales and treatises on criminology are not forbidden, and though publications made up of criminal deeds not characterized by bloodshed or lust are omitted from the interpretation of the court of Appeals, we think fair use of collections of pictures and stories would be interdicted because of the utter impossibility of the actor of the trier to know where this new standard of guilt would draw the line between the allowable and the forbidden publications. . . .

It does not seem to us that an honest distributor of publications could know when he might be held to have ignored such a prohibition [as is provided in the New York law]. . . . Where a statute is so vague as to make criminal an innocent act, a conviction under it cannot be sustained. . . .

Reversed.

National Broadcasting Co. v. Niemi (1977) (434 U.S. 1354)

The citation given here marks only one step in a long series of criminal and civil cases that began in the Superior Court for the County of San Francisco in 1977. Three years earlier, a nine-year-old girl, Olivia Niemi, was raped with a discarded beer bottle by a group of four boys. Niemi, through her parents, claimed that the assault had been inspired by a showing on the NBC television network four days earlier of the movie "Born Innocent." In the movie, a young girl is raped with a plumber's helper by four of her reform school roommates. The case is important in this book because it is the only one dealing with the effects of televised violence on viewers that reached the Supreme Court. The Supreme Court declined to issue a stay on the case scheduled at the time to be heard in the Superior Court for the City and County of San Francisco. Some of the comments made by the court of appeals in its two decisions on this case on 19 January 1978 and 2 February 1982 are as follows:

Analysis of this appeal commences with recognition of the overriding constitutional principle that material communicated by the public media, including fictional material such as the television drama here at issue, is generally to be accorded protection under the First Amendment to the Constitution of the United States. . . .

Specifically, television broadcasting is a medium which is entitled to First Amendment protection [citations omitted]. Thus, expression by means of television dramatization is included within the free speech and free press guarantees of the First and Fourteenth Amendments. . . .

The freedom of speech guaranteed by the First Amendment is not, of course, absolute. Certain narrowly limited classes of speech may be prevented or punished by the state consistent with the principles of the First Amendment.

The court then discusses the lower court's ruling on the Niemi complaint, which it had dismissed without a jury trial. The appeals court decided that this decision was improper and declared:

The judgment is reversed with directions to impanel a jury and proceed to trial of the action. (126 Cal.App.3d 488)

Four years later, the case was back in the same court of appeals before the same judge. In the meantime, a jury had been impaneled in San Francisco to hear the case. After the plaintiff's opening statement, however, the trial judge had granted the defendant's motion to dismiss the case. The plaintiff's appeal was then denied also. The primary reason for the appellate judge's decision was that the plaintiff's attorney was not able to prove that NBC intended to "incite" acts of violence, a fact that he himself admitted.

On remand, appellant's counsel in his opening statement to the jury indicated that the evidence would establish negligence and recklessness on respondent's part, rather than incitement. At the conclusion of appellant's opening statement, respondents moved for a judgment of nonsuit [citations omitted] on the grounds that appellant admittedly could not meet the test for incitement [citations omitted]. Appellant's counsel again acknowledged his inability to meet the incitement test; the trial court granted respondent's motion and rendered judgment dismissing the action.

The appeals judge then develops a complete argument as to the problem in restricting the depiction of violence on television.

First Amendment rights are accorded a preferred place in our democratic society [citations omitted]. First Amendment protection extends to a communication, to its source and to its recipients [citations omitted]. "[A]bove all else, the First Amendment means that government has no power to restrict expression because of its message, its ideas, its subject matter, or its content [citations omitted]." Applied to the electronic media, the First Amendment means that it is the broadcaster that has authority to make programming decisions [citations omitted].

The court then explains what might happen if viewers were able to successfully prosecute cases of this nature:

Appellant does not seek to impose a prior restraint on speech; rather, she asserts civil liability premised on traditional negligence concepts. But the chilling effect of permitting negligence actions for a television broadcast is obvious. . . . Realistically, television networks would become significantly more inhibited in the selection of controversial materials if liability were to be imposed on a simple negligence theory. "[T]he pall of fear and timidity imposed upon those who would give voice to public criticism is an atmosphere in which the First Amendment freedoms cannot survive.". . . The deterrent effect of subjecting the television networks to negligence liability because of their programming choices would lead to self-censorship which would dampen the vigor and limit the variety of debate [citations omitted]. . . .

Notwithstanding the pervasive effect of the broadcasting media [citations omitted] and the unique access afforded children [citations omitted] the effect of the imposition of liability could reduce the U.S. adult population to viewing only what is fit for children.

The court then reviews the arguments presented by plaintiff for allowing a negligence suit against NBC to proceed and explains why each one is invalid. Toward the end of its decision, the court finally states that in cases such as the present one:

Other methods of controlling violence on television must be found. . . . Imposing liability on a simple negligence theory here would frustrate vital freedom of speech guarantees. (126 Cal.App.3d 488)

Policy Statements and Recommendations

The problem of how to deal with violence in the media while insuring the right of free speech has been a dominant theme in the deliberations of many private and public governmental and non-governmental organizations. The policy statements, resolutions, and other recommendations for action taken by such groups often reflect this dilemma. A selection of such statements is reprinted below. Unless otherwise indicated, all of the following statements and recommendations have been taken verbatim from documents provided by the organization specified in each case.

National Foundation To Improve Television

SUMMARY OF RULES PROPOSED TO THE FEDERAL
COMMUNICATIONS COMMISSION BY THE
NATIONAL FOUNDATION TO IMPROVE TELEVISION'S
"PETITION FOR RULE MAKING"

Filed with the FCC
On March 25, 1993

1. CHILDREN'S VIEWING HOURS
   Broadcasters, cable operators and other television programming providers are prohibited from transmitting programming containing an "excessive amount of dramatized violence" between the hours of 6:00 A.M. and 10:00 P.M. [definition of "excessive amount of dramatized violence" appears at end of main petition]

2. VIEWER WARNINGS

Between the hours of 6:00 A.M. and 10:00 P.M., telecasters are required to provide audio and visual warnings of programming containing an "excessive amount of dramatized violence" immediately before and at the conclusion of commercial breaks during such programming.

3. SUPERIMPOSED WARNING SIGNAL

Telecasters are required to superimpose an appropriate visual warning signal over any programming containing an "excessive amount of dramatized violence" shown between the hours of 6:00 A.M. and 10:00 P.M.

4. VIOLENCE-FREE COMMERCIALS

Excessively violent commercials or promotions for upcoming shows cannot be shown between the hours of 6:00 A.M. and 10:00 P.M.

5. STANDARD VIOLENCE RATING SYSTEM

Telecasters are required to develop and classify their shows on the basis of their violent content according to a set of standards developed in consultation with the FCC and concerned public interest groups.

6. BENEFICIAL PROGRAMMING

Telecasters are required to provide programming designed to educate and inform children about violence and sponsor activities designed to enhance the value of such programming.

7. HEARINGS ON TELEVISION VIOLENCE

The Commission shall convene hearings to solicit public comment on the issue of televised violence, after which the Commission shall promulgate guidelines on programming containing dramatized violence telecast between the hours of 6:00 A.M. and 10:00 P.M., which guidelines shall provide telecasters with a clear understanding of their responsibilities.

FOR THE PURPOSES OF THE PROPOSED RULES, THE FOLLOWING PARAGRAPHS DEFINE THE TERM "EXCESSIVE AMOUNT OF DRAMATIZED VIOLENCE"

1. Television programming contains an excessive amount of dramatized violence if it contains dramatized portrayals of killings, rapes, maimings, beatings, stranglings, stabbings, shootings, or any other acts of violence which, when viewed by the average person, would be considered excessive or inappropriate for minors.

2. "Violence" means the use or threatened use of physical force against another or against one's self, whether or not such act or threat occurs in a realistic and serious context or in a fantastic and humorous context. Idle threats, verbal abuse, and gestures without credible violent consequences are not "violence" for purposes of the Petition.

3. "An excessive amount of dramatized violence" means an amount of dramatized violence inappropriate for minors or exceeding that

permitted by the guidelines developed by the Federal Communications Commission.

National Association of Secondary School Principals

STATEMENT OF POSITION

Violence in the Media and Entertainment Industry

Whereas, in 1979, the National Association of Secondary School Principals urged the broadcasting and motion picture industries to work with educators and parents in moving toward a significant reduction of violent acts in television and film programming;

Whereas, the nation is experiencing an unrivaled period of juvenile violent crime perpetrated by youths from all races, social classes, and lifestyles;

Whereas, the average American child views 8,000 murders and 100,000 acts of violence on TV before finishing elementary school, and by the age of 18, that same teenager will have witnessed 200,000 acts of violence on TV, including 40,000 murders; and,

Whereas, the entertainment industry (movies, records, music videos, radio, and television) plays an important role in fostering anti-social behavior by promoting instant gratification, glorifying casual sex, encouraging the use of profanity, nudity, violence, killing, and racial and sexual stereotyping; be it therefore known that,

The National Association of Secondary School Principals:

- appreciates the efforts of the U.S. Attorney General to focus on the problem of increasing violence in the media;
- stands in opposition to violence and insensitive behavior and dialogue in the entertainment industry;
- commends television broadcasters who have begun self-regulation by labeling each program it deems potentially offensive with the following warning: DUE TO VIOLENT CONTENT, PARENTAL DISCRETION IS ADVISED; and producers of music videos and records who use similar labeling systems;
- encourages parents to responsibly monitor and control the viewing and listening habits of their children with popular media products (records, videos, TV programs, etc.);
- calls upon advertisers to take responsible steps to screen the programs they support on the basis of their violent and profane content;
- supports federal legislation designed to decrease and monitor TV violence including;

   a. H.R. 288, sponsored by Representative Edwin Markey (MA)
      and Jack Fields (TX), requiring TVs to be equipped with a
      V-chip, enabling viewers to completely block programs
      classified as violent by the networks;
   b. S. 942, sponsored by David Durenburger (MN), requiring the
      Federal Communications Commission (FCC) to develop and
      codify standards to reduce TV violence; and,
 - calls upon the Federal Communications Commission to initiate
   hearings on violence in the media, and to consider as part of
   those hearings the establishment of guidelines for broadcasters
   to follow during prime time and children's viewing hours;
   furthermore, the FCC should use its licensing powers to ensure
   broadcasters' compliance with guidelines on violence and
   establish a strict procedure to levy fines against those licensees
   who fail to comply.

National PTA

RESOLUTION

(Adopted by the 1975 convention delegates,
reactivated and reaffirmed 1989)

VIOLENCE IN TV PROGRAMMING

WHEREAS, children spend countless unsupervised hours watching
TV; and

WHEREAS, the choice of program offerings often is less than
desirable, with much emphasis on violence; and

WHEREAS, children are known to imitate observed behavior and
actions; and

WHEREAS, statistics reveal an alarming increase in crime committed
by younger and younger children; and

WHEREAS, the Surgeon general's report states that there can be a
cause-and-effect relationship between watching violence on TV and
aggressive behavior in children and young people; and

WHEREAS, at this time TV programming is self-regulated by the
broadcasting industry through the National Association of Broadcasters
(NAB) TV Code, a *voluntary* code not subscribed to by all stations and
the provisions of which are repeatedly violated; be it therefore

   Resolved, That the National PTA urge its state congresses,
   districts, councils and local units to observe and monitor TV
   programming and commercials in their areas; and where an
   excessive amount of violence in programming is seen, to make
   known their views with documented reporting to sponsors of the
   program, with copies to the local TV stations, to the TV network,

to the NAB, to the Federal Communications Commission, and to their elected representatives; and be it further

Resolved, That the National PTA *demand* from networks and local stations reduction in the amount of violence shown on television programs and commercials during the entire day, with particular attention to viewing hours between 2:00 P.M. and 10:00 P.M. and weekend morning hours, when impressionable children and young people are most likely to be watching; and be it further

Resolved, That the National PTA through its state congresses, districts, councils, and local units *demand*, if the self-regulation of programming and commercials by the broadcasting industry does not result in better TV programming with less emphasis on violence, that the Federal Communications Commission establish and enforce regulations limiting the number and percentage of programs of violence to be presented each day.

Working Group on Media of the National Consultation on Safeguarding Our Youth

VIOLENCE PREVENTION FOR OUR NATION'S CHILDREN

The working group on media met in three breakout sessions over two days to consider issues related to mass media and our growing culture of violence. This was hardly time to exhaust the many complex and interrelated aspects of the current situation. Never-theless [*sic*], several key concepts emerged to help define the issues involved along with a number of recommendations for new directions that might lead to resolution.

Key Concepts:

1. **The issue of media and violence is much broader than television.**
    *   There's also cable, movies, video games, advertising, music and popular culture.
    *   Important to recognize that news is different from entertainment media. Violence in the reporting of current events, although it too can be portrayed gratuitously, may have more justification than violence for entertainment.
2. **Mass media may be accused of causing an increase of violence in society, but they are not the [only] cause.**
    *   Many factors are involved in creating our current culture of violence—circular poverty, decay of the inner city, breakdown of family life, lack of education and jobs, addiction to drugs, loss of purpose and self-esteem, etc.—along with, of course, the ready availability of guns. A further influence is an attitude of milita-

rism, domination of the weak and competition to win at all costs—which may be, in turn, portrayed by the media, making them appear normative and acceptable to society.

- This is not to excuse the media industry from accepting a share of the responsibility for the current situation. Continuing to deny *any* responsibility is unacceptable and even, unconscionable.
- It is important to distinguish, from research, the multiple and various effects of mediated violence. Most people focus their attention primarily on whether media violence "causes" some people to later commit violent acts, but the literature suggests there are at least four social effects that need to be considered:
  1. *Increased aggression and meanness*—that is, correlation between seeing mediated violence and being more violent now or in the future. May or may not involve influencing a person to commit criminal acts; the effect may also be a bullying attitude, hostility or mean-spiritedness toward others or society as a whole.
  2. *Victim effect*—the increase in fear and concern for self-protection—locks and security gates—fear of going out alone or at night. Result: staying home where we watch ever increasing ratios of violent entertainment thus perpetuating the paranoia. Gerbner's "mean world syndrome."
  3. *Bystander effect*—increased callousness and insensitivity to those around us who may be hurting. Decline of "community" and being a "Good Samaritan" to others in need.
  4. *Increased appetite for violence*—the more violence one sees, the more "jolts per minute" needed to keep viewers involved—and watching. Media violence can be addictive.
3. **All young people don't view mediated violence as influential.**
   - Many see poverty, joblessness, drugs, gangs or parental neglect as more influential on a life-style of violence or crime.
   - Research indicates that adults and children don't see the same TV—what is offensive or influential to one person of a specific age, gender, ethnic or class background may not be similarly offensive or influential to another.
   - It is also true that media are so pervasive in our lives that few are aware of the impact of media at all—positive or negative. Particularly in regard to television, Americans have generally bought the myth of media as mindless entertainment without much significance or consequence. Today's young people have not known a time when there was not television so they can hardly separate themselves from the image culture in which they are growing up.
4. **The civic community has a lot to learn about how to work with local media and how to use media formats to introduce or reinforce positive social messages.**

- There has been a sense of powerlessness about media and technology so media have not been used by community groups to set a community's social agenda; media set the agenda, in part, by portraying the negative rather than covering the positive.
- If media are part of the problem in creating our current culture of violence, they must be challenged to be part of the solution. We have not done enough to move beyond blame to involved local and national media leaders in "win-win" solutions.

Directions/Recommendations

1. **The mood in America is changing.**
   - An increasing number of American citizens no longer believe the myth of media as mindless entertainment. Particularly parents of young children see the enormous influence of media to convey to their children positive as well as negative behaviors and attitudes. This ground-swell cannot be ignored. The challenge is to direct it to positive action rather than extremist reaction.
   - The issue of media violence is really just the first phase of a major cultural debate about life in the 21st century. What kind of people do we want our children to become? What kind of culture will best give them the environment they will need to grow up healthy and whole?
   - We all have to examine our personal responsibility for contributing to the increase in media violence. Violence *does* attract an audience.
   - In the face of rising violence creating a clear public health crisis, First Amendment arguments no longer seem unassailable—and yet few are comfortable with any form of censorship. A new concept is to find regulatory standards that are "First Amendment friendly."
   - We *can* change the direction of media by a combination of audience education and effective organizing techniques. Such change will not happen quickly, however. We must be patient and have a long-term vision and multi-year strategies.
2. **Need to support a major public "movement" to challenge the corporate media of America to act more responsibly as good citizens in an increasingly mediated society.**
   - Take lessons from the environmental movement to form a "cultural environmental" movement. Hold media accountable for being an educator as well as a business and an entertainer.
   - Good solutions will not micro-manage the media industry. They will focus rather on a *vision* of what mass media can do to unify society rather than tear it apart. Reclaim concept of media as a public service rather than just a private investment; long term impact, not just short term thinking.

- Rather than using negative energy, e.g., boycotts, be pro-active, e.g., establish a Council of Excellence to reward corporations/ advertisers who resist sponsoring violence, who "do the right thing."
- Make it easy for citizens to express their views—"800" numbers, bilingual access.
- This is increasingly important as we face a technological future with 500 cable channels, interactive programming and "electronic superhighways." Who will set policies?

3. **Community groups/agencies need to become more effective in using communications media and working with local media institutions to create the safe, caring communities we all envision and desire.**
   - Though community institutions should not have to "kick down the door" to access print or electronic media outlets, it may be necessary at times.
   - Collaboration will be more effective if community leaders are well informed and understand the organizational structure and business needs of commercial vs. public media systems.
   - Mediated activities can complement and extend the impact of interpersonal programs, e.g., late night radio music/talk show to supplement gang intervention or violence reduction programs; videos for parenting education, computer networks, electronic forums, etc.
   - Local and national media could play a major role in educating the public about violence as a public health issue.

4. **Broad-based media literacy education needs to become a priority in the U.S. and implemented in an inter-agency, interdisciplinary approach.**
   - Media literacy education is a growing movement in the U.S. but is still many years behind most other countries, especially Canada.
   - Effective media literacy education involves four interrelated aspects:
     1. *critical thinking*—learning to uncover the explicit and implicit meanings of a media message, whether verbal, visual or aural.
     2. *critical analysis*—"making the connections" between what's in the media and its significance to one's daily life; identifying economic influences as well as political ideologies and values, such as racism or sexism.
     3. *creative production skills*—learning to produce a media message, to express oneself in various media forms from print to multimedia; creating alternative points of view to mainstream media.
     4. *preparation for "citizenship" in a media culture*—understanding

the economic and political structures and how mass media "works" in society; learning to take personal or public action to influence the use or challenge the abuse of media in society—from sending a postcard to the F.C.C. to teaching youngsters to decode alcohol or tobacco advertising to organizing a public access cable show.

- At the community level, organize media literacy not just in school classrooms but perhaps more effectively in afterschool programs for kids or parenting programs for adults. Involve churches, clubs, social workers, health care, youth and family serving agencies. All helping professions can make a "media connection."
- On the federal level, involve Departments of Education as well as Health and Human Services, the F.C.C., the F.T.C. and others in inter-agency investment in research and development of comprehensive as well as specifically targeted media literacy programs.

American Academy of Pediatrics

In 1984 the American Academy of Pediatrics Task Force on Children and Television issued a statement that cautioned pediatricians and parents about the potential for television to promote violent and/or aggressive behavior and obesity. The influence of television on early sexual activity, drug and alcohol use and abuse, school performance, and perpetuation of ethnic stereotypes was also stressed. Advances in our understanding of the effects of television on children have prompted this update of the Academy's policy.

In 1989 the average child in the United States still spent more time watching television than performing any other activity except sleeping. According to recent Nielsen data, children aged 2 to 5 years view approximately 25 hours of television per week, children aged 6 to 11 years watch more than 22 hours per week, and adolescents 12 to 17 years watch 23 hours of television per week. Although the amount of commercial television viewed by children has declined since 1980, the most recent estimates of television viewing do not include the use of video cassette recorders. Therefore, the amount of time that children in our country spend in front of the television set has probably not decreased significantly in the past 8 years.

Television's influence on children is a function of the length of time they spend watching and the cumulative effect of what they see. By the time today's child reaches age 70, he or she will have spent approximately 7 years watching television. Therefore, television may displace more active experience of the world. For some children, the world shown on television becomes the real world.

In the 6 years since the original statement was released, sufficient data have accumulated to warrant the conclusion that protracted television viewing is one cause of violent or aggressive behavior. Television viewing also contributes substantially to obesity.

Although there is no clear documentation that the relationship between television viewing and sexual activity or the use of alcohol is causal, the frequency of adolescent pregnancy and sexually transmitted diseases and the prevalence of alcohol-related deaths among adolescents and young adults represent major sources of illness, injury, and death. American teenagers see an estimated 14,000 sexual references and innuendos per year on television, yet only 150 of these references deal with sexual responsibility, abstinence, or contraception. Therefore, the many implicit and explicit messages on television that promote alcohol consumption and promiscuous or unprotected sexual activity are a cause for concern.

The Committee on Communications, therefore makes the following recommendations:

1. Efforts should be developed and intensified to teach pediatricians and parents about the influence of television and furthermore, new initiatives should be developed to promote involvement by parents as well as critical television viewing skills among children.

2. Pediatricians should advise parents to limit their children's television viewing to 1 to 2 hours per day. In addition, pediatricians should include advice regarding the effects of television on children and the importance of limiting television time as part of anticipatory guidance during health maintenance visits. Parents should be encouraged to develop television substitutes such as reading, athletics, and physical conditioning, as well as instructive hobbies.

3. Families should participate in the selection of the programs that their children watch. Parents should watch television with their children in order to help interpret what they see. Parents should take advantage of the acceptable programs offered on video cassettes for their children's viewing, if affordable.

4. Pediatricians should continue to support legislation making broadcast of high quality children's programming a condition of license renewal and seek a revival of legislation mandating at least 1 hour per day of programs of educational and instructional benefit to children.

5. Pediatricians should continue their efforts to ban toy-based programs, since such programs are designed to sell toys to children and constitute program-length commercials.

6. Pediatricians should continue to urge that sexuality be portrayed responsibly by the media.

7. Pediatricians should support efforts to eliminate alcohol adver-

tising on television and also encourage extensive counter advertising.

8. The Academy should support further research into the effects of television on children and continue to build coalitions with other groups to monitor and improve television for children.

Source: "American Academy of Pediatrics Committee on Communications: Children, Adolescents and Television," *Pediatrics*, June 1990, pp. 1119–1120. Reprinted with permission.

American Medical Association

RECOMMENDATIONS

In order to reduce violent behavior that may result from exposure to violent television and cable television programming and motion picture production, and to offer parents better information about the nature and content of media intended for their children, the Board of Trustees recommends that the following recommendations be adopted in lieu of Resolution 418 (A-93) and that the remainder of the report be filed:

1. That the AMA urge the entertainment industry to make fundamental changes in the rating system, which will give consumers more precise information about violent and sexual content of motion pictures, television and cable television programs, and other forms of video and audio entertainment, thereby enabling consumers to make more meaningful decisions for themselves and their children about what they view or hear;

2. That the AMA work with the entertainment industry and other groups interested in reducing violent content of media programming, to incorporate age classifications into the ratings system that reflect scientifically demonstrated developmental periods during childhood and adolescence such as ages 3- to 7-year-olds, 8- to 12-year-olds, and 13- to 17-year olds;

3. That the AMA urge the entertainment industry to develop a uniform ratings system that is easy for consumers to understand and which can be applied across existing and future entertainment technologies;

4. That the AMA urge physicians to counsel parents about the known effects of media violence on children's behavior and encourage them to reduce the amount of violent programming viewed by their children;

5. That the AMA monitor changes in the current ratings system and work through state medical societies to inform physicians and their patients about these changes;

6. That the AMA urge consideration be given to the potential

development of a Television Violence Code, with input from the government, the television industry, and the public, including the medical profession, to address issues relating to all television violence, including news reports and entertainment;

7. That the AMA support all other appropriate measures to address and reduce television, cable television, and motion picture violence;

8. That this report, along with its recommendations, be distributed widely to both professional and lay audiences, particularly those groups that work with youth.

Source: *Violence in Video Games: Hearing before the Subcommittee on Telecommunications and Finance of the Committee on Energy and Commerce,* House of Representatives, 103rd Congress, 2nd sess., 30 June 1994, pp. 41–42.

National Association of School Psychologists

Resolution on Children and Violence in Media and Toys

The Executive Board of the National Association of School Psychologists recognizes that children observe a large number of violent acts in television programming, videotapes, toys[,] electronic and video games, movies and cartoons. Research supports that exposure to violence in media and toys can have a negative impact on children's learning and development and can lead to harmful consequences.

Therefore, the Executive Board of the National Association of School Psychologists resolves to:

a. Inform public policy makers, leaders in media and toy industries, parents[,] educators, school psychologists, and others of research on the potential negative consequences that violence in media and toys may have for children;

b. Support public policies which effectively address children's exposure to violence in media and toys;

c. Promote the development of policies and practices within media and toy industries which effectively address children's exposure to violence;

d. Assist parents, educators, school psychologists, and others with developing effective practices for (1) evaluation and monitoring children's exposure to violence in media and toys and (2) responding to the day-to-day impact that exposure to media and toy violence may have on children;

e. Encourage media and toy industries to produce more developmentally appropriate, non-violent media and toys which can have a positive impact on children's learning and development, and encourage children, parents, and others to consider selection of these media and toys instead of more violent media and toys; and

f. Work collaboratively with other professional and advocacy groups in the implementation of the practices described in this resolution.

Adopted by the Executive Board on January, 1994.

The Institute for Mental Health Initiatives

We have worked with television writers, producers, directors and executives to help and encourage them to:

1) Show a variety of constructive anger management behaviors that serve to empower both the character and the viewers.
2) Depict violence as a last resort for heroes, who have used their wits in encountering danger.
3) Depict the perpetrators of "thoughtless" violence as villains and their use of weapons as weak and foolish.
4) Portray the devastating emotional consequences and impact of violence on the perpetrators, the victims and witnesses.

Source: *Violence on Television: Hearings before the Subcommittee on Telecommunications and Finance of the Committee on Energy and Commerce,* House of Representatives, 103rd Congress, 1st sess., 12 May, 25 June, 1 and 29 July, and 15 September 1993, pp. 38–39.

The National Coalition on Television Violence

NCTV 10-POINT PLAN TO SWEEP VIOLENCE OFF TV AND OFF OUR STREETS

1. No Censorship
    There should be no Governmental censorship of the media. It must be recognized that upholding the separation of government and media (as well as religion and media) is even more vital to the citizens of the United States, than curbing violence.
2. Ratings Systems for Violence
    A ratings system which describes the violent content of TV shows should be agreed upon by the networks and cable channels. Ratings would delineate the quantity of violence (in terms of violent acts per show) and the quality of violence (in terms of how graphic and lethal the violence is, whether the overall message is pro- or anti-violence, and how gratuitous the violence is). Ratings would be determined by an independent review board comprised of experts in the field of media violence.

3. Ingredient Labels
   Using the precedent of requiring labels on food products which
   detail the ingredients contained inside, TV shows should be required
   to broadcast ingredient labels and use them in TV publicity/listings.
   Such labels would reflect the results of the ratings system: the
   quantity and quality of the violence contained inside the show.

4. Warning Labels on TV Shows
   Using the precedent established for products such as cigarettes, TV
   shows should be required to flash a warning label before those
   shows rated high in violence. The warning label should read: "The
   TV show you are about to watch may be hazardous to your psychological and/or physical health due to its highly violent content."

5. Warning Labels on TV Ads
   Commercials for war toys (including, but not limited to: action
   figures, videogames, guns and other weapons) and other violent-
   themed products, would need to carry appropriate warning labels.
   These would read: "The toy you have just seen advertised may be
   hazardous to the psychological and/or physical health of a child
   due to its theme which inspires violent play."

6. Violence Advisors On Staff
   At least one psychiatrist and/or researcher on TV violence should be
   on staff at each network and cable channel to review its shows and
   determine the psychological impact of any violence portrayed. This
   person should then advise the producers and TV executives of the
   findings and make recommendations as to how the violence can be
   toned down without compromising artistic integrity.

7. Public Service Announcements
   Networks and cable channels should be strongly advised to carry
   PSA's which educate viewers about the harmful effects of media
   violence. Each channel would be advised to carry a number of PSA's
   per day which would be in proportion to how much violent programming it broadcasts.

8. "Just Say No" in Government Institutions
   No violent TV programming should be offered to residents of
   government institutions—such as jails and psychiatric hospitals.
   These residents are often exposed to countless hours of TV viewing,
   while in a condition where they are particularly vulnerable to its
   effects, instead of receiving more appropriate psychotherapy and
   rehabilitation. No children residing in government institutions
   should be exposed to TV violence.

9. Tax Breaks
   Tax breaks should be given to networks and cable channels, production companies, foundations, private donors, etc. who provide
   money to support:

- research and education on the effects of TV violence.
- development of non-violent TV programming for children.
10. Media Literacy Public Health Campaign
    A public health campaign should be launched, in the same spirit as
    the campaigns against drunk driving and against the consumption
    of alcohol by pregnant women, to promote awareness of the effects
    of media violence. Schools and TV itself would participate in this
    campaign to create better educated media consumers. Obviously,
    safeguards must be built in to disallow government and media
    sources from promoting self-serving agendas.

Source: *Violence on Television: Hearing before the Subcommittee on
Crime and Criminal Justice of the Committee on the Judiciary,* House of
Representatives, 102nd Congress, 2nd sess., 15 December 1992,
pp. 93–96.

Research Reports

Three national commissions have focused on the subject of violence in the mass media. Some major findings and summaries from
these three studies are summarized below. The section concludes
with a brief statement by Dr. Melvin S. Heller, who conducted an
important study for the ABC television network on the effects of
televised violence. Dr. Heller's statement is included to provide a
glimpse of the way in which media organizations tend to view
research on the presentation and role of violence in their profession. It is also included because media organizations uniformly
declined to provide the author with their own interpretations of
some of the research discussed in this book.

National Commission on the Causes and Prevention of Violence

In 1969, the National Commission on the Causes and Prevention
of Violence presented its report. Among the committees that contributed to that report was one that analyzed the research on the
portrayal of violence in the media and its effect on the general public. This committee prepared a very long and detailed report on its
findings on this issue. The report is of value because it presents in

a clear, succinct manner the research findings that were then available on the effects of violence in the mass media on viewers. The following excerpt presents only some of the most important of these findings.

General Conclusions

1. The weight of social science stands in opposition to the conclusion that mass media portrayals of violence have no effect upon individuals, groups, and society.
2. To the extent that mass media portrayals of violence have effects upon individuals, groups, and society, it is a variety that most persons would deem costly and harmful to individuals and society.
3. The direction of effects of mass media portrayal of violence is to extend the behavioral and attitudinal boundaries of acceptable violence beyond legal and social norms currently espoused by a majority of Americans.

a. Short-Run Effects

1. Exposure to mass media portrayals of violence stimulates violent behavior when—
   (a) Subjects are either calm or anxious prior to exposure, but more so when they are frustrated, insulted, or otherwise angered.
   (b) Aggressive or violent cues are presented (e.g., weapons of violence).
   (c) Subjects are exposed either to justified or unjustified violence, but more so when justified violence is portrayed.
2. The weight of relevant research evidence throws doubt on the tenability of the "catharsis" hypothesis.
3. Audiences exposed to mass media portrayals of violence learn how to perform violent acts.
4. Audiences who have learned violent behavior from the mass media are likely to exhibit that learning (i.e., engage in acts of violence) if they encounter a situation similar to the portrayal situation, expect to be rewarded for violent behavior, or do not observe disapproving reactions to the portrayed aggression from another person in the viewing situation.

b. Long-Run Effects

The following statements contain hypotheses which are clearly consistent with and suggested by established research findings and by the most informed social science thinking about the long-run effects of exposure to mass media portrayals of violence.

1. Exposure to mass media portrayals of violence over a long period of time socializes audiences into the norms, attitudes, and values for

violence contained in those portrayals. The probability of socialization increases as—

(a) The duration of exposure increases;
(b) The intensity of exposure increases (e.g., number of hours per day);
(c) The age of the viewer decreases;
(d) The number of other sources of socialization into violence decreases;
(e) The number of senses stimulated by the medium increases (e.g., sight or sound);
(f) The primacy of the part played by violence in media presentation increases.

2. Persons who have been effectively socialized by mass media portrayals of violence will under a broad set of precipitating conditions, behave in accordance with the norms, attitudes, and values for violence contained in media presentations. Persons who have been effectively socialized into the norms for violence contained in the television world of violence would behave in the following manner:

(a) They would probably resolve conflict by the use of violence.
(b) They would probably use violence as a means to obtain desired ends.
(c) They would probably passively observe violence between others.
(d) They would not be likely to sanction or punish others' use of violence.
(e) They would probably use a weapon when engaging in violence.
(f) If they were policemen, they would be likely to meet violence with violence, often escalating its level.

3. Persons exposed to mass media portrayals of violence over a long period of time are influenced by their exposure, especially when:

(a) The mass media are the sole or major sources of information about violence.
(b) There is ambiguity in the communities' norms for violence.
(c) There is ambiguity in audience members' minds about the violent or relatively non-violent character of groups which are portrayed.

4. Persons influenced by the television world of violence would be influenced in at least the following ways:

(a) Development of more positive attitudes toward violence as a means to fulfillment of individual ends.
(b) Support and extension of the attitude that young men can enhance their masculinity by displaying proficiency in the use of violence.
(c) Lowering the value of non-violent means of problem-solving.
(d) Development of the attitude that it is not the responsibility of

individual citizens to help each other out of violent situations.

(e) Development of and support for the belief that policemen are as violent as criminals.

(f) Development of and support for the attitude that successful people may or may not break the law as they please.

5. Distinctions between fantasy and reality presentations of media violence are not consistently perceived by child audiences.

6. Appearance in the media confers status upon those appearing, regardless of their portrayed behavior.

7. Long-term exposure to mass media portrayals of violence may make audience members insensitive or emotionally neutral in response to real acts of violence.

8. Long-term exposure to mass media portrayals of violence in which the physical, psychological, and social effects of violence are not realistically shown can lower inhibitions against the use of violence.

9. The effects of long-term exposure to goreless, unrealistic portrayals of violence and gory realistic presentations are probably both conducive to lowering emotional reactions to violence, making the audience more likely to use violence and to passively tolerate violence by others. There is some reason to suggest that periodic presentations of gory, realistic, violence would have more salutary effects than either completely unrealistic and goreless or realistic and gory portrayals.

10. The extent and intensity of mass media portrayals of violence, especially in the case of television, probably have the effect of creating and/or supporting a view of the world as totally violent. Such a world view tends to promote widespread tolerance of violence, a feeling that it is hopeless to try to control violence, and the belief that individuals must be violent in order to survive in a violent world.

11. The high value placed upon action, immediacy, and simple resolution of problems in the mass media works against the idea that one should react to problems and conflict by deliberation and communication.

12. To the extent that mass media portrayals of violence contain rigid "good-guy"-"bad-guy," right-wrong, and other either-or distinctions, young audiences are likely to develop and maintain psychological rigidity characteristic of adolescence.

13. Inaccurate portrayals of class, ethnic, racial, and occupational groups in mass media presentations retard productive communication between groups. To the extent that certain groups are portrayed as violent, members of those groups may emulate their portrayal, while non-members may react with fear, hatred, and other emotions conducive to intergroup conflict and violence. The effects of these portrayals are especially potent when members of those groups have no direct personal contact with one another.

Source: National Commission on the Causes and Prevention of Violence, *Mass Media and Violence*, volume IX of *To Establish Justice, To Ensure Domestic Tranquility* (Washington, DC: Government Printing Office, 1969), pp. 375–378.

General Summary

The final report of the National Commission on the Causes and Prevention of Violence attempted to encapsulate the above findings along with other information obtained by the committee on violence and the mass media. That report concluded that:

Some defenders of violence on television, however, contend that viewers "drain off" aggressive tendencies by their vicarious participation in violent media programs. According to this reasoning, the mass media serve a socially useful "cathartic" function: by displaying violence they provide harmless outlets for the violent impulses of audience members and thereby prevent overt actions that would be socially undesirable.

Laboratory experiments on the reactions of adults and teenagers to violent film content provide little support for this theory. In fact, the vast majority of experimental studies on this question have found that observed violence stimulates aggressive behavior, rather than the opposite. Moreover, the stimulation of aggressive responses from exposure to filmed aggression is more likely to occur when the witnessed aggression occurs in a justified rather than in an unjustified context. Further experimental elaboration has shown that stimulation of aggression is most likely when the context of the film is similar to the viewer's perception of his own situation. . . .

We believe it is reasonable to conclude that a constant diet of violent behavior on television has an adverse effect on human character and attitudes. Violence on television encourages violent forms of behavior, and fosters moral and social values about violence in daily life which are unacceptable in a civilized society.

We do not suggest that television is a principal cause of violence in society. We do suggest that it is a contributing factor. Television, of course, operates in a complex social setting and its effects are undoubtedly mitigated by other social influences. But it is a matter for grave concern that at a time when the values and the influence of traditional institutions such as family, church, and school are in question, television is emphasizing violent, antisocial styles of life.

Source: National Commission on the Causes and Prevention of Violence, *To Establish Justice, To Ensure Domestic Tranquility* (Washington, DC: Government Printing Office, 1969), pp. 198–199.

Surgeon General's Scientific Advisory Committee on Television and Social Behavior

The report issued by the Surgeon General's Scientific Advisory Committee on Television and Social Behavior in 1972 was highly controversial. Many authorities and journalists who read the committee's final report came away with vastly different ideas as to what it had concluded about the effects of televised violence. When the surgeon general, Dr. Jesse L. Steinfeld, appeared before the Senate Subcommittee on Commerce on 21 March 1972, Senator John O. Pastore asked him to "spell out as simply as possible" what the committee's major conclusions were. Dr. Steinfeld's response was as follows:

After review of the Scientific Advisory Committee's report and the five volumes of original research undertaken at the request of the Senate Subcommittee, as well as a review of the previous literature on the subject, my professional response is that the broadcasters should be put on notice. The overwhelming consensus and the unanimous Scientific Advisory Committee's report indicate that televised violence, indeed, does have an adverse effect on certain members of our society.

While the Committee report is carefully phrased and qualified in language acceptable to social scientists, it is clear to me that the causal relationship between televised violence and antisocial behavior is sufficient to warrant appropriate and immediate remedial action. The data on social phenomena such as television and violence and/or aggressive behavior will never be clear enough for all social scientists to agree on the formulation of a succinct statement of causality. But there comes a time when the data are sufficient to justify action. That time has come.

I would also emphasize that no action in this social area is a form of action: it is an acquiescence in the continuation of the present level of televised violence entering American homes.

In stating this causal relationship, it is important to keep in mind that antisocial behavior existed in our society long before television appeared. We must be careful not to make television programming the whipping boy for all of society's ills. Yet we must take whatever actions we can when we do identify factors contributing to antisocial behavior in our society.

Source: *Hearings on the Surgeon General's Report by the Scientific Advisory Committee on Television and Social Behavior: Hearings before the Subcommittee on Communications of the Committee on Commerce,* United States Senate, 92nd Congress, 2nd sess., 21–24 March 1972, p. 26.

National Institute of Mental Health

In 1979, a group of researchers suggested to then–Surgeon General Julius B. Richmond that it might be worthwhile for the government to support a follow-up study on the Surgeon General's Scientific Advisory Committee on Television and Social Behavior, which issued its report in 1972 (see above). The researchers claimed that there was a "growing need for collection, review, synthesis, and assessment of the new [since 1972] literature on television and behavior."

The committee formed by the surgeon general in response to this recommendation worked for nearly three years and finally submitted its report in 1982. The primary conclusions expressed in the General Summary and in the Technical Reviews are summarized below.

General Summary

. . . Most of the researchers look at the totality of evidence and conclude, as did the Surgeon General's advisory committee, that the convergence of findings supports the conclusion of a causal relationship between televised violence and later aggressive behavior. The evidence now is drawn from a large body of literature. Adherents to this convergence approach agree that the conclusions reached in the Surgeon General's program have been significantly strengthened by more recent research. Not only has the evidence been augmented, but the processes by which the aggressive behavior is produced have been further examined.

In the past 10 years, several important field studies have found that televised violence results in aggressive behavior. . . .

The report authors then point out that the single most troubling exception to the trend observed by researchers was a "large scale study sponsored by the National Broadcasting Company."

. . . But according to many researchers, the evidence accumulated in the 1970s seems overwhelming that televised violence and aggression are positively correlated in children. The issue now is what processes produce the relation.

Technical Reviews

. . . The major substantive legacy of that report [the 1972 report of the Surgeon General's Advisory Committee] and the research sponsored by the Surgeon General's program is the conclusion that a causal connection exists between violence shown on television and subsequent aggressive behavior by children. As Comstock notes, the Surgeon General's scientific committee reached a unanimous conclusion in 1972. Early press coverage on the report was misleading and stimulated controversy over the meaning of that conclusion.

But the controversy over that conclusion continues even today, despite the fact that most researchers in the field accept that causal relationship. It is the lay public and the television industry which are less persuaded. Indeed, the controversy will probably increase in the light of the new findings and conclusions of the study by Milavsky and his colleagues [the NBC study]. . . .

Thus, except for the Milavsky report, evidence for associations between television watching and some measures of aggressive behavior can now be identified across the age spectrum from 4 years of age through about age 15. . . .

Where does all this leave the field of research on television and violence? On the original question, the consensus still seems to uphold the original conclusion of a causal relationship found the by [*sic*] Surgeon General's committee. At the same time, methods of analysis and interpretation of the results have achieved new levels of sophistication. For example, cross-lagged correlation was a relatively new procedure when it was employed by Huesmann and his colleagues in their longitudinal study published in the report to Surgeon general in 1972. That study, because of the significance given to the cross-lagged correlations, was a major factor in the conclusion reached by the Surgeon General's committee. By 1980, cross-lagged correlation was no longer a novel procedure, having been joined by other statistical models for estimating causal inferences, including those employed by Milavsky and his colleagues and by Belson. All of these models have their proponents and critics.

It is ironic, but not unexpected, that with this increasing sophistication of analysis no unequivocal conclusion has been reached about the relationship between violence and aggression. While the case for the relationship has certainly been strengthened in the past 10 years, the full authenticity of cause and effect—let alone its power—is still subject to honest disagreement.

Source: National Institute of Mental Health, *Television and Behavior: Ten Years of Scientific Progress and Implications for the Eighties* (Rockville, MD: U.S. Department of Health and Human Services, Public Health Service, Alcohol, Drug Abuse, and Mental Health Administration, National Institute of Mental Health, 1982), vol. I, pp. 37–38 and vol. II, pp. 104–106.

Views of Melvin S. Heller, M.D.

Dr. Heller is a forensic psychiatrist who has done considerable research on the causes of violence. In an appearance before the National PTA Association in 1977, he announced his own views about
the role of television in engendering violent behavior.

We have searched hard, long, and carefully among a population of
known youthful and young adult offenders in order to identify the role
of television in their childhood, and in the development of their
subsequent criminal careers. We found out many things about how they
viewed television as children and adolescents, and what they got out of
it. . . . In the careful assessment of hundreds of violent offenders all of
whom grew up with a working television set in their homes, we have
never found one person whose criminal career was caused by television
viewing.
    The causes of violence are well known. Unfortunately, they are not
conveniently located in the television tube where they could be easily
eradicated. The causes of real-world violence—rather than laboratory
produced aggression—are to be found in the childhood experiences of
known violent offenders with the real persons in their early lives.
    In my view, it is a well meaning diversion, and distinct disservice to
the victims of violence for this great organization [the PTA] to deceive
both itself and the public by focusing on television rather than on the
social inequities, poverty, child neglect and abuse which have constituted the real violent experiences so often found in the childhood
backgrounds of our violent offenders. If this great organization would
focus its energies on controlling handguns, drugs, alcohol, and gang
formation among our youth and adolescents, then, in my view, we
would be doing something indeed to prevent and control violence.

Source: Remarks made to a National PTA Public Hearing on the
Effects of Television on Children and Youth, Los Angeles, 22 Feb-
ruary 1977, as reprinted in *Sex and Violence on TV: Hearing before the
Subcommittee on Communications of the Committee on Interstate and
Foreign Commerce*, House of Representatives, 95th Congress, 1st
sess., 2 March 1977, p. 324.

Opinions about Televised Violence

Any effort to present arguments for and against the level of violence in the media would seem doomed to failure. Certainly millions of words have been written and spoken over the past century

about the dangers—or lack of danger—posed by violence in various forms of the media. It might be of some interest, however, to reprint two examples of such arguments taken from one of the most recent public forums on this issue, a 1993 hearing held before the Subcommittee on Telecommunications and Finance of the House Committee on Energy and Commerce. Although they are only two such statements, they carry messages that have been repeated over and over again during past decades.

Statement by Warren Littlefield, President of Entertainment for NBC, Inc.

When one examines the facts rather than becoming distracted by the rhetoric, it becomes clear that network television is not an appropriate primary target for those concerned with violence in society.

First, the amount of programming on network television that could even arguably be said to contain some violent material is only a tiny fraction of the thousands of hours of entertainment programming offered to viewers each year. For example during the May Sweeps, which were harshly criticized for violent programming, the vast majority of NBC's programming consisted of news, sports, sitcoms, soap operas and game shows devoid of violence. Only a minuscule percentage of the roughly 400 hours of programming offered by NBC— all movies or serious dramas exhibited after 9:00 P.M.—contained some action material that could conceivably be labelled "violent," and, we submit, it was not gratuitous. More to the point, during the May sweeps all ten most watched programs on NBC among children (2–11) were non-violent situation comedies, like "Blossom," "Fresh Prince," and "Cheers."

Second, the limited depictions of violence on network TV are generally not inappropriate or excessive, but are essential to the development of drama, appear principally in programs for an adult audience, and generally are shown later in the evening.

Third, the primary concern is with the viewing of violent material by children and children simply do not watch network programs designed for adults. Of the top 30 network programs among children, none could reasonably be construed as violent. On the other hand, NBC's highest rated police drama, "Law & Order," ranks 141st among children.

Fourth, while there is enormous and justifiable concern about society violence, NBC has little evidence of widespread *public* concern about violent programming on *network* TV. We received 240,000 actual viewer calls and letters from viewers during the 1992–93 season, and only about 1% of these viewer contacts related to concerns about violence.

Fifth, to the extent there appears to be more violence on television, it is because of the proliferation of other channels—not network TV. In fact, a recent Roper study confirmed that the public believes that there is far *more* violence on cable than on broadcast TV. While the networks schedule programs with more violent content late in the evening where they attract few young viewers, many independent television stations and cable operators compete for the young audiences with extremely violent programs. In New York, the highest rated non-network program is usually the "8 O'Clock Movie" on WPIX Channel 11. It often attracts 200,000 2-11 year olds. As noted, only a very small percentage of NBC's May sweeps programming arguably contained violence. In contrast, most of the 24 movies shown by WPIX during the May Sweeps were violent action adventure or horror movies, such as "Blood Sport" and "Death Wish." Similarly, during May the highest rated programs on pay cable were mostly violent movies. In fact, of the top 30 pay cable programs, 19 were violent movies which were shown unedited.

. . . NBC always has recognized its responsibility to its viewers to broadcast programming which is entertaining but which avoids glamorous or excessive depictions of violence. Recent Congressional attention to television violence has riveted our attention. In response, NBC has redoubled its efforts in this area through a series of steps calculated to reduce TV violence and provide parents with the information necessary to enable them to assert more control over what children watch. Moreover, we believe that TV can be used affirmatively to promote anti-violence themes and messages and to shine the light of publicity to raise awareness of issues like child abuse and date rape.

Source: *Violence on Television: Hearings before the Subcommittee on Telecommunications and Finance of the Committee on Energy and Commerce,* House of Representatives, 103rd Congress, 1st sess., 12 May, 25 June, 1 and 29 July, and 15 September 1993, pp. 194–196.

Statement by William H. Dietz, M.D., Chair of the American Academy of Pediatrics Subcommittee on Children and Television

The violence in our society is driven by a variety of complex factors, including drugs, poverty, and violence in the home. Given the epidemic of violence that is upon us, it may be reasonable to ask where children acquire their information about problem solving, and why violence is the first rather than the last alternative selected.

Although none of us hold television solely responsible as the only origin of violence, any discussion of violence in the United States must consider the influence of television. We believe that televised violence has a clear and reproducible effect on the behavior of children, that televised violence contributes to the climate in which we live, the frequency with which violence is used to resolve conflict, and the passivity with which violence is perceived.

Violence is an act intended to injure or harm. Violent acts that meet this criterion occur about 20 times an hour on children's programming, and approximately 8 to 12 times an hour on prime time television. Children spend approximately 25 hours per week watching television. If we assume that two-thirds of this time is spent watching prime time television and one-third watching children's cartoons, we find that children are exposed to a conservative estimate of over 12,000 violent acts per year.

Violence on television is frequent, inconsequential, effective, and rewarded. The lingering psychological and physical effects of violence are rarely shown. Violence ends confrontations quickly and effectively, without a requirement for patience, negotiations, and compromise. Violence is practiced as often by the heroes as by the villains.

Both epidemiologic and experimental studies have demonstrated a clear relationship in children between the viewing of televised violence and violent or aggressive behavior. Although we cannot say with assurance that an individual child will respond to violence on television with violent behavior, I believe that an argument can be made that violence affects the child population as a whole. The association between violent television and aggressive behavior has been demonstrated in multiple studies. The more violent television children watch, the more likely they are to be violent or aggressive. Other societal factors, such as domestic violence and child abuse, may figure into the prevalence of violence in our society, but surely repeated exposure to televised violence must also be a contributing factor.

Because children learn from what they see, it should surprise no one that the violence on television clearly provokes violent or aggressive behavior in children. The absence of consequences of the violence that they see, and the rapidity with which difficulties are resolved by the use of violence, increase the likelihood that violence will be among the first strategies that a child selects, rather than the last. Also, the rewards that the heroes receive for their violent behavior legitimize and tacitly endorse violence as a means of solving problems. Finally, the frequency with which children view violence, and the lack of long-term consequences of the victims of violence, desensitizes children, and makes them more passive to acts of violence and less likely to intervene when violence occurs. . . .

The repeated denials by network executives that televised violence has no effect on the behavior of children or adolescents are inconsistent with the use of repetitive commercials to sell products. Children clearly respond to commercials. The inability of children to distinguish between commercial and program content led the Federal Trade Commission to require a break between cartoons and commercials. This decision recognizes that young children have difficulty distinguishing fantasy from reality. Therefore, we can expect no difference between the effect of a fantasy on human character or the development of early childhood behavior. It is illogical to argue that children will not also respond to the violence that they see, which occurs far more frequently on television than does any commercial.

Source: *Violence on Television: Hearings before the Subcommittee on Telecommunications and Finance of the Committee on Energy and Commerce,* House of Representatives, 103rd Congress, 1st sess., 12 May, 25 June, 1 and 29 July, and 15 September 1993, pp. 59–60.

Directory of Organizations

5

Organizations

Many organizations are concerned about the issue of violence in the media and have issued publications, taken public stands, participated in national and regional meetings on the subject, and have otherwise been active and involved with regard to this issue. As an example, 28 organizations were represented on the Citizens Task Force on TV Violence, which, in the mid-1990s, aided in the drafting of Senator Kent Conrad's Children's Media Protection Act of 1995. Included among these organizations were the National Sheriffs Association, the International Association of Chiefs of Police, the American Psychiatric Association, the National Association for Family and Community Education, and the National Child Care Association. The organizations listed below, however, have been chosen for inclusion in this chapter because they have expressed a major ongoing commitment to working on the issue of violence in the mass media. Organizations whose entry is preceded by an asterisk (*) did not respond to requests for information. Their entries have been prepared from generally available sources of information.

Alliance Against Violence in Entertainment for Children
17 Greenwood Street
Marlboro, MA 01752
Tel/Fax: (508) 481-6926
e-mail: NCTVma@aol.com

During the late 1980s, AAVEC evolved to its present form out of a local unit of the Unitarian-Universalist Church. The Alliance consists of professionals in the Boston area working to reduce the spread of violence in local communities and in the field of entertainment. It works in cooperation with other local and national groups, especially with the National Coalition on Television Violence (see below). Its current emphasis is to develop projects that will help children, teenagers, and parents develop critical viewing skills. AAVEC maintains a list of speakers for community organizations.

Publications: A pamphlet, *A Call to Action* (in English and Spanish), and four posters, "Every Day in Massachusetts," "Every Day Bullets Kill . . .," "Children Learn by Imitation," and "The Victims of Fictional TV Crimes Are Not *All* on the Screen."

American Civil Liberties Union
Arts Censorship Project
132 West 43rd Street
New York, NY 10036
Tel: (212) 944-9800, ext. 704
Fax: (212) 869-4314

The ACLU Arts Censorship Project was founded in 1991 in an effort to combat what the organization saw as increasing threats to artistic freedom. These threats seemed to be coming both from governmental bodies and from private pressure groups. The goal of the project is to carry out educational campaigns and legal challenges to protect artists from attacks on their First Amendment rights. The project also works with the national office of the ACLU in Washington on federal legislative issues relating to censorship of the arts. It provides legal assistance in censorship cases both to individual artists and to arts organizations.

Publications: A quarterly newsletter; a pamphlet, *The Creative Spirit Must Be Free;* a two-page flyer about the labeling of popular music, *Popular Music under Siege;* the "ACLU Briefing Paper on Artistic Freedom"; a paper by Project Director Marjorie Heins, "Media Violence and Free Speech"; and a book by Heins, *Sex, Sin & Blasphemy: A Guide to America's Censorship Wars.*

American Family Association
P. O. Drawer 2440
Tupelo, MS 38803
Tel: (601) 844-5036

The American Family Association was founded as a nonprofit organization in 1977 by Donald E. Wildmon, a minister in the United Methodist denomination. AFA believes that the entertainment industry has played a major role in what it sees as the decline of certain traditional values in the United States.

One of its most effective methods of making its case against programs that it deems objectionable is to contact advertisers and distributors of those programs, trying to convince those advertisers and distributors to discontinue any association with the programs in question. For example, AFA was successful in convincing the 7-Eleven chain of convenience stores to remove from their shelves certain magazines whose content the AFA found objectionable. Among the subsidiary groups working within AFA are more than 500 local affiliate groups, the AFA Law Center founded to defend the civil rights of Christians, and radio station WAFR-FM, a 24-hour-a-day station that broadcasts Christian teachings and Christian music.

Publications: A monthly journal, *AFA Journal;* a Bible-study course, "Christianity and Humanism: A Study in Contrasts"; pamphlets and brochures, such as *Public School Sex Education: A Report, Pornography: Problems and Solutions, The Fight Back Book,* and *Pornography: A Report.*

Americans for Responsible Television
P. O. Box 627
Bloomfield Hills, MI 48303
Tel: (313) 646-4248
Fax: (313) 646-4247

Americans for Responsible Television (ART) was founded in 1989 to encourage and promote the responsible use of public airwaves by its license holders. It works with advertisers, networks, media executives, creative people, legislators, educators, and health and other professionals to find ways of eliminating exploitative sex, violence, and "other indignities" from television.

ART currently has four immediate objectives, including restoration of the "Family Viewing Hour," restoration of program codes and self-regulation, reduction of "senseless violence and expletive [sic] sex," and improvement of the quality of children's television.

ART was founded by Terry Rakolta, mother of four children. The organization currently claims 350,000 members.

Publications: A pamphlet, *Protecting Your Child against TV Violence: What You Can Do*, and a regular newsletter that goes to all members, *Americans for Responsible Television Update.*

Center for Media and Public Affairs
2100 L Street, N.W., Suite 300
Washington, DC 20037
Tel: (202) 223-2942
Fax: (202) 872-4014

The Center for Media and Public Affairs was founded in 1986 for the purpose of studying the ways in which the media treat social and political issues. Much of its work is involved with analyzing the ways in which various media presentations affect public opinion on such issues.

One of the studies for which the Center has become best known is the investigation called "A Day of TV Violence," conducted originally on the first Thursday of April in 1992 and then again on the same day two years later. In these two studies, observers watched programs on ten television channels throughout an 18-hour day and noted the number and type of violent incidents that occurred during that time. The original study formed the basis of a special issue of *TV Guide* in 1992.

Publications: A monthly magazine, *Media Monitor*; regular reports on events taking place in the media; a number of books, monographs, and articles. A brief summary and a full report of "A Day of TV Violence" are both available from the Center.

Center for Media Education
1511 K Street, N.W., Suite 518
Washington, DC 20005
Tel: (202) 628-2620
Fax: (202) 628-2554
e-mail: cme@access.digex.net

The Center for Media Education was founded in 1991 as an advocacy group for children's media policy and as a means to provide access to the information superhighway for nonprofit groups. The Center's goals are to educate the public, the nonprofit community, and the press about critical policy choices in "the emerging 21st century information superhighway." One of the Center's main initiatives has been a program known as "Campaign for Kids' TV." Some of the primary elements of that campaign include research on children's television programming, advocacy work on behalf of better media policies for children, parental education about children's television, outreach to the media, and local campaigns to improve television programming for children. The organization claims that, since the closing of Action for Children's Television in 1992, its Campaign for Kids' TV has "emerged as the most effective voice on behalf of children's needs in the electronic media."

Publications: Descriptive material on The Campaign for Kids' TV, The Future of the Media Project, and Children and the Information Superhighway.

Center for Media Literacy
1962 S. Shenandoah
Los Angeles, CA 90034
Tel: (310) 559-2944
Fax: (310) 559-9396

The Center for Media Literacy grew out of a magazine-style newsletter, *Media&Values*, originally founded as a student project by Elizabeth Thoman in the late 1970s. In January 1994, *Media&Values* was "reinvented" with the goal of concentrating on national leadership and teacher training in the field of media literacy in the United States. The Center is now a nonprofit membership organization.

The Center's "vision" statement says that the organization is dedicated to "a new vision of literacy for the 21st century," a vision that includes the ability to communicate in all media forms as well as to gain access to, understand, analyze, and evaluate the messages provided by the media. The Center now claims to be the largest distributor of media literacy resources in the United States and Canada.

In March 1995, the Center announced the release of its new community education program, *Beyond Blame: Challenging Violence in the Media.* The program consists of 272 pages of lesson plans, 70 worksheets and handouts, a 55-minute audiocassette, and nearly 2 hours of video segments on five videocassettes. The purpose of the program, according to the Center, is "to get parents, pastors, teachers, caregivers, and all concerned citizens thinking *and acting* on the undeniable connection between make-believe violence and real violence."

In addition to the community education program, the Center provides training workshops for educators, parents, and community leaders, and works with other media literacy organizations and educational institutions on issues of common interest.

Publications: In addition to the curriculum program described above: a newsletter, *Connect*, that goes to all members; Media Literacy Workshop Kits, including *TV Alert: A Wake-Up Guide for Television Literacy*, consisting of lesson plans, handout masters, background article readings, and a 77-minute video, and *Living in the Image Culture*, consisting of 15 curriculum modules, illustrated handout masters, background material, and a *Media Literacy Resource Directory;* "Media and Violence," a two-part series taken from *Media&Values* magazine; "Exploring the Issues of Media and Violence," a study-discussion package; and a booklet, *Resources for Media Literacy.*

Comics Magazine Association of America
355 Lexington Avenue, 17th Floor
New York, NY 10017
Tel: (212) 661-4261

The Comics Magazine Association of America was founded in 1954 when complaints about violent, sexual, and other offensive themes in comic magazines had reached their peak. The association was formed for the purpose of developing an industry-wide code that would guarantee to prospective readers that their products would meet "high standards of decency and good taste and eliminate objectionable material in comics magazines." The association currently consists of 12 publishers, distributors, printers, and engravers of comic magazines.

Publication: Code of the Comics Magazine Association, periodically updated.

*Federal Communications Commission (FCC)
1919 M Street, N.W.
Washington, DC 20554
Tel: (202) 632-7000
TDD: (202) 632-6999

The FCC was created by the Communications Act of 1934 to regulate interstate and foreign communications by wire and radio in the public interest. It was assigned additional regulatory jurisdiction under the provisions of the Communications Satellite Act of 1962. The scope of its regulation now includes radio and television broadcasting; telephone, telegraph, and cable television operation; two-way radio and radio operators; and satellite communications.

The Commission consists of five members who are appointed by the president with the advice and consent of the Senate. Some of the subdivisions of the FCC include the Mass Media, Common Carrier, and Private Radio Bureaus. The Mass Media Bureau is responsible for the regulation of AM and FM radio, television, low-power TV translators, instructional TV, and other broadcasting media. This Bureau issues construction permits, operating licenses, and renewals or transfers of such licenses. It oversees compliance by broadcasters and cable TV operators with Commission policies and regulations. The Common Carrier Bureau administers the regulatory program for interstate and international telephone, telegraph, radio, and satellite operation. The Private Radio Communication Bureau regulates use of the radio frequencies by private business, state and local governments, and aircraft and ships.

Publications: A vast array of FCC rules and regulations are available through the Library (202-632-7100) and the News Media Division (202-632-5050).

Film Advisory Board, Inc.
1727 ¹/₂ N. Sycamore Avenue
Hollywood, CA 90028
Tel: (213) 874-3644
Fax: (213) 929-0635
Internet: http://www.loop.com/FAB/

The Film Advisory Board was founded by Elayne Blythe in 1975 as a nonprofit organization dedicated to recognizing and supporting entertainment of special quality and value for children and family. The Board's Award of Excellence is intended to acknowledge films that are not only of superior quality but that de-emphasize the importance of gratuitous violence.

The Board has also developed an alternative to the Motion Picture Association of America's film rating system. The six basic ratings in this system are C (for children ages 10 and under), F (for families of all ages), PD (parental discretion), PD-M (parental discretion/mature), EM (extremely mature), and AO (adults over the age of 18). The Board requires that any producer using its rating on an advertisement also include a content description to help viewers better understand the nature of the film being advertised.

Publications: None

Future WAVE
105 Camino Teresa
Santa Fe, NM 87505
Tel: (505) 982-8882
Fax: (505) 982-6460
e-mail: future@spy.org

Future WAVE, Inc. is a nonprofit educational organization that works with the entertainment industry to find ways of producing interesting drama without glorifying or trivializing violence. The organization is also involved in the development and distribution of alternative forms of mass media that can be produced for general consumption.

Members of the Future WAVE Advisory Board include Dennis Weaver, Martin Sheen, Jamie Farr, George Gerbner, Deborah Prothrow-Stith, and George McGovern.

One of the first products from Future WAVE was a film entitled *Ooops!* about a "brilliant young woman scientist who bungles her time-warp experiment, plunging the world into the Pentagon's worse nightmare: an outbreak of accidental . . . PEACE!" The next film, *Astrocops*, is a science-fiction film in which "bad guys" are disarmed and transformed rather than being "blown away."

Publications and Products: Two films *(Ooops!* and *Astrocops);* a play *(The Legend of Bullyproof Shields);* and ancillary toys, games, and related products.

KIDSNET, Inc.
6856 Eastern Avenue, N.W., Suite 208
Washington, DC 20012
Tel: (202) 291-1400
Fax: (202) 882-7315
e-mail: kidsnet@aol.com

KIDSNET is a national nonprofit computerized clearinghouse devoted to children's television, radio, audio, and video programming. It was created in the mid-1980s by a consortium of entertainment companies that includes the Arts & Entertainment Network, Bravo, Capital Cities/ABC, CBS, the Discovery Channel, the Disney Channel, the Family Channel, Fox Children's Network, Home Box Office, Jim Henson Productions, Lorimar Television/Warner Brothers Television, Mind Extension University, National Association of Broadcasters, National Geographic Society/Television, NBC, Nickelodeon, Showtime, Turner Broadcasting System, and USA Network. The organization publishes a monthly *Media Guide* that lists all programs of interest to children. KIDSNET is also involved in the development of print materials, such as study guides, that can be used in the viewing of children's television programs. The organization also conducts two- to three-hour workshops aimed at improving the viewing skills of children.

Publications: The monthly *KIDSNET Media Guide* (also available on America Online by choosing keyword KIDSNET) and many study guides prepared for use with specific children's television programs.

Media Action Research Center
475 Riverside Drive, Suite 1948
New York, NY 10115
Tel: (212) 870-2402
Fax: (212) 870-2171

MARC is affiliated with United Methodist Communications and is engaged in a variety of activities that are designed to educate the general public about the content and influence of television on consumers. In October 1994, MARC was one of the sponsors of a teleconference on violence in the media that included speakers from the Center for Media Literacy, the National Council of Churches, Hunter College, radio station WBAL, and the Canadian Radio-

Television and Telecommunications Commission, as well as Surgeon General Dr. M. Joycelyn Elders.

Publications: Program guidebooks, student leaflets, and packets for leaders containing information and instructional suggestions.

*Motion Picture Association of America
1133 Avenue of the Americas
New York, NY 10036
Tel: (212) 840-6161

The Motion Picture Association of America was founded in 1922 under the name Motion Picture Producers and Distributors of America. It assumed its new name in 1945. The primary reason for the creation of the MPAA was to provide a mechanism by which the motion picture industry could respond to increasing demands for a reduction in the amount of sexual and violent themes found in early films. Over time, the MPAA has developed, publicized, and attempted to enforce a series of industry codes and rating systems intended to maintain a high moral tone in its films. These codes and rating systems have met with an uneven degree of success, however. The organization currently consists of less than a dozen members, all of whom are major film producers in the United States.

Publications: None

National Alliance for Non-Violent Programming
1846 Banking Street
Greensboro, NC 27408
Tel: (910) 370-0407
Fax: (910) 370-0392

The National Alliance for Non-Violent Programming is a nonprofit network of ten national and international women's organizations created to address the issue of violence in the media without suggesting the imposition of censorship or interfering with the First Amendment rights of producers. The ten organizations include the American Medical Women's Association, the Association of Junior Leagues International, Inc., B'nai B'rith Women, Jack and Jill of America, Inc., the International Association of Women Police, the Links, the National Association of Minority Women in Business, the National Association of Women Business Owners, Soroptimist

International of the Americas, and Women's International League for Peace and Freedom.

The Alliance works with local groups such as schools and colleges, health departments, boys and girls clubs, religious organizations, and nonprofit organizations who are interested in suggesting positive programming to local media outlets. It makes available a packet of materials designed to promote awareness about violence in the media. The packet can be adapted for meetings, discussion groups, and other educational settings and is available from the Alliance for $15.

Publication: Education/awareness packet described above.

National Association for the Education of Young Children
1509 16th Street, N.W.
Washington, DC 20036-1426
Tel: (202) 232-8777 or (800) 424-2460
Fax: (202) 328-1846

NAEYC, with 90,000 members, is the largest organization of professionals in the United States dedicated to improving the quality of services for young children and their families. The work of the Association focuses on the first eight years of a child's life, which it believes to be crucial in a person's development. Much of the organization's work is done through a network of 450 affiliate groups in the United States and other countries.

One department of NAEYC, Information Services, collects information on national issues dealing with early childhood programs and provides personalized data for individuals and groups interested in these issues. The Public Affairs Department provides information on legislation affecting early childhood services, strategies for promoting high-quality early childhood programs, and communication with the general public.

For a number of years, the organization has been particularly active in helping parents deal with the problems of televised violence. NAEYC has adopted a "Position Statement on Violence in the Lives of Children," which it now makes available to the general public for a charge of 50 cents per copy.

Publications: These include a brochure, "Media Violence and Children: A Guide for Parents," a book, *Early Violence Prevention: Tools for Teachers of Young Children*, a video, *Confronting the Epidemic of*

Violence—A Community Strategy, a bimonthly journal, *Young Children*, a quarterly journal, *Early Childhood Research Quarterly*, and a list of more than 200 books, pamphlets, brochures, posters, and buttons.

National Association of Elementary School Principals
1615 Duke Street
Alexandria, VA 22314
Tel: (703) 684-3345
Fax: (703) 548-6021

NAESP is a professional association of 26,000 elementary and middle school principals in the United States, Canada, and other nations. Among its many professional activities, it has been active in support of efforts to make parents more conscious of the potential effects of televised violence on their children. Its 1993 "Report to Parents" on "How Parents Can Turn Off TV Violence" was distributed to all of its members with the suggestion that the report be duplicated and distributed to all of their students.

Publications: A newsletter, *Communicator*, distributed ten times a year; a magazine, *Principal*, published five times a year; other regular publications, such as *Focus on Finance* (three times a year); *Report to Parents* (bimonthly); *Research Roundup* (three times a year); and *Streamlined Seminar* (bimonthly).

National Coalition on Television Violence
23290 W. 14 Mile Road, Suite 498
West Bloomfield, MI 48322
Tel: (810) 489-3177
Fax: (810) 489-8696

5132 Newport Avenue
Bethesda, MD 20816
Tel: (301) 986-0362
Fax: (301) 656-7031

144 East End Avenue
New York, NY 10128
Tel: (212) 535-7275

17 Greenwood Street
Marlborough, MA 01752
Tel/Fax: (508) 481-6926
e-mail: NCTVma@aol.com

A nonprofit organization established in 1980, NCTV's primary goal it is to educate the general public about the amount of gratuitous violence on television and about the potentially harmful effects of televised violence. The organization consists of a group of concerned professionals from a variety of disciplines located in the four centers listed above. These individuals appear as expert witnesses before congressional hearings, speak at public forums and seminars, and provide interviews for the print and broadcast media.

Publication: Brochure describing NCTV for prospective members.

National Council of Churches of Christ in the U.S.A.
Mike Maus, Director of Communications
475 Riverside Drive, Room 852
New York, NY 10015-0050
Tel: (212) 870-2049
Fax: (212) 870-2030

The National Council of Churches of Christ in the U.S.A. was established in 1950 by the action of 29 denominations within the Protestant, Anglican, and Eastern Orthodox faiths. Its goal is to carry out activities that reflect common beliefs among the member denominations—activities such as providing disaster relief, promoting interfaith meetings, providing resources for religious education, and strengthening family life. In 1995, the General Board of the Council adopted by a 145 to 0 vote a statement on "Violence in Electronic Media and Film," which called for, among other things, programs for improved media literacy and a higher level of social consciousness among members of the mass media.

Publications: A newsletter, *Ecu-Link; Yearbook of American and Canadian Churches;* policy statement, "Violence in Electronic Media and Film."

National Foundation to Improve Television
60 State Street, Suite 3400
Boston, MA 02109
Tel: (617) 523-6353
Fax: (617) 523-4619

NFIT is a nonprofit, public-interest, educational organization founded in 1969. It is dedicated to bringing about responsible change and improvements in the quality of television viewing, with particular emphasis on reducing the amount of televised violence to which children are exposed. The Foundation has undertaken a three-pronged approach to accomplishing its goal: (1) raising public awareness about the dangers to children of television violence; (2) working with business leaders to limit advertising that keeps violent programming on the air; and (3) seeking regulatory and legislative remedies for the problem of televised violence.

Publications: None

National Political Congress of Black Women, Inc.
600 New Hampshire Avenue, N.W., Suite 1125
Washington, DC 20037
Tel: (202) 338-0800
Fax: (202) 625-0499

NPCBW is a nonprofit, nonpartisan organization created in 1984 by a number of prominent black women, including Shirley Chilsholm, former congresswoman from Texas; Mary Frances Berry, then-chair of the Civil Rights Commission; Sharon Pratt Kelly, former mayor of the District of Columbia; and Eleanor Holmes-Norton, representative to the U.S. House of Representatives from the District of Columbia. The organization was founded in order to educate and train young African American women so that they will be prepared for leadership positions in the twenty-first century.

One of the organization's major campaigns is the current effort to eliminate gangsta rap from the recording industry. A leader in that program has been the current chair of NPCBW, DeLores Tucker.

As evidence of its progress, NPCBW points to a 100 percent increase in the number of African American women elected and appointed to positions of importance in the United States over the past decade, and a 300 percent increase in the number of such women appointed by the U.S. president.

Publications: No regular publications

National PTA
Public Relations Department
330 N. Wabash, Suite 2100
Chicago, IL 60611-3604
Tel: (312) 670-6782
Fax: (312) 670-6783

The National PTA was founded on 17 February 1897 by Alice McLellan Birney and Phoebe Apperson Hearst. In its long history, the organization has been involved in a number of social issues relating to the welfare of children, including efforts to secure child labor laws, compulsory public education, a national public health service, improved school libraries, and education for children with special needs.

For nearly three decades, the PTA has also been addressing the issue of violence in the media. Its first position statement on this issue, "Improvement of the Quality of TV Programs for Children," was adopted in 1968 and was then reaffirmed in 1989 and 1994. The organization has also adopted other position statements on the issue in 1970 ("Mass Media," reaffirmed in 1981, 1989, and 1994), in 1975 ("Violence in TV Programming," reaffirmed in 1989), and in 1982 ("Television Viewing Skills Development").

In 1995, the PTA announced the formation of the Family and Community Critical Viewing Project in conjunction with the National Cable Television Association and Cable in the Classroom. The purpose of this project is to provide parents and teachers with the information and skills they need to help families make better choices in the television programs they watch and to improve the way they watch those programs. During the first year of the project, 17 workshops were scheduled at state and local PTA meetings and at special sessions operated by the Cable Industry Training Program.

Publications: A large number of books, booklets, posters, videos, and brochures on parenting, health, education, and safety issues as well as leadership development materials for state and local PTAs. Some relevant publications include the magazine *PTA Today*, published five times a year; the booklet *Outreach* that contains reproducible articles; a newsletter, *What's Happening in Washington*, on federal legislative issues (published six times a year); *Taking Charge of Your TV*, a guide to critical viewing for parents and children; and two brochures, *Television and Your Family* and *What Do Parents Need To Know about Children's Resources Television Viewing*.

Parents Music Resource Center
1500 Arlington Boulevard
Arlington, VA 22304
Tel: (703) 527-9466
Fax: (703) 527-9468

The Parents Music Resource Center is a nonprofit organization that was founded in 1985 to educate the public, especially parents, about the importance of being aware of the messages contained in the popular music that is marketed to children and adolescents. The Center encourages public discussion and research on messages of violence, suicide, racism, misogyny, satanism, and the glorification of drugs and alcohol in music lyrics, videos, and concert performances. One of the Center's primary roles is to act as a clearinghouse for information about these issues. Early in its history, the Center was largely responsible for the adoption of a system by which audio recordings are labeled to indicate the presence of explicit sexual, violent, or drug references. The Center has the resources to respond to only a limited number of requests from children and adolescents about the issues in which it is interested.

Publications: A pamphlet, *Music—A Health Issue?* and a video, *Rising to the Challenge,* that is accompanied by a booklet, *Let's Talk Rock.*

Stop War Toys Campaign
Youth Peace Campaign of the War Resisters League
339 Lafayette Street
New York, NY 10012
Tel: (212) 228-0450
Fax: (212) 228-6193
e-mail: wrl@igc.apc.org

The Campaign attempts to educate the general public about what it sees as the harmful effects of war toys (guns, tanks, soldiers, and other devices that glorify violent action) as well as the potential harm from violence in the media, such as cartoon programs broadcast on television.

Typical activities of the Campaign include collecting statistics on violence in the media, providing speakers on war toys and related topics, organizing demonstrations aimed at companies that produce war toys and violent television cartoons, and producing informational packets that describe protest strategies for grassroots organizations.

Publications: A periodic newsletter; a quarterly literature list, "Books That Make a Difference"; buttons, pins, posters, stickers, tags, cards, videos, and other materials publicizing the importance of nonviolent activism.

Writers Guild of America, West
Department of Public Affairs
8955 Beverly Boulevard
W. Hollywood, CA 90048-2456
Tel: (310) 550-1000
Fax: (310) 550-8185

The Writers Guild of America, West is a labor union representing writers in the motion picture, broadcast, cable, and new technologies industries. It is the sole collective bargaining representative for writers in these fields. The approximately 7,000 members of the Guild write for news, entertainment, interactive, CD-ROM, and new media production.

The Guild grew out of the Writers Guild of America, organized in 1912 as an association concerned with the proprietary rights of authors of books, short stories, articles, and other types of publication. Today, the Guild sponsors seminars, panel discussions, and other events dealing with issues of interest to writers. With regard to issues involving violent themes in media programming, the Guild has long taken the position that writers should have a free hand in producing manuscripts free of governmental regulation. It was a party in 1979 to the lawsuit that resulted in the discontinuation of the family-viewing-hour concept.

Publications: A monthly publication, *The Journal;* pamphlets and booklets dealing with topics of interest to writers, including *Professional Writers' Teleplay/Screenplay Format Guide, Plagiarism & Copyright Infringement, Creative Rights,* and *Guidelines for Writers, Producers & Executives.*

Industry Information

The following is a directory of organizations responsible for the production of broadcast and cable television programming.

A&E (Arts and Entertainment Network)
P. O. Box 1610, Grand Central Station
New York, NY 10163-1610
Tel: (212) 210-1328
Fax: (212) 949-7147

ABC-TV
Capital Cities/ABC
77 W. 66th Street, 18th Floor
New York, NY 10023
Tel: (212) 456-7777

AMC (American Movie Classics)
Rainbow Programming
150 Crossways Park, West
Woodbury, NY 11797
Tel: (516) 364-2222
Fax: (516) 364-8929

BET (Black Entertainment Television)
1700 N. Moore Street, Suite 2200
Rosslyn, VA 22209
Tel: (800) 229-2388

Bravo
150 Crossways Park, West
Woodbury, NY 11797
Tel: (516) 364-2222

CBS-TV (Columbia Broadcasting System)
51 W. 52nd Street
New York, NY 10019
Tel: (212) 975-4321

Corporation for Public Broadcasting
Education Office
901 E Street, N. W.
Washington, DC 20004-2006
Tel: (202) 879-9724

The Discovery Channel
7700 Wisconsin Avenue
Bethesda, MD 20814-3522
Tel: (800) 321-1832

The Disney Channel
3800 W. Alameda
Burbank, CA 91505
Tel: (818) 569-7500
Fax: (818) 566-1358

The Family Channel
1000 Centerville Turnpike
Virginia Beach, VA 23463
Tel: (804) 523-7301
Fax: (804) 523-7880

Fox Broadcasting Co.
P.O. Box 900
Beverly Hills, CA 90213-0900
Tel: (310) 369-1000

Galavision (Spanish-language programs)
2121 Avenue of the Stars, Suite 2300
Los Angeles, CA 90067

HBO (Home Box Office)
HBO/Cinemax
1100 Avenue of the Americas
New York, NY 10036
Tel: (212) 512-1000
Fax: (212) 512-5517

Lifetime
3612 35th Avenue
Astoria, NY 11106
Tel: (718) 482-4127

MTV (Music Television)
1515 Broadway, 23rd Floor
New York, NY 10036
Tel: (212) 258-8560

NBC-TV (National Broadcasting Company)
30 Rockefeller Plaza
25th Floor
New York, NY 10112
(212) 644-4444

Nickelodeon
1515 Broadway
New York, NY 10036
Tel: (212) 258-7773

PBS (Public Broadcasting Service)
Elementary/Secondary Service
1320 Braddock Place
Alexandria, VA 22314
Tel: (703) 739-5038

Showtime
The Movie Channel
1633 Broadway
New York, NY 10019
Tel: (212) 708-1600

TBS Superstation
Turner Educational Services
1 CNN Center
Atlanta, GA 30348-5366
Tel: (800) 344-6219

TNT (Turner Network Television)
Turner Educational Services
1 CNN Center
Atlanta, GA 30348-5366
Tel: (800) 344-6219

Univision (Spanish-language programs)
603 3rd Avenue
New York, NY 10158
Tel: (212) 455-5312

USA Network
1230 Avenue of the Americas
New York, NY 10020
Tel: (212) 408-9100
Fax: (212) 408-3606

Selected Print Resources 6

The number of books dealing with the media and its effects on children and adults runs into the hundreds. A large percentage of these contain at least one chapter on violence in the media. It would hardly be practicable in a book of this size to list even the majority of such books. Thus, this chapter focuses on works that are totally devoted to the subject of violence in the media or that include a significant number of chapters on that topic. The bibliography by Signorielli and Gerbner (see page 186), although now somewhat outdated, is of particular value in locating individual books, chapters, reports, and articles dealing with violence in the media.

Bibliographies

Atkin, Charles K., John P. Murray, and Oguz R. Nayman. **Television and Social Behavior: An Annotated Bibliography of Research Focusing on Television's Impact on Children.** Washington, DC: Government Printing Office, 1971. 150pp. No ISBN.

This bibliography was prepared in connection with the work of the Surgeon General's

Scientific Advisory Committee on Television and Social Behavior. It consists of approximately 300 annotated and 250 unannotated citations taken from sources such as *Psychological Abstracts*, *Sociological Abstracts*, *Current Contents*, the National Clearinghouse for Mental Health, and earlier bibliographies on this subject. Although the work is now, of course, very much out-of-date, it is a valuable resource for many hundreds of articles, books, reports, and other materials written before 1970.

Schramm, Wilbur, ed. **The Effects of Television on Children and Adolescents: An Annotated Bibliography with an Introductory Overview of Research.** Paris: UNESCO, 1964. 54pp. No ISBN.

This bibliography covers 165 books and articles dealing with the effects of television (and to some extent, films) on children and adolescents. The effects of televised violence are included in the annotations. The overview to the book summarizes some important points about the research evidence that existed at the time, including such topics as "Why these effects are hard to study," "Why children watch television," "Television's effect on a child's leisure time," and "When does television affect a child's outlook and values?" Interestingly enough, the study draws roughly the same conclusions as those reported by most such studies over the following three decades, namely that televised violence appears to have relatively modest effects on either the production or amelioration of aggressive behavior in children.

Signorielli, Nancy, and George Gerbner. **Violence and Terror in the Mass Media.** New York: Greenwood Press, 1988. 233pp. ISBN 0-313-26120-2.

This extensive bibliography began as a research project commissioned by the United Nations Educational, Scientific, and Cultural Organization in 1984. The compilers sent out over 4,600 requests for research reports, papers, articles, and other publications dealing with the subjects of violence and terrorism. Their final product lists 784 annotated titles. Of particular interest is the inclusion of a number of publications from nations other than the United States. The book is an invaluable resource for material written prior to the late 1980s.

Books

Anderson, Kristin, and Nancy Dennis, eds. **Television and Children: Priorities for Research.** New York: The Ford Foundation, [1976]. 38pp. No ISBN.

This short book is a report of a conference held early in November 1975 at Reston, Virginia, and sponsored by the Ford Foundation, the John and Mary R. Markle Foundation, and the National Science Foundation. The purpose of the meeting was twofold: (1) to consider the various ways in which future research in this field might go, and (2) to develop guidelines for formulating television policies based on research findings. The report consists of speeches by George Comstock and Lloyd Morrisett and the reports and recommendations of workshop participants.

Arons, Leon, and Mark A. May. **Television and Human Behavior: Tomorrow's Research in Mass Communication.** New York: Appleton-Century Crofts, 1963. 307pp. No ISBN.

In the fall of 1960, the Television Bureau of Advertising announced a competition for "exceptional plans in the field of television research." The competition was designed to produce fresh approaches to the question of how television affects viewers. This book presents the 18 award-winning plans. Plan 6, "The Effects of Aggressive Content in Television Programs upon the Aggressive Behavior of the Audience," and plan 7, "Television Viewing and the Norm-Violating Practices and Perspectives of Adolescents," deal specifically with the issue of the effects of televised violence on young viewers.

Barcus, F. Earle. **Saturday Children's Television: A Report of TV Programming and Advertising on Boston Commercial Television.** Newtonville, MA: Action for Children's Television, 1971. 55pp. No ISBN.

This book details one of the early studies supported by Action for Children's Television. The study demonstrated the extent to which children's television was a "wasteland" in the early 1970s: About a quarter of all time spent on children's programs was devoted to commercial advertising. Nearly a third of all dramatic programming involved some form of violence.

Barcus, F. Earle, with Rachel Wolkin. **Children's Television: An Analysis of Programming and Advertising.** New York: Praeger, 1977. 55pp. No ISBN.

This book is an expanded version of the earlier studies carried out by Barcus and commissioned by Action for Children's Television. The authors watched a total of 1,530 minutes of television programming and advertising on three major networks (ABC, NBC, and CBS) and two independent television stations (channels WSBK and WLVI in the Boston area). They provide very detailed and comprehensive data on the time, setting, subject matter, popularity, and general nature of programs and advertisements, with particular attention to the role of violence in both areas of television broadcasting. A particularly interesting section of the report provides detailed examples of the various forms of violent actions they observed during their studies.

Barker, Martin. **Comics: Ideology, Power and the Critics.** New York: St. Martin's Press, 1989. 321pp. ISBN 0-7190-2588-5.

This history of the comics is especially interesting since it focuses on that form of the media in Great Britain. Interestingly enough, many of the issues of violence in British comic strips parallel those that arose in the United States during the 1950s.

Barlow, Geoffrey, and Alison Hill, eds. **Video, Violence & Children.** New York: St. Martin's Press, 1986. 182pp. ISBN 0-3403-8917-6.

This volume reports the findings of the Parliamentary Group Video Enquiry (PGVE) created in July 1983 to obtain evidence on the effects resulting from children's viewing of violence on television. After reviewing a host of earlier research conducted in both the United States and Great Britain, the book documents a number of research studies carried out as part of the PGVE.

Barnouw, Erik. **A Tower in Babel: A History of Broadcasting in the United States. Volume 1: To 1933.** New York: Oxford University Press, 1966. 344pp. No ISBN.

This volume is useful as a general reference to the development of radio broadcasting as a form of the mass media in the United States.

Interestingly, radio appears to be the one form of mass media about which relatively little concern has been expressed vis-à-vis its role in the instigation of violent behavior among the general public. A valuable chronology is included along with the complete text of the Radio Acts of 1912 and 1927.

Barwise, Patrick, and Andrew Ehrenberg. **Television and Its Audience.** London: Sage, 1988. 206pp. ISBN 0-8039-8154-6.

This book deals with issues of televised violence to only a modest degree, but it is an excellent general reference on the subject of television itself and the impact of the medium on viewers. Specific sections of the book deal with topics such as how viewers select the programs they watch, how television is paid for, how programs are broadcast, and what issues television faces in the future.

Belson, William A. **Television Violence and the Adolescent Boy.** Farnborough, England: Saxon House, 1978. 529pp. ISBN 0-566-00211-6.

This study was financed by the Columbia Broadcasting System (CBS) in the United States, but carried out in England. The author investigated a number of hypotheses about the supposed effects of violence in television and other forms of media (for comparison) on boys. His strongest finding was that "high exposure to television violence increases the degree to which boys engage in serious violence." He suggests that some forms of television violence (gratuitous violence, violent Westerns, and violence in a good cause, for example) have a stronger effect than do other forms (science fiction and slapstick comedy, for example).

Bogart, Leo. **The Age of Television.** New York: Frederick Unger, 1972. 515pp. ISBN 0-8044-5159-1.

This book is primarily of historical interest. It was published first in 1958, when television was still something of a novelty. In his book, Bogart presents a massive review of research evidence bearing on the subject of television and other forms of mass media. The new edition, released in 1972, consists largely of the original version, with some notes intended to bring the text up-to-date. It is of some interest to see that issues of televised violence, and uncertainty surrounding the effects of such violence, were almost as much of an issue in the late 1950s as they are today.

Bryant, Jennings, and Daniel R. Anderson, eds. **Children's Understanding of Television: Research on Attention and Comprehension.** New York: Academic Press, 1983. 370pp. ISBN 0-12-18160-9.

The book's stated goal is to "bring together for the first time most of the major contributors to research on the *fundamental nature of children's television viewing.*" The various articles in the book, therefore, deal with a wide range of topics, but they serve as an excellent introduction to what research has to say about the way children respond to television programming. Of special interest is chapter 11, "Implications of Childhood Television Viewing for Cognition, Imagination and Emotion," by Jerome and Dorothy Singer.

Burnet, Mary. **The Mass Media in a Violent World.** Paris: UNESCO, 1971. 44pp. No ISBN.

This short book summarizes a symposium on the impact of violence in the mass media on youth and adults convened by the United Nations Educational, Scientific, and Cultural Organization from 29 June to 7 July 1970 at Geneva. The symposium's task was to search for answers to three questions: (1) What is meant by violence? (2) What is commonly assumed and what is actually known about the relation between violence in the mass media and violence in real life? and (3) What are the most effective means of preventing the media from being, however unintentionally, instrumental in increasing the amount of violence in the world?

Cater, Douglass, and Stephen Strickland. **TV Violence and the Child: The Evolution and Fate of the Surgeon General's Report.** New York: Russell Sage Foundation, 1975. 167pp. ISBN 0-87154230-X.

The Russell Sage Foundation supported this study of what has probably been the most thorough and most controversial study of television violence ever completed in the United States, the surgeon general's report of 1972. The authors explain the background leading to the study, outline its major findings, and discuss reasons that the study's findings became so controversial and so poorly understood by the general public.

Charters, W. W. **Motion Pictures and Youth: A Summary.** New York: Macmillan, 1933. 102pp. No ISBN.

This books summarizes a series of 12 research projects funded by the Payne Foundation in the late 1920s and early 1930s. The impetus for these studies was a meeting held in 1928 between members of the Motion Picture Research Council (formerly the National Committee for the Study of Social Values in Motion Pictures) and a group of university psychologists, sociologists, and professional educators. The purpose of the studies was to find out how children and youth are influenced by moving pictures.

The findings from those studies were reported in ten books, the summary volume cited above, and nine additional titles listed below. The author's overall impressions of motion pictures are expressed in his opinions that the movies "are an unsavory mess" and that producers "ought to have a heart" with respect to their influence on children.

In general, the conclusion of most studies carried out with Payne Fund money appeared to be that moving pictures do have some effects on the knowledge, attitudes, and behaviors of young people, but that the specific effects are complex and difficult to sort out. Interestingly enough, the conclusions appear to presage those reported in studies of televised violence many years later, namely that some individuals are influenced in some ways by some kinds of violence. In addition to Charters's general summary of the Payne studies, the volume cited above also includes one of those studies, "Getting Ideas from the Movies," by P. W. Holaday and George D. Stoddard. The popular summary of the Payne studies was reported in the volume by Forman, listed below. Other volumes in the series or research studies include the following.

Blumer, Herbert. **Movies and Conduct.** New York: The Macmillan Company, 1933. 257pp. No ISBN.

Blumer, Herbert, and P. M. Hauser. **Movies, Delinquency, and Crime.** New York: The Macmillan Company, 1933. 233pp. No ISBN.

Cressey, Paul G., and Frederick M. Thrasher. **Boys, Movies and City Streets.** New York: The Macmillan Company, 1933. No ISBN.

Dale, Edgar. **The Content of Motion Pictures.** New York: The Macmillan Company, 1933. 234pp. No ISBN.

Included in this volume is "Children's Attendance at Motion Pictures," by Edgar Dale.

————. **How To Appreciate Motion Pictures.** New York: The Macmillan Company, 1933. 243pp. No ISBN.

Dysinger, W. S., and Christian A. Ruckmick. **The Emotional Responses of Children to the Motion Picture Situation.** New York: The Macmillan Company, 1933. 153pp. No ISBN.

This volume also includes "Motion Pictures and Standards of Morality," by Charles C. Peters.

Forman, Henry James. **Our Movie Made Children.** New York: The Macmillan Company, 1935. Reprinted by Arno Press (New York), 1970. 288pp. ISBN 0-405-01646-8.

This volume contains the popular summary of the results of the studies supported by the Payne Fund. The author concludes that, while some children appear to be led into criminal acts as a result of watching films, the precise conditions under which such behaviors occur are still not well understood. In addition, he points out that viewing motion picture films can also have salutary effects on the behavior of children.

Peterson, Ruth C., and L. L. Thurstone. **Motion Pictures and the Social Attitudes of Children.** New York: The Macmillan Company, 1933. 75pp. No ISBN.

This volume also includes "The Social Conduct and Attitudes of Movie Fans," by Frank K. Shuttleworth and Mark A. May.

Renshaw, Samuel, Vernon L. Miller, and Dorothy Marquis. **Children's Sleep.** New York: The Macmillan Company, 1933. 242pp. No ISBN.

Clifford, Brian R., Barrie Gunter, and Jill L. McAleer. **Television and Children: Program Evaluation, Comprehension, and Impact.** Hillsdale, NJ: Lawrence Erlbaum Associates, 1995. 264pp. ISBN 0-8058-1682-8.

This book addresses the general question of how television affects children: how they view it, what they think of specific programs, and how these likes and dislikes affect learning of the content presented.

Cline, Victor B., ed. **Where Do You Draw the Line? An Exploration into Media Violence, Pornography, and Censorship.** Provo, UT: Brigham Young University Press, 1974. 365pp. ISBN 0-84250-986-0.

Attorneys, civil libertarians, government officials, social scientists, and other scholars examine the question as to where the depiction of violence and pornography becomes an intrusion on the civil rights of citizens. Section 3, "Violence in the Media," presents research findings on the issue and a variety of opinions on the relationship between free speech and the use of violence in the media.

Clutterbuck, Richard. **The Media and Political Violence.** London: The Macmillan Press, 1981. 191pp. ISBN 0-333-34492-8.

This book provides one of the relatively few resources that discuss the role of the media in the development of political violence among adults, in contrast to the instigation of aggressiveness in younger viewers. The question raised by the author is whether the potential for encouraging violence by broadcasting it is great enough to justify some form of external censorship by the government, or internal censorship by broadcasters themselves.

Combs, James, ed. **Movies and Politics: The Dynamic Relationship.** New York: Garland Publishing, 1993. 304pp. ISBN 0-8153-0043-3.

Moving pictures and political systems interact in a variety of ways, with each sphere having its own effects on the other. In this book, eight authors consider questions such as the depiction of women in film, the Hays code, and political propaganda in the movies. Chapter 5 provides an especially interesting review of the creation and significance of the Hays code.

Comstock, George. Rand Corporation monographs, 1972–1977.

George Comstock has been a most prolific writer on the effects of television on human behavior. In the 1970s, he wrote a series of monographs on various aspects of this issue for the Rand Corporation in Santa Monica, California. Most of these papers were also presented as speeches to professional conferences. The papers that make up the series are listed below. They have no ISBN, but do carry a Rand Corporation report number, such as P-5550.

"Effects of Television on Children: What Is the Evidence?" April 1976, P-5412. 16pp.

"Television and the Young: Setting the Stage for a Research Agenda." November 1975, P-5550. 16pp.

"Research and the Constructive Aspects of Television in Children's Lives: A Forecast." March 1976, P-5622. 12pp.

"Television and Its Viewers: What Social Science Sees." May 1976, P-5632. 26pp.

"The Evidence of Television Violence." October 1976, P-5730. 14pp.

"Television and the Teacher." October 1976, P-5734, 15pp.

"The Long-Range Impact of Television." October 1976, P-5750, 11pp.

"Television Portrayals and Aggressive Behavior." December 1976, P-5762. 15pp.

"Priorities for Action-Oriented Psychological Studies of Television and Behavior." August 1977, P-5879. 14pp.

Comstock, George. **Television Violence: Where the Surgeon General's Study Leads.** Santa Monica, CA: The Rand Corporation, 1972. 18pp. No ISBN.

The author has written extensively on issues of television and its effects on human behavior (see following entries). In this short report, he attempts to outline the major implications that result from the surgeon general's report on televised violence.

Comstock, George, ed. **Public Communication and Behavior.** Volume 1. Orlando, FL: Academic Press, 1986, 319pp. ISBN 0-12-543201-1.

This book is a collection of scholarly articles dealing with the general question of how public communication affects human behavior. Two of the chapters, "The Myth of Massive Media Impact: Savagings and Salvagings" and "The Found Experiment: A New Technique for Assessing the Impact of Mass Media Violence on Real-World Aggressive Behavior," deal directly with the issue of violence in the media. However, other chapters are also of some interest in the general information they provide about the way mass media affects human behavior.

Comstock, George, Steven Chaffee, Nathan Katzman, Maxwell McCombs, and Donald Roberts. **Television and Human Behavior.** New York: Columbia University Press, 1978. 581pp. ISBN 0-231-04420-8.

The first author of this book, a longtime worker in the field of the effects of televised violence, describes the research reported in this volume as a new way of looking at studies in this field. He points out that the amount of information available is so large that no one researcher is able to become familiar with it all. In attempting to deal with this problem, the Rand Corporation established an information service whose task it was to search through all existing literature and summarize the evidence found there. This book presents the results of that research. Three additional books produced in conjunction with this study are as follows:

> Comstock, George, et al. **Television and Human Behavior: The Key Studies.** Santa Monica, CA: The Rand Corporation, 1975. 251pp. No ISBN.
>
> This volume provides summaries of about 450 studies and other items that the reviewers have judged to be of "key importance" on the effects of television on human behavior. For each study, the following items are included, where appropriate: Principal findings; Design and methodology; Theory and discussion; Principal conclusions; and Theory and conclusions.
>
> Comstock, George, and Marilyn Fisher. **Television and Human Behavior: A Guide to the Pertinent Scientific Literature.** Santa Monica, CA: The Rand Corporation, 1975. 344pp. No ISBN.
>
> This large reference contains 1 master bibliography and 11 specialized bibliographies on topics such as

"Television's Messages," "Audience Behavior," "Television and Children and Youth," "Television and Psychological Processes," "Communicator Behavior," and "Current Research."

Comstock, George, and George Lindsey. **Television and Human Behavior: The Research Horizons, Future and Present.** Santa Monica, CA: The Rand Corporation, 1975. 120pp. No ISBN.

The focus of this volume is on works in progress. It summarizes approximately 50 studies not yet completed at the time of this project. The volume also provides an analysis of the priorities held by scientists with respect to research on television and human behavior.

Comstock, George, with Haejun Paik. **Television and the American Child.** San Diego: Academic Press, 1991. 386pp. ISBN 0-12-183575-8.

The authors provide an extensive and readable summary of hundreds of research studies on the effects of television on children. They begin with a review of the statistics on television viewing by children and then go on to examine the evidence relating to the many ways in which children's scholastic achievement, knowledge, beliefs, perceptions, and behavior appear to be affected by their exposure to television programming and advertising. The issue of violence on television is analyzed in some detail in various sections of the book. An extensive bibliography of nearly a thousand books, articles, and research reports is particularly useful.

Cook, David A. **A History of Narrative Film.** New York: W. W. Norton, 1981. 721pp. ISBN 0-393-01370-7.

In addition to being a fascinating history of the motion picture industry, this text provides an excellent review of the many political issues involved in the industry's use of violent and sexual themes in its products. See especially chapters 6 and 12 dealing with the introduction of various film codes and their eventual restructuring in the last three decades.

Cowan, Geoffrey. **See No Evil: The Backstage Battle over Sex and Violence on Television.** New York: Simon & Schuster, 1979. 323pp. ISBN 0-671-23091-3.

The author, whose father was an executive with a major national television network, examines the dramatic changes that took place in the nature of television programming at the end of the 1970s. He describes the growth of "provocative themes" in television series such as *All in the Family, Laugh-In,* and *The Smothers Brothers Comedy Hour.* He shows how these changes came about at the same time that the family viewing policy was adopted and that a number of viewer groups were beginning to launch boycott campaigns against advertisers who sponsored such "provocative" shows.

Cullingford, C. **Children and Television.** New York: St. Martin's Press, 1984. 239pp. ISBN 0-5660-0655-3.

This book reports on a study of the television viewing habits of more than 5,000 children in the United States and the United Kingdom. The study covered many aspects of the subject. Chapter 2 deals most directly with the question of how children respond to televised violence.

Dalziel, Margaret. **Popular Fiction 100 Years Ago: An Unexplored Tract of Literary History.** London: Cohen and West, 1957. 188pp. No ISBN.

The author reviews the nature of popular fiction that developed in the mid-nineteenth century as well as some of the public reaction to this new form of the mass media. In comparing the literature of this period with comparable works from the mid-twentieth century, the author draws one interesting conclusion. She claims that the modern writings of her time show a form of "deterioration" compared to popular fiction of the 1850s. One of the most serious manifestations of that deterioration, she claims, is "the treatment of violence" in contemporary works compared to those of a century earlier. She is troubled, she says, because contemporary depictions of "silly stupid" violence are "more deliberate and more deliberately delineated" than those of earlier periods.

Davis, Robert Edward. **Response to Innovation.** New York: Arno Press, 1976. 725pp. ISBN 0-40507-533-2.

The author examines the argument that the introduction of a new form of mass media tends to bring about a negative reaction from members of the general public. He first reviews the history of that controversy for three forms of the mass media: motion pictures, radio, and television. He then examines the reasons that such a phenomenon exists.

deKoning, T. L., D. P. Conradie, and E. M. Nel. **The Effects of Different Kinds of Television Programming on the Youth.** Pretoria, South Africa: Institute for Communication Research, Human Sciences Council, 1980. 71pp. No ISBN.

This book is of interest because it documents a long-term experiment dealing with the effects of television on preschool children's pro-social and aggressive behavior as a result of watching television. In general, the authors concluded that exposure to television may have both positive and negative effects on young children, although the nature of those effects is very much dependent on age, sex, home background, nature of the program, and other factors.

Doerken, Maurine. **Classroom Combat: Teaching and Television.** Englewood Cliffs, NJ: Educational Technology Publications, 1983. 316pp. ISBN 0-87778-186-9.

The author argues that television now competes with the formal classroom as the most important influence in educating young children. Chapter 2 presents a detailed discussion of the nature of televised violence, its possible effects on the behavior of children, and the responses to this problem from the television industry.

Edgar, Patricia M. **Children and Screen Violence.** St. Lucia, Australia: University of Queensland Press, 1977. 275pp. ISBN 0-70221-403-5.

Three groups of teenagers were exposed to three types of films showing violence within the family setting. Responses were strongly affected by a number of factors, such as age, sex, and level of self-esteem. The author concludes that filmed violence may have some affect on a teenager's emotional state, but that other factors are probably more important.

Eisenberg, Azriel L. **Children and Radio Programs.** New York: Columbia University Press, 1936. 240pp. No ISBN.

This book recounts a study of 3,345 pupils in grades 5 through 8 of the New York Public School system. The research was relatively primitive and depended primarily on a series of written questions to which students were asked to reply. It is of some interest that the researcher found certain "weird stories and tales of crime and detection" to be troublesome enough to many children to cause them to have nightmares. He decided that the problem was serious enough to recommend that radio broadcasters present such programs "during daylight hours, on Sunday mornings, or very late at night" when, presumably, children were less likely to hear the programs.

Eysenck, H. J., and D. K. B. Nias. **Sex, Violence, and the Media.** London: Maurice Temple Smith, 1978. 306pp. ISBN 0-85117-161-3.

Eysenck and Nias review a massive amount of experimental evidence—both field studies and laboratory experiments—as well as the reports of a number of commissions appointed to study sex, violence, and the media. They come to the conclusion that the evidence quite clearly points to a causative relationship between the viewing of violence on television and the display of aggressive behavior by viewers. Their first recommendation, based on this conclusion, is that "makers of films and TV programmes, producers of theatre plays and others concerned with the portrayal of violence should show more social responsibility than they have done so far."

Feshbach, Seymour, and Robert D. Singer. **Television and Aggression.** San Francisco: Jossey-Bass, 1971. 186pp. ISBN 0-87589-083-0.

This book describes a study conducted on the effects of television viewing on a group of preadolescent and adolescent boys in various private schools and boys' homes over a period of six weeks. The authors conclude from that research that "Although we had predicted that a significant subgroup of participants would become more aggressive as a result of exposure to the aggressive TV diet, we did not find this change to occur . . . we found consistent evidence in particular and identifiable groups of reduced aggression as a result of exposure to the aggressive television diet."

Geller, Evelyn. **Forbidden Books in American Public Libraries, 1876–1939.** Westport, CT: Greenwood Press, 1984. 234pp. ISBN 0-313-23808-1.

This study examines an important change that took place within the library profession between 1876 and 1939. Prior to that period, librarians usually saw their role as that of a moral censor in which offensive books were to be kept from the public's eyes. By the end of the period, however, librarians had become among the primary spokespersons for the freedom of speech and the right of individuals to obtain books on nearly any subject, no matter how controversial it might be.

Gilbert, James. **A Cycle of Outrage.** New York: Oxford University Press, 1986. 258pp. ISBN 0-19-503721-9.

The mid-1950s saw the growth of a social theory about the relationship between the mass media and juvenile delinquency. A number of experts expressed the view that the media had taken over many of the responsibilities of parents and that the resulting estrangement of parents from their children led to what appeared to be an epidemic of juvenile delinquency. This theory received what may have been its most public airing in a series of hearings by Senator Estes Kefauver. Gilbert analyzes the events that took place during this period and points out that they represent a recycling of similar views about the effect of the media on children's behaviors that had been expressed during earlier historical periods.

Gore, Tipper. **Raising PG Kids in an X-Rated Society.** Nashville, TN: Abingdon Press, 1987. 219pp. ISBN 0-687-35283-5.

The author explains that she has written this book because she had begun "to see the kinds of record lyrics that my children were being exposed to." She was shocked and angry, she said, to find the level of sexual explicitness and violence depicted in these lyrics. The book outlines the problem that Gore believes certain forms of modern music present to parents today and suggests a number of actions that parents can take to protect their children from the most offensive forms of modern music. The book contains an excellent list of resources for parents to consult as well as information about record production companies.

Goulart, Ron, ed. **The Encyclopedia of American Comics.** New York: Facts on File, 1990. 408pp. ISBN 0-8160-1852-9.

An excellent resource book on nearly every aspect of comics in the United States, this book's major drawback is that it contains no general overview of the field to guide the uninformed reader to topics of particular interest in the history of the comics. A better choice for the general reader might be a similar text by Maurice Horn (see below).

Greenfield, Patricia Marks. **Mind and Media: The Effects of Television, Video Games, and Computers.** Cambridge, MA: Harvard University Press, 1984. 210pp. ISBN 0-674-57620-9.

Professor of psychology for the University of California at Los Angeles at the time she wrote this book, the author suggests that society needs to take an enlightened and balanced view of the potential educational value of electronic media such as television, video games, and other interactive forms of media. She acknowledges and reviews the problems of violence in these forms of the media, but goes beyond criticism to point out ways in which they can contribute more positively to a child's development.

Gunter, Barrie. **Dimensions of Television Violence.** Aldershot, England: Gower Publishing, 1985. 282pp. ISBN 0-566-00617-0.

The author was appointed as a research fellow in 1980 by the Independent Broadcasting Authority for the purpose of studying violence on British television and its effects on viewers. The ultimate goal of the study was to determine the feasibility of constructing a system by which the amount and seriousness of violence on television could be measured objectively. The author's conclusions are summarized in chapter 16, "Implications of a Perceptual Analysis of Television Violence for Monitoring of Programme Content."

Halloran, James D., Roger L. Brown, and David Chaney. **Television and Delinquency.** Leicester, England: Leicester University Press, 1970. 221pp. ISBN 0-7185-1088-7.

The authors report on a study carried out in Great Britain on the television viewing patterns among a group of juvenile delinquents. The results of that study were unable to confirm any causal relationship between the viewing of violence and the development of delinquency in viewers.

Hefzallah, Ibrahim M. **Critical Viewing of Television: A Book for Parents and Teachers.** Lanham, MD: University Press of America, 1987. 205pp. ISBN 0-8191-6107-1.

The author, a professor of educational media at Fairfield University, has written a handbook for teachers and parents on the art of television viewing. Chapter 9 deals with the question of "Violence on Television" and focuses on six major reasons for being concerned about the quality and quantity of violence in the medium.

Heller, Melvin S. and Samuel Polsky. **Studies in Violence and Television.** New York: American Broadcasting Company, 1976. 503pp. No ISBN.

This volume recounts a group of studies sponsored by one of the major television networks. These studies were aimed at determining the influence of television viewing on children who were classified as "disturbed," that is, children from broken homes, young male offenders, and emotionally disturbed youngsters. The results appear to demonstrate that televised violence is more likely to stimulate violent fantasies than violent behaviors and that some "disturbed" children may actually develop pro-social attitudes and behaviors as a result of watching televised violence.

Himmelweit, Hilde T., A. N. Oppenheim, and Pamela Vince. **Television and the Child: An Empirical Study of the Effect of Television on the Young.** London: Oxford University Press, 1958. 522pp. No ISBN.

This study examined the effects of televised violence in Great Britain on children ranging in age from less than six years of age to teenagers. There appeared to be no evidence that violence on television was a causative factor in the development of aggressive behavior in the children studied, although the authors suggest that it may result in children's being more willing to accept aggression as a way of solving disputes and other problems.

Hodge, Robert, and David Tripp. **Children and Television: A Semiotic Approach.** Stanford, CA: Stanford University Press, 1986. 233pp. ISBN 0-80447-1352-9.

Semiotics is a fairly new field of scientific inquiry that investigates the way signs and symbols, including linguistics, are used to convey meanings. The authors use the science of semiotics to study the way that children interpret messages that are sent out on television programs. They pay special attention to the way televised violence is interpreted in chapter 7, "The Violence Debate." The authors conclude that efforts to limit the depictions of violence on television are "based on a radical misconception of how the media work." They admit, however, that violence can be disturbing to young children and that the "world-view" presented by some kinds of violence may be sufficiently offensive to require limitations.

Horn, Maurice, ed. **The World Encyclopedia of Comics.** New York: Chelsea House Publishers, 1976. 6 vols. 895pp. ISBN 0-87754-323-2.

This remarkable work covers just about every aspect of comics that one could want to know. Of particular interest for those interested in the issue of violence in the media is the 28-page "Comics of the World: A Short History." This section provides a thorough and insightful analysis of the political problems faced by the industry with the rise of "horror" comic books in the 1950s.

Howitt, Dennis, and Guy Cumberbatch. **Mass Media, Violence and Society.** New York: Wiley, 1975. 167pp. ISBN 0-470-41745-5.

The authors point out in their introduction to this book that they have reviewed the "available social scientific research" on the question of violence in the media and have come to the conclusion that "the Mass Media do not have any significant effect on the level of violence in society." The book is especially interesting in that these conclusions fly in the face of the vast majority of research published by other scholars who are not associated with one of the media corporations. The authors conclude that the value of their book is to help the general public understand existing research in this field and thus not be "duped" by social scientists who appear to give easy answers to complex problems.

Hudson, Robert V. **Mass Media: A Chronological Encyclopedia of Television, Radio, Motion Pictures, Magazines, Newspapers, and Books in the United States.** New York: Garland Publishing, 1987. 435pp. ISBN 0-8240-8695-3.

Although this work has relatively little in it dealing directly with the issue of violence, it is a fascinating story of the development of the mass media in the United States and of the interaction between the media and other aspects of society. Of particular interest is the continuing controversy over the role of government in the monitoring and control of media products.

Huesmann, L. R., and L. D. Eron, eds. **Television and the Aggressive Child: A Cross-National Comparison.** Hillsdale, NJ: Lawrence Erlbaum Associates, 1986. 314pp. ISBN 0-89859-754-4.

This volume collects a series of papers from five nations—Finland, Poland, Australia, Israel, and the United States—concerning the way in which television is related to aggressive behavior in children. The editors attempt to show how the results of these studies are alike.

Huston, Aletha C., et al. **Big World, Small Screen: The Role of Television in American Society.** Lincoln: University of Nebraska Press, 1992. 195pp. ISBN 0-8032-2357-9.

In 1986, the American Psychological Association appointed a task force to conduct a comprehensive review of the literature on the relationship of television to society. This book reports the results of that study. The section devoted to violence on television is fairly modest in size, but its straightforward conclusions about the effects of televised violence are well worth reading, especially pages 52 to 58. The extensive bibliography is also of considerable value and interest to those interested in reading more about the effects of television in all parts of human society.

Jowett, Garth. **Film: The Democratic Art.** Boston: Little, Brown, 1976. 518pp. ISBN 0-316-47370-7.

The author has written a brilliant and scholarly history of the motion picture that provides one of the best descriptions of the social and moral issues that arose in the early twentieth century as films became more popular.

Lange, David L., Robert K. Baker, and Sandra J. Ball. **Mass Media and Violence.** Washington, DC: Government Printing Office, November 1969. 614pp. No ISBN.

This book is the ninth volume in the report of the National Commission on the Causes and Prevention of Violence. It is organized into three major sections. Part 1 provides a historical perspective on the development of the print medium in the United States and its expansion to nonprint media such as movies, radio, and television. Part 2 focuses on "The News Media" and considers issues such as the functions and credibility of news media, communications among various subgroups within society, the coverage of civil disorders (a major cause for the appointment of the Commission), journalism education, and media practices and values. Seven extensive appendices deal with issues such as media codes and guidelines, the canons of journalism, and employment data.

Part 3 of the report deals with television entertainment and violence. The longest chapter, chapter 15, focuses on topics such as "Dimensions of Violence," "The Nature of Violence," and "The People of Violence." Chapter 19 compiles a number of recommendations about televised violence, the most important of which is that a Center for Media Study be established to study media violence and to make recommendations as to how society is to respond to its presence. Eleven additional appendices contain research reports commissioned for the study.

Among the many conclusions drawn by the authors of the study are the observations that "The weight of social science stands in opposition to the conclusion that mass media portrayals of violence have no effect upon individuals, groups, and society," and "To the extent that mass media portrayals of violence have effects upon individuals, groups, and society, it is a variety that most persons would deem costly and harmful to individuals and society."

Larsen, Otto N., ed. **Violence and the Mass Media.** New York: Harper & Row, 1968. 310pp. No ISBN.

This anthology contains a collection of articles reprinted from academic journals and popular magazines. The articles are divided into seven general topics: the context of controversy, inciting social sensitivity to media violence, the content of mass media violence, effects of mass media violence/empirical studies, regulation and control/public participation, regulation and control/governmental participation, and regulation and control/media participation.

Lefkowitz, M. M., L. D. Eron, L. O. Walder, and L. R. Huesmann. **Growing Up To Be Violent: A Longitudinal Study of the Development of Aggression.** Elmsford, NY: Pergamon Press, 1977. 236pp. ISBN 0-080-19514-8.

This book documents a famous study that analyzed the relationship between televised violence and aggressive behavior in a large sample of eight-year-olds. The study began in 1960 and was completed ten years later with a sample of about half the size of the original group.

Liebert, Robert M., Joyce N. Sprafkin, and Emily S. Davidson. **The Early Window: Effects of Television on Children and Youth,**

2nd edition. New York: Pergamon Press, 1982. 255pp. ISBN 0-080-27547-8.

The editors describe the purpose of this book as to "provide an account of the theory and research which now bears on television and children's attitudes, development, and behavior, and to explore the social, political, and economic factors that surround these issues." Individual chapters deal with topics such as the nature of television as a business, the surgeon general's report of 1972 and its aftermath, the portrayal of race and sex on television, and the effects of television advertising on children.

Lodziak, Conrad. **The Power of Television: A Critical Appraisal.** New York: St. Martin's Press, 1986. 217pp. ISBN 0-312-63397-1.

Probably the most useful section of this book is found in the first chapter, "Studying the Power of Television." In this chapter, the author begins by pointing out, "There has been more research into the effects of the portrayal of violence on television than any other area of television research." He then goes on to point out what he regards as fundamental flaws in the vast majority of the scientific research in this area.

Madden, Denis J., and John R. Lion, eds. **Rage/Hate/Assault and Other Forms of Violence.** New York: Spectrum Publications, 1976. 265pp. ISBN 0-470-15022-X.

Only one chapter of this book, "Violence in the Media," deals specifically with the issue at hand. However, the presentation is complete and intriguing.

Mass Media Hearings. Washington, DC: Government Printing Office, December 1969. 463pp. No ISBN.

This volume is a transcript of the hearings conducted before the National Commission on the Causes and Prevention of Violence. It includes the personal testimony of 24 witnesses from the media, academia, and public interest groups along with an additional 22 letters, responses, and memos to the Commission.

Milavsky, J. Ronald. **TV and Violence.** Washington, DC: U.S. Department of Justice, National Institute of Justice, [1988?]. 4pp. No ISBN.

This short study guide provides a useful albeit brief summary of the television/violence issue up to 1988. It was written to accompany a videotape, *TV and Violence*, produced by the National Institute of Justice as one of its Crime File series on critical issues in criminal justice.

Milgram, Stanley, and R. Lance Shotland. **Television and Antisocial Behavior: A Field Experiment.** New York: Academic Press, 1973. 183pp. No ISBN.

The authors conducted a series of field experiments in four cities, Chicago, Detroit, New York, and St. Louis, to test the hypothesis that viewing violence on television would produce antisocial behavior among viewers. None of their results were statistically significant, making it impossible to validate the original hypothesis.

Mitchell, Alice M. **Children and Movies.** Chicago: University of Chicago Press, 1929. 181pp. No ISBN.

Under a grant from the Wiebodt Foundation, the author studied the moving picture viewing practices of some 10,000 children. These children were selected from three groups: (1) institutions housing juvenile delinquents, (2) public school students, and (3) members of the Boy Scouts and Girl Scouts. Mitchell studied a number of factors relating to movie attendance, including choice of movie, frequency of attendance, time of attendance, movie companions, relative attractiveness of other forms of recreation, and so on. One of her conclusions was that "the delinquent child's contact with the movie far exceeds that of other children," but she was unable to conclude whether delinquency results from movie-going or vice versa.

Murray, J. P. **Television and Youth: 25 Years of Research and Controversy.** Boys Town, NE: Boys Town Center for the Study of Youth Development, 1980. 183pp. ISBN 0-93851-000-2.

The author provides a detailed review of the existing research dealing with the relationship among televised violence, pro-social behavior, and aggression. The bibliography provided is especially useful.

National Commission on the Causes and Prevention of Violence. **To Establish Justice, To Ensure Domestic Tranquility.** Washington, DC: Government Printing Office, 1969. 338pp. No ISBN.

The National Commission on the Causes and Prevention of Violence was established by President Lyndon Johnson in an Executive Order of 6 June 1968. The Commission's work covered a wide range of topics, including the history of violence in the United States, the nature of violent crime, firearms and violence, assassinations, and campus disorders. Chapter 8 of the report deals specifically with the question of how, if at all, violence in television entertainment programs affects human behavior, especially that of the young. The recommendations made by the commission in this area closely parallel those made by many other public and private groups, namely that the amount of violence on television programming, especially children's programming, should be reduced.

National Institute of Mental Health. **Television and Behavior: Ten Years of Scientific Progress and Implications for the Eighties.** Rockville, MD: U.S. Department of Health and Human Services, Public Health Service, Alcohol, Drug Abuse, and Mental Health Administration, National Institute of Mental Health, 1982. 2 vols. 017-024-01129-1 and 017-024-01141-0.

A follow-up study on the surgeon general's report of 1972 (see below), outlining changes that have taken place in the decade since. In the final report of the NIMH review, committee members present an even stronger statement than was made in the surgeon general's report of a decade earlier that televised violence does indeed cause aggressive behavior in at least some individuals under some circumstances. For a large majority of researchers in the social sciences, this report provides the definitive body of evidence linking violence in television and aggressive behavior in children. Network executives reject the committee report, however, and continue to argue that the evidence does not support any link between these variables.

Noble, Grant. **Children in Front of the Small Screen.** London: Constable and Company, 1975. 256pp. ISBN 0-09-460250-6.

The author examines the general relationship between television viewing and child development. He begins by reviewing methods of research that have been used for the study of television and its effects and then outlines some of the results of that research dealing with the way in which children identify with television characters, the development of deviant behavior, the media as a means of escaping from the real world, and the connection between television viewing and aggressive behavior.

Nye, Russel. **The Unembarrassed Muse: The Popular Arts in America.** New York: Dial, 1970. 497pp. No ISBN.

In his chapters on "Murderers and Detectives," "Sixshooter Country," and "Culture at the Bijou," Nye shows how deeply ingrained violent themes are in popular American cultural forms such as literature, motion pictures, and television. A fascinating survey of the issue of violence in the mass media from a somewhat earlier period.

Oskamp, Stuart, ed. **Applied Social Psychology Annual: Volume 8. Television as a Social Issue.** Newbury Park, CA: Sage, 1988. 390pp. ISBN 0-8039-3069-0.

Part 3 of this collection of scholarly papers deals with violence on television. The five chapters in this section include "Television Violence and Aggression: What the Evidence Shows," "Television and Aggression Once Again," "Some Hazards of Growing Up in a Television Environment," "Beyond Cartoon Killings," and "Television Research and Social Policy." Other chapters in the book also deal with issues of violence on television in less specialized ways.

Palmer, Edward L. **Children in the Cradle of Television.** Lexington, MA: Lexington Books, 1987. 176pp. ISBN 0-669-11299-2.

Palmer provides a general overview of the rise of television and its manifold effects on young viewers. He concentrates on the issue of violence in television primarily in chapter 4, "Winds of Change," in which he describes the rise of citizen concerns about televised violence and the responses (and nonresponses) of industry and government to those concerns.

Palmer, Edward L, and Aimée Dorr, eds. **Children and the Faces of Television: Teaching, Violence, Selling.** New York: Academic Press, 1980. 360pp. ISBN 0-12-544480-X.

The editors explain in the preface to this book that their goal is to provide a single source that will introduce readers to the many complex facets of the ways in which television "does for, to, or in collaboration with children." The subtitle of the book describes the three major parts into which it is divided: "The Teaching Face of Television," "The Violent Face of Television," and "The Selling Face of Television." Part 2 consists of seven chapters dealing with topics such as "Television Violence: A Historical Perspective," "Research Findings and Social Policy," "New Emphases in Research on the Effects of Television and Film Violence," and "Concomitants of Television Violence Viewing in Children."

Pearl, David, Lorraine Bouthilet, and Joyce Lazar, eds. **Television and Behavior.** Rockville, MD: National Institute of Mental Health, 1982. 362pp. No ISBN.

This book is volume 2 in the 1982 NIMH study on **Television and Behavior: Ten Years of Scientific Progress and Implications for the Eighties,** a follow-up study of the 1972 report of the Surgeon General's Scientific Advisory Committee on Television and Behavior. The 24 research papers included in the volume are divided into six major groups: "Cognitive and Affective Aspects of Television," "Violence and Aggression," "Social Beliefs and Social Behavior," "Television and Social Relations," "Television and Health," and "Television in American Society."

In the overview of the section on violence and aggression, author Eli Rubenstein reminds readers that the surgeon general's scientific committee reached a unanimous decision about the effects of televised violence in 1972, but that press coverage was misleading, and controversy about the subject remained. He then adds that the confidence in the findings of the surgeon general's report "will probably increase in the light of the new findings and conclusions" reported in this volume.

Reitberger, Reinhold, and Wolfgang Fuchs. **Comics: Anatomy of a Mass Medium.** Boston: Little, Brown, 1972. 264pp. No ISBN.

The section of this historical book most applicable to the issue of violence and the media is chapter 5, "Criticism and Censorship." In this chapter, the authors review the history of crime comics, the role of Frederic Wertham in drawing public attention to violence in the comics, and the development of the comics code of ethics.

Rivers, William L. and Wilbur Schramm. **Responsibility in Mass Communication.** 3rd edition. New York: Harper & Row, 1980. 378pp. ISBN 0-06-013594-8.

Members of the mass media are constantly confronted with questions about the professional responsibilities they have for the transmission of information, while staying within the bounds granted them by the First Amendment right of free speech. These professionals have debated this question for at least as long as has the general public itself. This book discusses issues such as the role of the government and the mass media, the influences of business on the mass media, questions of truth and fairness in the media, and treatment of minorities by the media. A particularly valuable portion of the book is its six appendices that include the professional and ethical codes of conduct for organizations such as the American Society of Newspaper Editors, the Society of Professional Journalists, the Radio Code, the Television Code, and the Standards of Practice of the American Association of Advertising Agencies.

Roberts, Donald F., and Nathan Maccoby. "Effects of Mass Communications," in Gardner Lindzey and Elliot Aronson, eds., **Handbook of Social Psychology,** Vol. 2. New York: Random House, 1985, pp. 539-598. ISBN 0-394350-502.

This article is general in character, providing both theoretical approaches to the effects of mass communication as well as a review of research results. The article is very comprehensive and provides an excellent background for the subject. The extensive bibliography is also extremely useful.

Rowland, Willard D., Jr. **The Politics of TV Violence: Policy Uses of Communication Research.** Beverly Hills, CA: Sage, 1983. 320pp. ISBN 0-8039-1953-0.

The foreword of this book describes it as a critical review of the way in which the mass communication industries developed after World War I and the way that change has "alter[ed] the industrial and cultural terrain of America." Part 1 is devoted to a review of the way in which research on the effects of mass communication has developed in the United States. Part 2 concentrates on the history of violence-effects research, ranging from the earliest Payne Fund Studies of the late 1920s and early 1930s to the surgeon general's report of 1972. Part 3 discusses some of the reactions from government, industry, and the general public to the research described in the second part of the book. Overall, this book is a good summary of the research on televised violence up to the early 1980s.

Royal Commission on Violence in the Communications Industry. **Report of the Royal Commission on Violence in the Communications Industry.** 7 volumes. Toronto: The Royal Commission, 1977. No ISBN.

The LaMarsh Commission was appointed to examine the extent of televised violence in Canada and its effects on viewers. The seven volumes that make up this work provide an overall summary as well as extensive studies in connection with the issue. The Commission held 61 public hearings and consultations and commissioned 28 independent studies on the nature, extent, and effects of violence in various forms of communication. The second volume in the series is of special interest in that it summarizes about 3,000 research studies conducted in 26 countries on violence in the print media, motion pictures, radio, music, and television.

Sabin, Roger. **Adult Comics: An Introduction.** New York: Routledge, 1993. 321pp. ISBN 0-415-04418-9.

This history focuses specifically on the development of comic strips for adults. The text is especially interesting because of its description of the pervasive role of sex and violence in such productions. Chapter 12 deals particularly with the issues of violence in the comics that arose during the 1950s.

Sanders, Barry. **A Is for Ox: Violence, Electronic Media, and the Silencing of the Written Word.** New York: Pantheon Books, 1994. 369pp. ISBN 0-679417117.

The author is a professor of English at Pitzer College in Claremont, California. He argues that a phenomenon known as "the self" came into existence in human culture in the fifth or sixth century B.C. as the result of the development of the written word. With the abandonment of reading and writing skills by the current young generation of humans, he claims, the classic meaning of that "self" is disappearing, with consequences that most of us can hardly begin to appreciate. In his discussion of televised violence, for example, he suggests that the amount of exposure to such violence that most young people report "thoroughly debilitates" them. "It short-circuits the natural, emotional development they need," he writes, "to become healthy human beings; it strangles the development of their own voices, and denies them their own imaginative powers." This is a powerful and thought-provoking book.

Schneider, Cy. **Children's Television: The Art, the Business, and How It Works.** Lincolnwood, IL: NTC Business Books, 1987. 228pp. No ISBN.

The author explains that he has set out to write a "positive book" about children's television because "no one else did. Or would, I suspect." The tone of the book reflects this somewhat aggressive defensiveness about the complaints that have been raised regarding the way television affects the lives of children. His discussion of the issue of televised violence in children's programming, for example, occurs in the chapter entitled "The Do-Gooders, Politicos, Pedagogues, and Assorted Other Ax Grinders." In that chapter, he argues that the hearings held by Senators Dodd and Pastore in the 1960s and 1970s are "historically important because they became rallying points for a group of ladies in Boston, a handful of pedagogues, and professors of human development whose subsequent efforts were to make some tangible change in network policy during the years following the '60s—changes the Senators were unable to make."

Schramm, Wilbur, Jack Lyle, and Edwin B. Parker. **Television in the Lives of Our Children.** Stanford, CA: Stanford University Press, 1961. 324pp. No ISBN.

This book recounts the results of what one critic has called "the first major study done in the United States" on the effects of televised violence on children. Included in the report are a number of incidents in which children attempted to re-create acts of violence that they had witnessed on television. The study is of historical interest only, however, since the specific and discrete effects of certain types of televised events on certain types of children had not yet been adequately recognized.

Seabury, William Marston. **The Public and the Motion Picture Industry.** New York: The Macmillan Company, 1926. Facsimile reprint by Jerome S. Ozer, Publisher, 1971. 340pp. No ISBN.

The author, once general counsel to the Motion Picture Board of Trade and the National Association of the Motion Picture Industry, provides a fascinating overview of the motion picture industry as a business at a very early stage. Of particular interest to the study of violence in the media is a review of efforts to monitor the content of films at both the state and federal level. The author entitles one of his chapters "The Futility of Censorship," while still acknowledging the need for some kind of governmental control over the content of films as well as the way the industry operates. The major portion of his book is devoted to analyzing a solution to this problem for the United States, the League of Nations, England, France, and other European nations. Chapter 10 of the book provides a "cursory review" of federal and state laws affecting the motion picture industry.

Singer, Jerome L., and Dorothy Singer. **Television, Imagination, and Aggression: A Study of Preschoolers.** Hillsdale, NJ: Lawrence Erlbaum Associates, 1981. 213pp. ISBN 0-89859-060-4.

The authors report on a two-year study that compared the television viewing patterns of preschool children with their spontaneous behavior, play, aggression, and language use. The study also made an effort to modify children's viewing patterns and behavior through work with parents and special training procedures. The authors report that "the link of heavy viewing to attacking other children or property as a consistent pattern cannot be denied. Frankly, we had not anticipated so clear a result as we obtained."

Sparks, Richard. **Television and the Drama of Crime: Moral Tales and the Place of Crime in Public Life.** Buckingham, England: Open University Press, 1992. 185pp. ISBN 0-335-09328-0.

A contribution to the New Directions in Criminology series, this book examines the relationship between watching "cop shows" such as *Hill Street Blues* and *Miami Vice* and the extent and intensity of public fear and alarm about crime. Although the primary emphasis is on the way in which crime is portrayed on television, the author does devote some attention to the debate over the effects of televised violence on viewers.

Starker, Steven. **Evil Influences: Crusades against the Mass Media.** New Brunswick, NJ: Transaction Publishers, 1989. 212pp. ISBN 0-88738-275-4.

The author's thesis is that the development of any new form of communication is accompanied by the appearance of critics who anticipate deep and widespread moral decay as a result of the use of that medium. Starker traces this attitude to the very beginnings of the written word itself and then follows its development through the rise of newspapers, the novel, comic magazines, the radio, television, music videos, the VCR, and computer games. This thesis places criticisms of televised violence in a somewhat unusual and very interesting context.

Surgeon General's Scientific Advisory Committee on Television and Social Behavior. **Television and Growing Up: The Impact of Televised Violence.** Washington, DC: Government Printing Office, 1972. 279pp. No ISBN.

This study is one of the most famous of those dealing with the issue of televised violence. The final version consists of six volumes in addition to a final report: "Television and Social Behavior: Media Content and Control" (volume 1); "Television and Social Behavior: Television and Social Learning" (volume 2); "Television and Social Behavior: Television and Adolescent Aggressiveness" (volume 3); "Television and Social Behavior: Television in Day-to-Day Life: Patterns of Use" (volume 4); "Television and Social Behavior: Television's Effects: Further Explorations" (volume 5); and "Television and Social Behavior: An Annotated Bibliography of Research Focusing on Television's Impact on Children" (volume 6).

Tebbel, John. **The Media in America.** New York: Thomas Crowell, 1974. 422pp. ISBN 0-690-00500-8.

Tebbel's book is included in this bibliography not because it has anything to say about violence—it doesn't—but because of its importance as a written history of the mass media in the United States. Anyone interested in the subject of violence in the mass media should have some familiarity with the way in which the media grew up in this country and of the way issues of free speech have constantly been at the forefront of this growth. This book is without parallel for its day in this respect.

Twitchell, James B. **Preposterous Violence: Fables of Aggression in Modern Culture.** New York: Oxford University Press, 1989. 338pp. ISBN 0-19-505887-9.

This is a remarkable book that traces the use of violent themes in all forms of the media throughout the long history of human culture. The author claims that the use of violence in modern literature, films, television programming, and other forms of the media is nothing new in human culture, and he shows how a writer such as Stephen King is not a new phenomenon, but that he has a clear place in a centuries-old tradition. A fascinating book.

Van Evra, Judith. **Television and Child Development.** Hillsdale, NJ: Lawrence Erlbaum Associates, 1990. 239pp. ISBN 0-8058-0585-2.

This book is divided into three main sections. The first discusses the way in which television contributes to the cognitive development of children, particularly the specific elements from television that affect children's learning experiences. The second section describes the impact of television on children's emotional and social development, and the third section recounts the theories that have been developed to explain the impact of television on children's cognitive, emotional, and social development. Chapter 5, "Television and Social Behavior," discusses in some detail the effects of televised violence on a child's social development.

Wekesser, Carol, ed. **Violence in the Media.** San Diego: Greenhaven Press, 1995. 192pp. ISBN 1-56510-27-1.

This book is one in the Greenhaven Press Current Controversies series, which presents the pros and cons of important current issues. This book explores both sides of such "yes or no" questions as "Does Media Violence Affect Society?," "Should Media Violence Be Censored?," "Can the Media Effectively Regulate Violence in Their Products?," and "Does Music Promote Violence?"

Wertham, Frederic. **A Sign for Cain: An Exploration of Human Violence.** New York: Macmillan, 1966. 391pp. No ISBN.

Wertham's book is a wide-ranging analysis of the nature of various forms of violence and their possible causative factors. In chapter 10 he analyzes the ways in which he thinks that the mass media are responsible for certain kinds of aggressive behaviors. His earlier book (following) discusses this aspect of violence in much more detail.

Wertham, Frederic S. **Seduction of the Innocent.** New York: Rinehart and Company, 1954. 397pp. No ISBN.

The author was a psychiatrist and a longtime critic of the effects of violence in the media on children. In this book he documents seven years of research on comic magazines and their effects on young children. Various chapters deal with topics such as "The Effects of Comic Books on the Child," "The Influence of Comic Books on Reading," "The Contribution of Crime Comic Books to Juvenile Delinquency," and "Comic Books and the Psychosexual Development of Children." A late chapter in the book presents a preliminary discussion of the effects of televised violence on children under the title "Homicide at Home."

Wildmon, Donald E. **The Home Invaders.** Wheaton, IL: Victor Books, 1986. 192pp. ISBN 0-89693-521-3.

Wildmon is the founder of the American Family Association, a Mississippi-based Christian group that monitors the entertainment business for what it regards as violations of public morality. Wildmon's premise in this book is that the media in the United States pose "the greatest threat" to organized religion in the United States "since our country was founded." Wildmon attacks many facets of television viewing, one of which (discussed in chapter 6, "Violence Takes a Toll in Suffering and Pain") is the violence it includes.

Williams, Tannis Macbeth, ed. **The Impact of Television: A Natural Experiment in Three Communities.** New York: Academic Press, 1986. 446pp. ISBN 0-12-746290-7.

The experiments described in this book were carried out in three different communities: one in which there was no television available, one in which only one television station existed, and one in which more than one station was available. The researchers' general conclusion was that the greater the exposure of a child to television, the more negative the results that could be identified. Chapter 7, "Television and Children's Aggressive Behavior," is of special interest.

Withey, Stephen B., and Ronald P. Ables, eds. **Television and Social Behavior: Beyond Violence and Children.** Hillsdale, NJ: Lawrence Erlbaum Associates, 1980, 356pp. ISBN 0-89859-014-0.

This book summarizes the work of the Committee on Television and Social Behavior of the Social Sciences Research Council, undertaken as a result of the research carried out by the Surgeon General's Scientific Advisory Committee on Television and Social Behavior (1972). The Committee's original goals were to assess the

current state of research in the field of television and violent behavior and to suggest a scientific basis for carrying out the further
research needed to develop a profile of violence. This final product consists of two sections, one of which comprises a series of
general essays on topics relating to the subjects at hand and the
other, the reports of study groups organized by the Committee. Of
special interest is the chapter entitled "On the Nature of Media
Effects," by Jack M. McLeod and Byron Reeves.

Woods, L. B. **A Decade of Censorship in America.** Metuchen, NJ:
Scarecrow Press, 1979. 183pp. ISBN 0-8108-1260-6.

This thoughtful and comprehensive review of censorship of books
and magazines in the United States between 1966 and 1975 says
little overtly about the subject of violence. However, it presents a
valuable discussion about the right of free speech in marginal areas such as those involving sexuality, ethnicity, and political viewpoints. The majority of the book is devoted to detailed tables
showing items that were censored in the period under study, the
reasons for censorship, and the groups calling for their censorship.
Violence was cited as a reason for censoring publications only 1
percent of the time during the period under study.

Congressional Hearings

Crime and Violence in the Media. Hearings before the Subcommittee on Crime of the Committee on the Judiciary, House of Representatives, 98th Congress, 1st sess., 13 April 1983.

**Hearings on the Surgeon General's Report by the Scientific Ad-
visory Committee on Television and Social Behavior.** Hearings
before the Subcommittee on Communications of the Committee
on Commerce, United States Senate, 92nd Congress, 2nd sess., 21–
24 March 1972.

**Implementation of the Television Program Improvement Act of
1990.** Joint Hearings before the Subcommittee on the Constitution
and the Subcommittee on Juvenile Justice of the Committee on the
Judiciary, United States Senate, 103rd Congress, 1st sess., 21 May
and 8 June 1993.

Investigation of Juvenile Delinquency in the United States. Hearings before the Committee on the Judiciary, United States Senate, 84th Congress, 2nd sess., 13 January 1956.

Investigation of Radio and Television. Hearings before the Committee on Interstate and Foreign Commerce, House of Representatives, 82nd Congress, 2nd sess., 3 June to 5 December 1952.

Juvenile Delinquency (Television Programs). Hearings before the Subcommittee to Investigate Juvenile Delinquency of the Committee on the Judiciary, United States Senate, 83rd Congress, 2nd sess., 5 June to 20 October 1954.

Juvenile Delinquency (Television Programs). Hearings before the Subcommittee to Investigate Juvenile Delinquency of the Committee on the Judiciary, United States Senate, 84th Congress, 1st sess., 6 and 7 April 1955.

Juvenile Delinquency: Part 10: Effects on Young People of Violence and Crime Portrayed on Television. Hearings before the Subcommittee to Investigate Juvenile Delinquency of the Committee on the Judiciary, United States Senate, 87th Congress, 1st and 2nd sessions, 8 June 1961 to 14 May 1962.

Juvenile Delinquency: Part 16: Effects on Young People of Violence and Crime Portrayed on Television. Hearings before the Subcommittee to Investigate Juvenile Delinquency of the Committee on the Judiciary, United States Senate, 88th Congress, 2nd sess., 30 July 1964.

Media Violence. Hearings before the Subcommittee on Juvenile Justice of the Committee on the Judiciary, United States Senate, 98th Congress, 2nd sess., 25 October 1984.

Music Lyrics and Commerce. Hearings before the Subcommittee on Commerce, Consumer Protection, and Competitiveness of the Committee on Energy and Commerce, House of Representatives, 103rd Congress, 2nd sess., 11 February and 5 May 1994.

Sex and Violence on TV. Hearing before the Subcommittee on Communications of the Committee on Interstate and Foreign Commerce, House of Representatives, 95th Congress, 1st sess., 2 March 1977.

Sex and Violence on TV. Hearings before the Subcommittee on Communications of the Committee on Interstate and Foreign Commerce, House of Representatives, 94th Congress, 2nd sess., 9 July and 17 and 18 August 1976.

Social/Behavioral Effects of Violence on Television. Hearing before the Subcommittee on Telecommunications, Consumer Protection, and Finance of the Committee on Energy and Commerce, House of Representatives, 97th Congress, 1st sess., 21 October 1981.

Television Violence Act of 1989. Hearing before the Subcommittee on Economic and Commercial Law of the Committee on the Judiciary, House of Representatives, 101st Congress, 1st sess., 10 May 1989.

Television Violence Act of 1989. Report to the House of Representatives, together with dissenting views, 7 July 1989. 101st Congress, 1st sess.

Violence in Video Games. Hearing before the Subcommittee on Telecommunications and Finance of the Committee on Energy and Commerce, House of Representatives, 103rd Congress, 2nd sess., 30 June 1994.

Violence on Television. Hearing before the Subcommittee on Communications of the Committee on Interstate and Foreign Commerce, House of Representatives, 95th Congress, 1st sess., 1977.

Violence on Television. Hearing before the Subcommittee on Crime and Criminal Justice of the Committee on the Judiciary, House of Representatives, 102nd Congress, 2nd sess., 15 December 1992.

Violence on Television. Hearings before the Subcommittee on Telecommunications and Finance of the Committee on Energy and Commerce, House of Representatives, 103rd Congress, 1st sess., 12 May, 25 June, 1 and 29 July, and 15 September 1993.

Youth and Violence: The Current Crisis—A Fact Sheet. Select Committee on Children, Youth, and Families of the House of Representatives. Washington, DC: Government Printing Office, n.d.

Periodical

Parents' Choice. P. O. Box 185, Waban, MA 02168. (617) 965-5918. $18 per year.

This magazine describes itself as "the only nonprofit consumer guide to children's books/toys/video/audio/computer programs/television/magazines/rock 'n' roll." It is an excellent guide for parents who are interested in knowing, among other matters, about the level of violent content in programs designed for children in one of these formats.

Nonprint Resources

7

Relatively little in the way of nonprint materials has been produced on the subject of violence and the media. The items below constitute nearly the whole body of such materials. The reader is especially directed also to the extensive collection of multimedia programs on violence and the media available from the Center for Media Literacy. See the entry for that organization in chapter 5, which includes a brief summary of some of the materials available from the Center.

Videos

The Killing Screens:
Media and the Culture of Violence

Type: Videocassette
Age: High school and adult
Length: 37 min.
Cost: Universities and colleges: $195;
    nonprofit social-service agencies:
    $125; high schools: $97.50
Date: 1994
Source: Media Education Foundation
    26 Center Street
    Northampton, MA 01060
    Tel: (413) 586-4170; (800) 659-6882

The Killing Screens is divided into seven parts:
(1) Stories of Power; (2) Happy Violence; (3)

Accelerating Violence; (4) Violence Is a Social Responsibility; (5) The Lessons of Violence; (6) Citizenship in the Cultural Environment; and (7) What Parents, Teachers and Schools Can Do. The video features Dr. George Gerbner, one of the nation's most highly respected scholars in the field of mass communication. It presents examples of violence shown in films and television, outlines some of the effects that these depictions of violence may have on viewers, and discusses some ways in which parents, children, and social and educational organizations can affect the prevalence of violence in the media.

On Television: The Violence Factor
Type: Videocassette
Age: Grades K through 12 and adults
Length: 56 min.
Cost: $49
Date: 1984
Source: California Newsreel
San Francisco
149 Ninth Street, Room 420
San Francisco, CA 94103
Tel: (415) 621-6196

Clips from action-adventure series, Saturday morning cartoons, the nightly news, and MTV are interwoven with analyses by Dr. George Comstock and Dr. George Gerbner on the effects of televised violence on viewers. Network executives and producers of violent programming respond to charges made against their products by claiming that existing research is "flawed" and that their work is nothing more than fantasy that has little or no effect on viewers. The program argues that people can make a difference by assuring that they view television carefully and critically and that they not allow themselves to be programmed by networks and producers.

Rising to the Challenge
Type: Videocassette
Age: Not specified, but parents are advised to review before sharing with children and teenagers as contents "may be very shocking"
Length: 38 min.
Cost: $27.45
Date: 1991 (third edition)

Source: Vision Videos/Parents Music Resource Center
1500 Arlington Boulevard, Suite 300
Arlington, VA 22209
Tel: (703) 527-9466
Fax: (703) 527-9468

The Parents Music Resource Center first produced this video in 1986, and it has now been updated three times. The video shows album covers, lyrics, music videos, and concert footage taken from performing groups that promote everything from suicide to bigotry. The video is accompanied by a free copy of the booklet *Let's Talk Rock* that presents further discussion of issues raised in the video.

TV and Violence
Type: Videocassette
Age: High school and adult
Length: 28 min.
Cost: $17 for VHS and Beta; $23 for 3/4 tape
Date: n.d.
Source: Crime File
National Institute of Justice/NCJRS
Box 6000
Rockville, MD 20850
Tel: (800) 851-3420; (301) 251-5500

This videotape is one of 32 in the Crime File series on critical issues in criminal justice produced by the National Institute of Justice of the U.S. Department of Justice. The videotape presents a discussion about television and violence moderated by James Q. Wilson, professor of government at Harvard University, among L. Rowell Huesmann, University of Illinois; J. Ronald Milavsky, NBC News and Social Research; and David Phillips, University of California at San Diego. A four-page study guide provided with the videotape outlines the research on television and violence, suggests some better methods for studying television and aggression, lists a small number of print references, and concludes with five discussion questions based on the video program.

TV and Violence
Type: Videocassette
Age: High school and adult
Length: 60 min.
Cost: $20

Date: 1991
Source: War Resisters League
              339 Lafayette Street
              New York, NY 10012
              Tel: (212) 228-0450

This is a video recording of a live cable call-in show broadcast in November 1991. The topic of the show was the impact of warlike toys on children in society, with particular emphasis on the kinds of violence that such toys engender. There is also a discussion of the kinds of ways in which individuals can respond to this problem in their own settings.

Violence in the Media Teleconference
Type: Videocassette
Age: High school and adult
Length: 120 min.
Cost: $28.70
Date: 1994
Source: EcuFilm
              810 Twelfth Avenue South
              Nashville, TN 37203
              (800) 251-4091

This two-hour teleconference was originally sponsored by a number of groups interested in the issue of violence in the media. The teleconference included research information about the effects of media violence on children and adults, violence prevention strategies that make use of media literacy education, legislation under consideration in the United States and Canada, and strategies available to families for using television in a positive way.

Musical Play

The Legend of Bullyproof Shields
Type: Musical play
Age: Junior/senior high school
Length: Two hours, but can be adapted to 50- or 60-minute
              classroom length
Cost: Stageplay and promo video: $30
              Rap audiocassette: $5
              Photo poster: $30
              Violence prevention packet: $10

Date: 1994
Source: Future WAVE
105 Camino Teresa
Santa Fe, NM 87505
Tel: (505) 982-8882
Fax: (505) 982-6460
e-mail: future@spy.org

The Legend of Bullyproof Shields is subtitled *A Musical Violence-Prevention Play*. It makes use of native spirituality, childhood fantasy, and "hard-boiled realism" to show children and teenagers how they can respond to threatening situations. The play includes the character Breakout Bear—who says, "Break away from the current fray. When tempers cool, then make your play. Why ram right through the middle. Try an end-run to solve your riddle"—and others such as Understanding Unicorn, Listening Lynx, Loving Lion, and Yang Yak.

Glossary

M ost of the terms of special interest in discussions of violence in the media are taken from the fields of psychology and sociology, the area of mass communications, or the field of First Amendment rights and issues. This chapter lists the terms one is most likely to encounter in discussions of violence and the media at an introductory level.

affiliates   Broadcast stations that, by contractual agreement, receive most of the programs they transmit from a given network, but are not actually owned by the network.

aggression   A somewhat ambiguous term that expresses hostility. The term has been used to describe a wide range of behaviors ranging from mild verbal criticism to physical assault.

antisocial (behavior)   Behavior that violates generally accepted rules of behavior. Those rules may be stated explicitly or may be generally understood, but only implicitly. Antisocial behavior may be directed toward either personal or property rights.

art   Any form of human activity that is a result of or that appeals to the human imagination.

attention span   The period of time during which a person can concentrate on one specific event or item.

audience ratings   See **ratings.**

bandwidth   That section of the electromagnetic spectrum used by a station in broadcasting its program. The bandwidth for a color television channel, for example, is about six megahertz.

Bill of Rights   A term that refers to the first ten amendments to the Constitution of the United States, as adopted in 1791. The Bill of Rights is regarded as a statement of the fundamental rights of any American citizen.

Bobo doll   A doll invented by Dr. Albert Bandura for use in his studies on aggression in children. The doll is designed so that, once it is knocked down, it springs back up again.

broadcast   Any communication sent out by means of radio waves intended for reception by the general public. Originally the term referred to radio broadcasting, but now refers also to television broadcasting.

broadcast advisory   A brief statement made on television prior to the broadcasting of a program that may contain content that is unsuitable for certain viewers, especially young children. The most common broadcast advisory is "Parental Discretion Advised."

broadcast media   Those forms of communication, such as radio and television, that make use of public airwaves. The broadcast media differ from the print media in that the number of frequencies available for the former is limited and, therefore, the number of possible companies who may become part of the broadcast media is also limited. For comparison, see **print media.**

cable television   A system that transmits both original programming and programming from other sources (such as films and broadcast television) by means of a cable buried underground or suspended in the air, rather than by means of airwaves.

cartoon   A form of art that depicts a particular scene with exaggerated figures. The term is also widely used to refer to a comic strip.

catharsis   The release or purging of emotions.

causation   The notion that an event takes place because something has caused it to occur, in contrast to its having been a random event.

censorship   The practice by which one person or organization controls the materials that other individuals may see. Censors may actually change or delete words, phrases, or longer sections of spoken or written or visual documents or they may prevent the production or release of those documents entirely.

channel   The means by which some service, such as a television program, is transmitted from producer to consumer. The term also applies to specific stations that provide this service, such as the ESPN channel.

character score   A measure developed by Dr. George Gerbner that is used in calculating the violence index for a set of television programs. The character score for a given program is defined as the percent of all characters involved in any violence in the program plus the percent involved in any killing. Also see **violence index.**

civil liberty   The right of an individual to enjoy certain fundamental rights guaranteed by the Constitution, federal, state, or other laws without the interference of any governmental agency.

clear-and-present danger   The principle that some individual freedoms may need to be restricted if there is a serious and immediate threat to the general welfare.

code   With respect to the mass media, a set of statements that outline behaviors and practices that are and are not acceptable in the industry. Thus there is a comic books code that lists text and drawings that may or may not be included in comic books published under the code.

comic magazine   A magazine that contains artwork and text presenting a series of events that may or may not be humorous.

commercial-free programming   Programming (usually television programming) during which no paid commercial messages or advertisements are included. Commercial-free programming is sometimes recommended as a means of reducing the amount of advertising—some of it containing violent elements—to which children are exposed.

common carrier   Any telecommunications company that provides communication transmission services to the general public.

content analysis   Research in which a large number of programs, films, or other events are examined to find out what proportion of time is devoted to each of various topics, such as violence, sex, and business.

control group   One of the two groups used in many forms of experimentation. The control group is the one that receives no particular special treatment, in comparison with the experimental group, which does receive that treatment.

convergence   In general, the movement of two or more objects or events toward a single common point. In psychological theory, convergence refers to the notion that a person's behavior results from some complex mixture of both hereditary and environmental factors.

correlation   A statistical concept that shows the extent to which any two variables are associated with each other, other than randomly. A high correlation means that two variables follow a similar pattern to a greater extent than would be expected on the basis of chance alone. A correlation between two variables is not proof that one variable is dependent on the other.

cultivation analysis   A technique developed by Dr. George Gerbner and his colleagues for measuring the impact that television has on a viewer's outlook on life. Two groups of television viewers, "heavy" and "light" viewers, are asked a series of questions about everyday issues. The questions have "real-life" and "television" answers. By measuring the differences in answers given by the two groups, an estimate can be made of the impact of viewing on a person's perception of social reality.

cultural indicators   A term originally coined in 1969 by Dr. George Gerbner to describe a method for measuring the impact of the mass media—especially television—on the view of social reality that people have. Gerbner's cultural indicators studies involved three approaches: (1) institutional process analysis; (2) message system analysis; and (3) cultivation analysis. Also see **cultivation analysis, institutional process analysis,** and **message system analysis.**

DBS   An acronym for direct broadcasting by satellite, a system by which up to a dozen separate channels can be downloaded from a satellite directly to private homes. DBS signals can be captured by relatively small dish or plate antennas.

dehumanization   Any process that tends to strip a person of those qualities that distinguish humans from other animals, qualities such as compassion, sympathy, and kindness.

deregulation   The process by which broadcasters are freed from supervision by governmental agencies. Deregulation is favored by those who believe in open market or laissez-faire economics.

desensitization   Any behavior that tends to make a person less sensitive to the emotions of other people. For example, some people have argued that watching violence on television causes viewers to become less concerned about the violence they see in their daily lives.

disinhibition   The loss of some inhibition that had been previously learned. For example, children normally learn to control their natural violent impulses as they grow up. In some cases, however, a child (or an older person) may lose some of this control, a process known as disinhibition.

electronic media   A term used to describe any form of communication that delivers its message by electronic or electrical means, such as by radio or television waves.

empirical evidence   Any data that are collected as the result of experiments and/or observations.

experimental group   One of the two groups used in many forms of experimentation. The experimental group is the one to which some kind of treatment is applied, in comparison with the control group, which does not receive the same treatment.

extended definition TV (EDTV)   A television system that contains more lines per inch than traditional television (but fewer lines than HDTV) and that can, therefore, provide a clearer picture than do traditional television systems. Also known as enhanced definition television. Also see **high definition television.**

extrapolation   The process of predicting some future state of a system on the basis of past and current data. For example, one may try to extrapolate how viewers will respond to watching four hours of violent programming on television based on studies that show how they respond to watching one, two, and three hours of such programming.

family viewing time   A guideline established by the National Association of Broadcasters in 1975 suggesting that the broadcast period from 8:00 to 9:00 P.M. be free of themes that would be objectionable for young viewers. At times, a two-hour family viewing time has also been proposed. Also known as the family viewing hour.

fantasy (vs. reality)   Imaginary events and images created by the human mind that may or may not have any basis in the real world. Critics of violence in the media sometimes claim that young children cannot tell the difference between imaginary characters and stories created for the media (such as television programs) and characters and events in the real world.

field research   Experiments that take place in nonlaboratory settings, such as in schools, hospitals, and mental institutions.

First Amendment rights   The rights of free speech and expression, as laid out in the First Amendment to the United States Constitution.

free market   An economic and political term that refers to the philosophy that all goods and ideas should have equal access to the general public and that survival of those goods and ideas should depend on unhindered competition among them.

freedom of speech/expression/press   Freedoms guaranteed to all American citizens in the First Amendment to the United States Constitution. Also see **Bill of Rights** and **First Amendment rights.**

gangsta rap   A form of rap music that emphasizes sexual, violent, drug, and misogynistic themes.

grass roots   A term used to describe political actions planned and carried out by ordinary citizens in contrast to those of centralized organizations or professional politicians.

gratuitous violence   Violence that takes place or is presented without any specific reason other than to entertain the audience.

Gresham's Law   Originally a law of economics stated by Sir Thomas Gresham in the sixteenth century stating that money of lesser value will drive money of greater value out of circulation. More generally, the term is now used to suggest that cheap and shoddy items, entertainment programs, or other events will survive in competition with better-quality items, programs, and events.

habituation   The process of becoming accustomed to some stimulus so that a response is no longer given to that stimulus. For example, a television viewer might become so accustomed to watching murders on television that the thought of murder might no longer produce feelings of horror, disgust, or disapproval.

heavy viewers   People who tend to watch television more than 40 hours per week, on an average. In comparison, the average viewing time among Americans is about 25 hours per week. Also see **light viewers.**

high definition television (HDTV)   A technologically new form of television reception in which more lines per inch can be squeezed onto the television screen than is the case with traditional or extended definition television. HDTV promises to present much better pictures than are available with current technology, but it is likely to be much more expensive. Also see **extended definition TV.**

hip-hop   A form of rap music. See **rap music.**

identification   The process by which a person begins to associate his or her own life with that of someone or something else. Some authorities believe that people who read about, hear about, or see characters in the media begin to imagine that they are similar to those characters.

imitative learning   A pattern of behavior adopted by one person as the result of watching another person or thing and trying to be like him or her or it.

independent television   Any television station that is not affiliated with a network such as ABC, CBS, or NBC, and that does not depend on a network for a major portion of its programming.

information superhighway   A proposed nationwide electronic system by which any two computer terminals would allow the exchange of information between two or more individuals or businesses. When completely in place, the information superhighway would allow access to an essentially unlimited source of data, entertainment, and other information that can be transmitted by an electronic system.

instigation theory   A theory in social science that exposure to violent programming in the media brings about an immediate and aggressive response in some viewers.

institutional process analysis   An aspect of Dr. George Gerbner's cultural indicators research in which researchers attempt to discover the process by which policies are formulated and decisions made within mass media organizations. Also see **cultural indicators.**

interactive media   Forms of public communication in which the observer is able to respond to and be responded to by the particular medium. Video games are a form of interactive media since people who play the games are able to influence what happens in the games and, conversely, the game itself influences the player's behavior.

laissez-faire   A French expression meaning "allow it to happen," which describes a particular economic and political theory. That theory says that individuals and organizations should be allowed to do almost anything they want to do within certain general limitations.

legitimacy   The quality of being recognized as proper and lawful.

licensing   The granting by the Federal Communications Commission of the right to use some portion of the electromagnetic spectrum for radio or television broadcasting to some entity in the private or public sector.

light viewers   People who tend to watch a relatively modest amount of television, approximately 10 to 15 hours per week. Also see **heavy viewers.**

longitudinal study   A type of research that is carried on over long periods of time. Longitudinal studies attempt to determine how specific factors in the life of a person or some other organism affect the way that person's life develops.

market forces   Those factors that operate to control supply and demand in a free market. As originally expressed by Adam Smith in 1776, the concept of market forces argues that, left to their own free play, market forces will interact in such a way as to ensure the most satisfactory combination of price, quality, and quantity of goods and services for consumers.

mass culture   A term that has been used to describe all of the forms of cultural expression—such as clothing, hair styling, books and magazines, television, films, and music—that appeal to a very wide segment of the general public.

mass media   A form of communication that is designed to reach a very wide segment of the general public.

mean-world syndrome   A term suggested by George Gerbner reflecting a perception among the general public that crime is growing much more rapidly than statistics actually indicate to be the case. Gerbner claims that heavy television viewing "is the largest single contributor to the feeling of rampant criminality and the threat of violence lurking around every corner."

media   The term media is the plural form of the word medium, which means the channel through which information, ideas, and art are distributed to the public. Most linguists now acknowledge that the term can also be used as a singular form, as "the mass media," in referring to a cultural industry.

message system analysis   A technique developed by Dr. George Gerbner and his colleagues to discover "the composition and structure of the symbolic world" presented by television. In order to accomplish this goal, the whole range of television programming, including cartoons, movies, and television series, is analyzed to yield a summary of the kinds of characters presented on television, the kinds of action in which they are involved, the way they spend their time, the nature of their personalities, and so forth.

methodological flaws   The errors that occur during the design or execution of some experiment. In conducting a series of interviews on a particular subject, for example, an investigator might choose to talk with only white, middle-class males between the ages of 21 and 31. If the investigator were studying a question concerning the general population, limiting the people interviewed in this way would constitute a methodological flaw in his or her research.

modeling   The act of shaping one's behavior along the lines of some other admired and respected person's behavior.

moving pictures   A series of still photographs projected on a screen in rapid sequence so that objects in the photographs appear to be in motion. Moving pictures are also known as motion pictures or films.

National Endowment for the Arts   A federally funded program that makes grants to individuals, state and regional arts agencies, and nonprofit organizations in the fields of design, dance, folk arts, literature, media arts, museums, music, theater, and visual arts.

natural experiment   A research program in which investigators attempt to study some problem, such as the effect of televised violence, in naturally occurring conditions, such as in the homes of viewers.

observational learning   A theory of social learning first proposed by Albert Bandura that says that people can learn by watching and imitating the behavior of others. An important feature of Bandura's theory is that it suggests that learning can occur without reinforcement (reward or punishment) but simply by modeling the behavior of others.

pandering   The act making it possible for people to indulge in their lowest desires, passions, or vices.

parental advisory   See **broadcast advisory.**

pay-per-view   See **pay-TV.**

pay-TV   A system in which a given household is charged for the right to watch a particular television channel. Pay-per-view is a particular type of pay-TV in which the household is charged for watching a particular program or during a particular period of time.

peak viewing   That period of the day during which the largest number of people are watching television. Also see **prime time.**

post-video-game trauma   A state of emotional or psychological disturbance that may develop in an individual as a result of playing a (usually violent) video game.

predisposition   A previous inclination. Some people would argue that a person who watches gratuitous violence on television over long periods of time develops a predisposition, or a tendency, to engage in such behaviors himself or herself.

prevalence   The extent to which something occurs.

prime time   That period of the day during which the television audience reaches its highest level. It commonly refers to the period between 8:00 and 11:00 P.M.

print media   A form of communication in which information is produced and distributed to the general public. The print media includes books, newspapers, magazines, films, photographs, phonograph records, CDs and audiotapes. A key feature of the print media is that anyone can enter this field without restricting the participation of others. In comparison, see **broadcast media.**

prior restraint   A legal term meaning that a particular behavior is banned before it has ever occurred. The law normally operates by taking action against behaviors that have occurred and have been found to be illegal. In prior restraint, a behavior is prohibited from ever occurring in the first place because of the anticipated negative effects that behavior would have.

profit motive   One possible reason for taking some specific action or actions. One might imagine writing a book, for example, for many different reasons: to resolve long-held intrapersonal conflicts, to become famous, to change the way people think, to get revenge on someone else, or to make a lot of money. The last of these is the profit motive.

program score   A measure developed by Dr. George Gerbner to be used in calculating the violence index for a set of television programs. The program score includes three distinct measurements: (1) the percentage of programs in a set of programs that contain violence; (2) the rate of violent episodes for all programs; and (3) the rate of violent episodes per hour of performance. Also see **violence index.**

programming   The selection of presentations to be offered on a radio or television station or network.

pro-social programming   Programming that is developed specifically for the purpose of promoting socially desirable behaviors in listeners and viewers.

public interest   That which is to the greatest advantage to the greatest number of people.

public radio/television   A radio or television station or network that is operated as a noncommercial venture.

public service announcement (PSA)   An announcement advertisement carried by a radio or television station on some theme of general public interest. Both the production of the advertisement and its airing are donated—the production by a nonprofit organization or an organization such as the Ad Council, and the airing by the station carrying the ad.

rap music   A patter style of music that often consists of rhymed couplets recited rapidly and without melodic line.

ratings   The percentage of some given population that is watching a television program, advertisement, or channel during a given time period.

read-only memory (ROM)   An electronic system in which the user is allowed access to information stored on a disk, but to which he or she can not add new information. Also see **read-write memory.**

read-write memory   An electronic system that allows the user to both retrieve data and add data of his or her own to a disk.

reality/fantasy distinction   The ability to recognize when a particular depiction of a person or event is taken from or corresponds with real life and when it is a fiction created by someone's imagination.

redeeming social value   A trait that makes something worth protecting because it has significance for some group in society. A painting of a nude woman might be considered to be offensive by some individuals, for example, but if that painting inspired feelings of awe, admiration, respect, and other positive qualities in a number of individuals, the painting could be said to have redeeming social value.

reliability   A term used in statistics to indicate the likelihood that a particular result would be achieved each time an experiment were repeated. If an experiment is done 100 times with almost the same results every time, those results are said to be reliable. If widely different results are obtained in the 100 repetitions, the results are said to be unreliable.

response   Any behavior that occurs as the result of exposure to a stimulus. When a light is shined into a person's eye (the stimulus), the person is likely to blink (the response).

role model   Any person whose patterns of behavior influence the attitudes and behaviors of others.

sadism   The love of cruelty. The term is derived from the name of a famous French noble, the Marquis de Sade, who was reputed to have taken great pleasure in inflicting pain on others.

satiation   The experience of having repeated a given act so many times that a person becomes "filled up" with the act and attempts to avoid any further exposure to the act. A person who eats too much of any one kind of food may become satiated with the food and refuse to eat any more of it. Similarly, a person who watches too much violence on television may become satiated with violence and try to avoid being exposed to any further televised violence.

self-regulation   The policy that people and organizations whose products need to be monitored can do the necessary monitoring themselves. One way to deal with a child who eats too many cookies, for example, is to ask the child to place limits on the number of cookies he or she will eat in the future.

sexual violence   Acts in which any form of human sexuality is linked with violence. Rape is an example of sexual violence.

social learning   A theory from the social sciences that argues that children's personalities develop as the result of their interaction with culture, specific subcultures, family, and peers.

standard broadcasting   Radio broadcasting that makes use of AM (amplitude-modulation) transmission.

Standards for the Depiction of Violence in Television Programs   A set of standards developed and voluntarily accepted by the three major television networks in 1992.

standing   A legal term indicating that a particular person or organization has the legal right to make its opinions known on some issue before a court of law or a regulatory agency.

statistical significance   A mathematical measure that indicates that some particular event occurs more commonly in a situation that would be expected purely on the basis of chance.

stimulus   Anything that evokes a response.

superstation   A local television station that transmits its signal via satellite to cable systems that reach beyond its own local viewing area.

susceptibility   The state of being easily influenced by the thoughts or actions of another person or group of people.

television   A form of broadcasting in which both sound and visual signals are transmitted by means of radio waves.

Television Violence Act of 1990   An act of Congress that was passed in order to allow representatives of the three television networks to meet and discuss common standards for the depiction of violence on television without violating antitrust laws.

third-variable problem   A research issue raised by the possibility that some factor, often unknown, may be responsible for the observed correlation between two other factors. For example, a researcher may observe that children who watch a lot of television exhibit aggressive behavior. Besides saying that the viewing caused the behavior, one might argue that a third factor exists that causes both a high level of television viewing and aggressive behavior.

translator   A broadcast station that does not produce original programming, but rebroadcasts signals from other stations.

V-chip   A computer chip that has been proposed as a way of allowing parents to control the programs their children watch on television. Although critics of televised violence were calling for laws requiring the installation of V-chips in all newly manufactured television sets as early as the late 1980s, no such device has actually been made generally available to consumers to date.

validity   A statistical concept that says how likely it is that an answer or series of answers are close to the correct answer. If one knows from an independent source, for example, that the true answer to a research experiment is 400 people per day, then the closer the results of that experiment are to 400, the more valid they are.

video games   Forms of entertainment in which an observer can manipulate the characters and objects shown on a television or computer screen, affecting the way events are eventually played out on the screen. Also see **interactive media.**

violence   Any form of action that causes harm to another person. The term has been defined quite differently by various authorities. In some cases, violence is said to refer only to physical acts, such as striking, shooting, or stabbing another person. In other cases, violence is said to include harsh or unkind words or physical gestures.

violence index   A measure developed by Dr. George Gerbner to estimate the amount of violence presented in any set of television programs, as in a week or season of television. The violence index is defined as the sum of the program score and character score for the programs that make up that set of programs. Also see **character score** and **program score.**

violence profile   A set of indicators first developed by Dr. George Gerbner designed to measure the way in which television programming affects the conceptions of social reality developed by viewers. Also see **cultural indicators** and **violence index.**

Index

David E. Newton holds B.A. and M.A. degrees from the University of Michigan and an Ed.D. in science education from Harvard University. He taught mathematics and science at the secondary level in his hometown of Grand Rapids, Michigan, and then courses in chemistry, physical science, teacher education, and human sexuality at Salem State College in Salem, Massachusetts. He has also held appointments as visiting professor at Western Washington University and as adjunct professor at the University of San Francisco.

He has more than 400 publications to his credit, including about 50 books on topics such as science and social issues, gun control, hunting, global warming, the gay and lesbian civil rights movement, ozone depletion, and the chemical elements. He and his partner own a nine-room bed-and-breakfast inn in Ashland, Oregon.